OPENING TO THE INFINITE

OPENING TO THE INFINITE

HUMAN MULTIDIMENSIONAL POTENTIAL

By

Alice Bryant

Rev. Linda Seebach M.S.W.

Wild Flower Press
P.O. Box 190
Mill Spring, NC 28756

Library of Congress Cataloging-in-Publication Data
Bryant, Alice, 1924-
Opening to the Infinite: Human Multidimensional Potential by
Alice Bryant, Linda Seebach
p. cm
Includes bibliographical refernces and index.
ISBN 0-926524-43-7
1. Consciousness--Miscellanea.
2. Hyperspace
I. Seebach, Linda, 1945-
II. Title
BF1999.B7247 1997
131--dc21
97-27079
CIP

Cover Artwork:
Maynard Demmon, Imark Design, Portland, OR
Manuscript editor:
Brian Crissey

Printed in the United States of America.

Address all inquiries to:
Wild Flower Press
an imprint of Blue Water Publishing, Inc.
P. O. Box 190
Mill Spring, NC 28756
U.S.A.

Blue Water Publishing, Inc., is committed
to use 100% recycled or tree-free paper.

DEDICATION

This work is dedicated to:

Tomorrow's Children

That they may receive the love, honor,
support and validation they
both need and deserve

Opening to the Infinite

Foreword

The concepts presented in this book at first might seem entirely new, certainly strange and probably "far out."

But, in fact, they are neither new nor strange. For the elements of the concepts have been considered by many earlier scientists and thinkers—albeit under the different idioms and nomenclature characteristics of past generations.

*

Most central to the concepts, past or present, is the understanding that the human being is what we today would call a carrier of information which can also process new information and somehow store the new information in memory.

The kind of memory referred to here, though, is not of the kind we normally use and rely on in our mundane daily affairs while we are consciously awake.

All past scientists and thinkers have more or less agreed that it is a deeper and more profound type of memory, largely stored in subconscious or nonconscious layers of the human psyche.

And many in the past have felt that this particular kind of "deep memory," including both its old and new elements, is genetically passed down through the generations in some kind of collective form.

*

This book, however, is not meant to be a scientific one—but rather one of broad human interest. In this sense, the book deals with real people—largely because the modern sciences are quite weak in explaining what people experience regarding deep memory, or deep experiencing, to say nothing of "traveling in hyperspace."

Along these lines, other researchers and writers are referring to "exceptional human experiencing," a generic form of nomenclature, but which is closely related to the experiences of the spontaneous multidimensionally aware which constitute the backbone of this book.

*

None the less, there are some past scientific precedents, at least in general outlines, which are relevant to the complicated phenomena discussed in this book

In one of its aspects, the deep memory referred to in this book is DNA memory—since science now largely agrees that our species DNA carries memory of experiences and adaptations to them, and which accounts for gradual or sudden evolutionary developments.

DNA (Deoxyribonucleic acid) is composed of cell nucleic acids and nucleoproteins. Nucleic acid is any of a group of organic substances found in the chromosomes of living cells that play an important role in the storage and replication of hereditary information and in protein synthesis.

Many complex processes are involved in the replication of hereditary information—the whole of which are summarized as the genetic code.

There is little doubt that the genetic code somehow "remembers" how to replicate heredity information—although how it contains this "memory" is not very well understood.

*

The fact that DNA (or the genetic code) reproduces our biological bodies is now universally accepted. But this acceptance has not yet explained how and why developmental changes come about in the DNA codes.

But these changes need to be understood in order to account for slow or sudden evolutionary steps, since these steps automatically involve changes in the DNA codes.

*

Before DNA was discovered, many earlier scientists occupied themselves with the problem of evolutionary developing.

The founder of invertebrate paleontology, Jean Baptiste Lamarck (1744-1829), proposed the theory that evolution is based upon the belief that characteristics acquired by an organism in its adaptation to its environment are passed on to its offspring, the result being the gradual evolution of a new species.

This concept, today known as that of inheritance of acquired characteristics, has been seriously disputed by modern biologists.

*

Lamark's work was, however, important as a forerunner to that of Charles R. Darwin (1809-1882), who established the theory of organic evolution known as Darwinism.

The theory suggested that the variations which prove helpful to a plant or an animal in its struggle for existence enable it to survive and reproduce. These favorable variations are thus transmitted to the offspring of the survivors and spread to the entire species over successive generations.

The transmission requires the existence of some kind of transferable genetic "memory imprints" in order that the variations can replicate down into successive generations.

Darwin's theory, however, applied only to biological variations. It did not address psychological or other more subtle traits found in the thinking types of species, and which also seem to be handed down into successive generations.

*

In speaking of some kind of memory imprints, one might just as well bite the bullet and speak of some kind of thought—for memory of any kind can be conceived of as thought.

But this was a sore issue regarding biologists who generally focused only on bio-physical aspects of our species and avoided or ignored its bio-mental aspects.

As a result, two issues arose. Was it matter over mind, or mind over matter?

These issues were for a long time held separate and the advocates of each defended them as such. But obviously a bridge between mind and matter had to be constructed. This bridge ultimately surfaced during the 1970s as the holistic mind/body concept, which held that body and mind interacted to result in the whole human organism or being.

*

Mind/body holism is, of course, widely accepted today. But the route to the acceptance has been very bumpy and many of its details are forgotten. Some of these are important to the concepts and substance of this book.

*

Various early psychologists were concerned with the issues, and many of them made tentative concepts regarding the interrelationship of body and mind.

Among these was the young Immanuel Velikovsky, whom many came to consider science's greatest heretic of all time after he published in 1950 his famous book, *Worlds In Collision*.

None the less, Velikovsky's credentials were of high order. He had studied the natural sciences at the University of Edinburgh; history, law, and medicine in Moscow; biology in Berlin; worked on physical and mental aspects of the brain in Zurich; and was a psychoanalyst in Vienna. As a young scholar, he produced a collective work out of which grew Jerusalem University.

*

In 1930, Velikovsky produced a paper entitled "On the Physical Existence of the World of Thought." In this paper he postulated that engram in brain cells were carriers of memory, and which could be reawakened or stimulated by suitable mechanical, mental or experiential impulses.

By "engram" Velikovsky and other biologists referred to a bio-mind imprint which, in some unknown way, is passed down to succeeding generations—and which transmission results in "racial memory" as it was termed back then. Today, we probably would refer to "racial memory" as species memory, rather than as regards the different races per se.

*

Velikovsky also claimed the existence of a collective mind in the early stages of the development of the species. Individuation, he wrote, accompanies the evolution from lower to higher forms.

Yet the collective mind is never fully erased in man—meaning that its constituents are passed along into each successive generation on a species-wide basis. Various elements of the collective mind can come to the fore preferably in excited states of mind but also in crowds swept by emotions.

Today, we would probably refer to Velikovsky's "excited states of mind" as altered states of consciousness—during or because of which people experience perceptual or cognitive phenomena which extend beyond the known limits of the physical perceptions.

Velikovsky eventually collected his thinking along these lines in his book titled *Mankind in Amnesia*, published in 1982.

*

Velikovsky passed his 1930 paper around, especially to the three most noted psychologists of his time—Eugene Bleuler, Sigmund Freud, and Carl Gustav Jung—all of which found favor with it. All wrote to him that they, too, had formed various independent opinions on the subject, and which came very close to Velikovsky's own.

*

None of these, however, linked "racial memory" to DNA, since the important constituents of DNA were not known at the time. Instead, racial memory was used interchangeably with cellular memory and genetic memory. But since DNA is now known as the fundamental building blocks of the genetic code, it would now be appropriate to substitute DNA memory.

In other words, DNA memory would include not only genetic codes for building the human biological anatomy, but imprints, cellular or otherwise, of acquired traits and past mind-experiencing relevant to the evolution and on-going development of our species.

Here, then, is not only a basis for the later body/mind holism, but another bridge into cellular or DNA memory of our species—and which, by hypothesis anyway, could be accessed by special states of altered consciousness.

*

Now a number of very meaningful questions arise. And it is these which are the substance and focus of this book.

The first of these questions concerns whether each member of our species individually possesses complete DNA memory, or at least some parts of it, in their genetic coding.

If so, then 'memory' of our species ought to include the collective memory of not only our species, but of its development in history from a very long time back.

This prospect is, of course, a *very* far out one, but largely only because it is alien to our education and direct experiencing only of the three-dimensional, physical world around us.

*

But there is a scientific principle which needs to be considered, one with which few are familiar except biologists.

This refers to a biogenetic law, one which is universally accepted, that species advanced in the evolutionary process such as humans, resemble at various stages the embryos of ancestral species, such as fish.

The law refers only to embryonic development, and not to adult stages. As development proceeds, the embryos of different species become more and in most dissimilar—but which means that their developmental ontology (embryonic development) is similar to other species at early stages.

So in a certain sense, it can be said, as it often is, that the embryo undergoes a temporary DNA replication of earlier species which presumably figure into its developmental DNA codes.

*

But here we now have to think not about the physical cellular development of embryos, but about the DNA codes which are the source or cause of the developmental stages.

Thus, it could be said, if only theoretically, that the DNA of a developing embryo is remembering, or at least echoing, and going through its accumulated DNA memory codes.

*

There is another factor which is probably important in considering all of this—recent advances in genetic research, especially those having to do with the constituents of the human species genome. The genome is described as constituting an identification of all the genes which comprise our entire species—and is often referred to as the human gene "pool."

The genome will not be completely mapped until sometime early in the next century. But enough is known to permit geneticists to say that about 98 per cent of all genetic (DNA) materials are identical in all members of our species. It is the remaining 2 per cent which make for the differences we see among individuals. Obviously, it is a very important 2 per cent.

Further, our species shares over 90 per cent of its DNA codes in common with all of the higher primates—higher primates include man, apes and monkeys.

*

Thus, if DNA memory is possible, we are presented with a rather large perspective, most of which is completely unknown—except to individuals who appear to have accessed various aspects of it.

In this regard, the authors have interviewed and worked with a number of such individuals, while the experiential phenomena of eight of them have been included in detail.

As might be expected, the experiential realities of such people ought to differ exceedingly—as they do—from what might be called average or normal experiencing.

And from what the authors have discovered concerning these individuals, it is apparent that they access much more than DNA memory—*or*, that DNA memory consists of much, much more than merely memory encoded in our species DNA.

*

The nomenclature which must be selected to describe these unknown realms, the DNA-memory "realms" (as it were), is a complex issue. But the authors have taken their views from those they have interviewed and studied.

For example, many of the individuals interviewed say that they experientially transcend time and space, and speak of other or additional dimensions other than the third-dimension which constitutes our normal space-time continuum.

Out of this has arisen the concept of "multidimensionality" as it is presented and discussed in this book, as well as the concept of "hyperspace" having to do with spatial dimensions beyond space and time. These two terms, however, have been used by other writers examining other contexts.

A very competent glossary is provided, and probably should be studied before reading the text.

*

It may be not quite correct to say that the multidimensional types collide with parapyschological and psychical phenomena. But in effect, what the multidimensionally aware indicate they experience bears close, even if not exact, relationship to what the modern Western cultures have blithely stereotyped as the "psychic paranormal."

Clearly, though, the term "psychic" is too limited regarding multidimensional types, and the authors have been correct in not leaning on it too much.

*

If we accept, as we do by now, that other or altered states of consciousness do exist, and that different kinds of phenomena are encountered which are appropriate to the states, then the contents of this book should not come as a surprise.

Rather, the contents should come as a revelation regarding the experiencing of the multidimensionally aware.

This book will easily fit as a seminal, ground-breaking one into the future of the kinds of trans-consciousness approach which is already under way in other places and in other forms.

I believe that most readers will, in fact, recognize parts of themselves in it.

Ingo Swann
New York, July 1996

Chapter One

The Multidimensionally Aware

Unless you have had the opportunity to sit down face to face with a multidimensionally aware person, it is hard to grasp the incredible implications of what these people represent. Profound is one of the most applicable descriptions. Mind boggling is another.

A multidimensionally aware individual is a person who can consciously access the regions beyond what we know as the third dimension, or the everyday world which is physically visible by human eye or mechanical aid. These vast regions are known as hyperspace.

Nothing is as it appears to be in third dimension, for there are layers upon layers of energy at work which humankind has forgotten exist. The multidimensionally aware have a highly advanced understanding of the deeper order and workings of all things. They see the multidimensionality of existence.

The one constant among the multidimensionally aware is that seldom do they go to the same space and almost never do they report the same type of experiences. This does not make one experience more valid than the other, but it does add to the confusion of the person who desires to compare their personal experiences with that of others.

The focus of this book is to reveal and respect their unusual experiences, to in some way fit the many anomalies into an overview that will encourage tolerance and understanding and to lay a basic ground work for other experiencers.

The material presented in this book was given over a three-and-a-half-year period by very sincere and dedicated people who can access hyperspace.

It is not channeled material in the most common utilization of the term. The multidimensionally aware actually travel in hyperspace. They see with an almost normal vision. It is only that the perspective from which they view it is so different from the known third-dimensional perspective.

Not every multidimensionally aware person is visual. Very often there is simply a knowing that is reached and it is very difficult to translate into third-dimensional terms how this knowledge is obtained.

The multidimensionally aware clearly point the way for the evolution of humankind. They already journey where the rest of us must learn to go, if we want to survive and evolve as a species. This is not an impossibility. It can be done.

In order to get there, we must let go of our belief systems that what we see, hear, feel, touch and smell is all that exists. Vast unimaginable regions are accessible to all of us; we must only be willing to believe they exist in order to find them.

In the eighteenth century, the English poet William Blake spoke of the infinite perception available if the consciousness doors were only opened by learning to see. The infinite, he believed, was not hiding from us, we were simply the ones who could not find it.

This may sound ultimately impossible, but each and every one of us flies through these unknown places in our dreams. This may be as close as our conscious mind will allow us to come. We then awaken to the illusion and call it reality.

In time, more and more people will be born to, or learn the arts of, the experience of hyperspace, to know what is available in the limitless multitude of dimensions. If we are very lucky, these people will be able to have the internal resources and support systems to know who and what they are.

Already too many multidimensionally aware minds have been lost, as society has not appreciated, nor valued, nor understood their extraordinary abilities.

The loving multidimensionally aware are here to anchor a new reality firmly into the Earth plane. By doing this, they open the doorways for the rest of humanity to follow.

Being alone and a forerunner for evolution is an unimaginably hard task.

The material herein was generously given by eight of the multidimensionally aware. As authors, we are deeply indebted to them for sharing their lives, their ideas and their world views with us.

Some of the aware, because of their chosen role in society, requested confidentiality, which we respected.

We present frameworks of reference upon which others may build. Our great desire is that this book be of assistance to the many multidimensionally aware who do not yet know what they are, that they would come to understand and be honored and blessed for their contributions to our world.

A Multidimensionally Aware View of Life[1]

Contributed By Carol Lynn White[2]

> "The only validation of my precognitive dreams, telepathy and clairvoyance was from my dad, a physician. He was an extremely strong diagnostician, felt he had ESP, and used those abilities. That was how he diagnosed so brilliantly. Later he would receive verification in the lab results. We had that in common, but it was never really a part of life, it was just something he mentioned. Everything else, as I was growing up, was buried and hidden, never out in the open.
>
> "All of my life I have had a huge sense of destiny. I just didn't know how it was going to manifest, but I felt that when the time was right it would happen.
>
> "Between ages 14 and 15 I thought I might be a witch, because I was able to create a reality. I would throw out a thought process and people would do what I wanted them to do, such as call, or show up. That worried me, but then I realized that was another form of nepotism.
>
> "My present form is to manifest reality in other ways than through manipulation, to manifest through the highest and best, never interfere with anybody else's reaction, but do what is right. I consider myself to be spiritually oriented and I teach people to do for themselves, to know what they know, trust it, and make it happen. This allows people to develop their perceptual abilities and strengths, then to manifest that in their lives.

---

1. Case histories are, of necessity, second-hand accounts of happenings that occurred when the children were very small. Names have been changed throughout to protect identities.
2. It was with great sadness that we learned that Carol Lynn White passed over in October, 1996. Correspondence to Mr. White may be addressed to Wild Flower Press and will be forwarded.

Power and Powerlessness

"I find the common thread in many people is a feeling of powerlessness. When they feel they cannot do anything, then they go to other people and give their power away.

"I am on a crusade to assist others to become their own guru, their own source of power, to be the director of their lives and be in tune at all times while in a physical body.

"People will say they just can't wait to go home, don't want to be here, hate living in this body. That is not the way to be in tune.

"If you seek that all the time, you are going to have to keep coming back here. I teach people that to learn to be a multidimensional person in the physical body is to have really ascended. Then you are doing it on all levels at once.

"Be here, be in the now, integrate on all levels. Do not just be in your spiritual plane or astral plane, be here. Value the physical plane, do not continue to devalue being human while pretending to be spiritual. Each is equally sacred.

Developing in a Different Way

"Though I had known as early as I could remember what I was, it was only in my twenties that I decided to truly be that, and do what I was to do.

"Again, that was a very traumatic time. I got very sick physically with a chronic fatigue virus and was in bed for about a year and a half. During that time, reading and talking to people, I did a lot of shifting on all levels. I was led to people I could relate to, people who were like me.

"I learned to develop in a different way. Prior to that, I did not know how to control the mishmash of information that came to me. I found a teacher and began to develop very quickly as far as knowing what I knew, trusting that, and knowing it was good and for healing. Once I knew my path of service was teaching, I was better able to cope.

"I teach spiritual principles with my own material. I have developed a combination of my own intuitive counseling and healing. Ian taught me how to be with people, how to teach, which I might never have done otherwise.

"I have always worked with telepathy and clairsentience. I see that as a physical capability, not necessarily an inspired state. My emphasis has always been, especially with students, to work from an inspirational space, completely open to Source, however that may come in. I never work through entities, because I feel that would be giving my power away. I am my own best source of information.

"Every being is connected with Source and Universal Truth and if I go direct, I am in touch with truth and that is a basis I can trust. I can trance, but I feel that is moving away from Source to a third party. Why not bring it through directly?

"When I work with my own guides, it is to assist me on a daily life basis, to give me instruction as to what is best in situations pertaining to me. When I work with people, I get information from their guides and teachers that will assist them, plus what I bring in.

Living in the Dimensions

"I live in the dimensions. I have always felt, if I had a problem at all, it was in being fully present in any one dimension. I am always so fragmented because of my awareness. I love to have my ears open and my eyes open and my senses open. I have one foot in one world and one foot in another two, or three, worlds.

"I do not go out to look at planets such as the recent impaction of Jupiter because I know it does not need my attention. Many things that concern other people, I have yet to be concerned about for myself. I know my own personal experience and I can only talk about what is real for me.

"When I hear of things of interest, I check in, and if it resonates with me, if it is something for me to be concerned about, I will interact. My strength is in knowing when something is going to happen. I will know. Often I will dream an event the night before it happens.

"We are all multidimensional beings whether we know it or not."

Incredible Journeys

The most incredible journeys ever taken have been made within the realms of the human mind. Perhaps for some, these journeys are simply pleasant day dreams, mental travels to far-away places on earth.

But for people who can mentally access other space/time continua, the multidimensionally aware, the journeys consist of far more than just imaginings.

The implications of multidimensional experiences for the future of humankind are staggering—for these mind journeys allow fantastic amounts of very different, advanced technological information to be brought into the third dimension.

The Spectrum of Consciousness

Robert Monroe, founder of the Monroe Institute of Applied Sciences, wrote in his book, *Ultimate Journey,* "The spectrum of consciousness ranges, seemingly endlessly, beyond time-space into other energy systems. It also continues 'downward' through animal and plant life, possibly into the sub-atomic level. Every human consciousness is active commonly in only a small segment of the consciousness continuum."[3]

The multidimensionally aware can actually travel into hyperspace and have conscious visualization and perceptions of other time/space dimensions, including accessing information through their own DNA. Often they speak of formulas, mathematical equations and atomic structure in ways quite different from current scientific thought.

The multidimensionally aware know that they see, feel and experience dimensions in addition to, and very different from, the every day third dimensional world. Advanced concepts often come to the multidimensionally aware in the form of a universal communication system, carried by light, seen as visions, symbols, numbers or heard through unusual, and not yet quite understood, sound mechanisms.

One multidimensionally aware individual we interviewed, explains:

> "The message I related to you was given to me by these impulses that are difficult to perceive, as our current condition and language interfere with meaning.
>
> "As I visualized the need for a new energy source, it was shown visually, interpreted poetically and named in linear fashion for integration into third dimensional use."

Pitfalls of Being on the Frontier

Once properly understood, nurtured and cultivated, the multidimensionally aware have much to offer humanity. They are the forerunners of a new world.

Their experiences are often difficult to verbalize for there is little common ground with third dimensional reality. The translation of these experiences is one of the most difficult challenges encountered.

---

3. Monroe, 1994. p. 100.

Yet, those multidimensionally aware people who could interpret their findings, such as Michelangelo, Leonardo Da Vinci, Albert Einstein and Nikola Tesla, were considered the geniuses who changed the world.

Hyperspace is so incredibly vast that there is no limit to the number of space/time continua that can be accessed. A multidimensionally aware individual might access the fifth or higher dimensions, or they could travel inside the very atoms of the third dimensional reality.

The Complexities of Hyperspace

The complexities of knowing their exact location within hyperspace are overcome with training and diligent effort. The position in hyperspace dictates both what will be encountered and how it should be interpreted.

Due to the high strangeness of hyperspace, each will interpret what they see in terms of their own past experiences and knowledge. The dimensions are teeming with life forms of all description, from balls of light to very concrete civilizations to completely unfamiliar objects and intelligences.

Hyperspace has not yet had any type of comprehensive study such as those of out-of-body experiences (OBEs) and dream interpretation and, indeed, such a study is virtually impossible.

Known objects and familiar third dimensional landscapes are easily comprehended, but when faced with an unknown perspective, the mind must formulate new ways of comprehension. The multidimensionally aware must expand their image building concepts to integrate the new information and also be able to correlate this new knowledge to the third dimension.

Setting Up the Right Energy

Because there is very little known about hyperspace and the intelligences who inhabit these realms, it is advisable for people, regardless of religious persuasion, to utilize an affirmation when accessing other dimensions. An affirmation is used as a means of protection for the individual, to attract the right experiences and repel the wrong ones. Setting up the right vibration and intent is important.

Monroe utilized an excellent affirmation in which he stated that he was more than his physical body, and asked for guidance from higher order beings.[4]

4. Monroe, 1985, p. 26-27.

Until much more is known about the inhabitants of hyperspace, it is not wise to be open to any and all energies which could be encountered.

Music of the Infinite

Changing mental focus between dimensions can occur instantaneously, and is often the result of outside stimuli—a harmonic resonance or key phrase, which can also act as a guide.

This harmonic resonance may come in the form of any number of things (a sound, a word, a flash of light, a sentence or an event) that acts as the opening key to a specific range of knowledge in hyperspace.

Journeying into hyperspace can be random, but specific key phrases seem to delineate given areas.

Large amounts of information can result when a multidimensionally aware individual is directed in a definite way to a given area by a harmonic resonance (activating mechanism or key phrase) which serves the same function as a query into a computer.

Although there may be unlimited data available, the query sets the parameters for specific information concerning a given topic. These key phrases can come at any time, from anywhere, such as memories, written material, TV, other people, etc.

Tones are one of the most common mechanisms for causing or enabling a person to access another dimension.

Monroe, among others, was a pioneer in exploring the effects of tones on the human brain and hyperspace experiencing. He discovered that the brain will respond or resonate by producing similar electrical signals when certain types of sound frequencies are heard.

Alternate or special states of awareness—sleep, tranquility, etc.—can be produced by hearing a certain sound pattern. A tone is heard with which the brain will resonate, and a corresponding state will ensue.

Monroe discovered that both sides of the brain could be brought into synchronization by the introduction of two tones, one in each ear. He termed this hemispheric synchronicity.[5]

Negotiating Life on Many Levels

Once the multidimensionally aware understand that they are, indeed, accessing information which exists outside known reality, the second, and

5. Monroe, 1985, p. 19

perhaps largest, challenge comes in mastering their abilities, integrating these aspects with their third dimensional selves.

Many of the multidimensionally aware are extremely advanced when they are born. Others live normal, almost ordinary, lives in their early years, until one or more events open the doors within their minds, and they are whisked, totally unprepared, through the dimensional doorway. They have entered the next stage in humanity's ability to access hyperspace.

People who are born with the awareness of hyperspace capabilities have a much easier time with integration of the experience than those who come into awareness later in life.

The multidimensionally aware have many well-developed psychic abilities, but not all psychics have developed hyperspace skills.

Multidimensionally aware experiencers differ from people who receive telepathic or mechanically forwarded information from various sources. They access philosophical and technical information, mathematics and advanced concepts within all the known disciplines by direct experience.

Gifted psychics are very highly evolved people who are beginning to come into the next stage of evolution, that of multidimensionality, with greater awareness.

The Next Step Up the Ladder

In general, our extended research seems to indicate that a statistical increase of multidimensional awareness and hyperspace experiences is taking place. However, this increase is difficult to determine because our sample is limited (as all samples are) and because past assessments of this kind are absent.

Many of the multidimensionally aware that we have interviewed seem to know that an increase of this kind of awareness is taking place—and also that the current influx of multidimensionally aware individuals is part of a greater plan to help correct the many ills now afflicting planet Earth.

A Multidimensionally Aware View of Life

Contributed By Ian Phillip White

Ian and Carol White are unique in that they are both multidimensional and have a loving relationship. When they met, both heard abbey bells and Carol saw Ian in a great burst of white light. Both feel they have had many previous lifetimes together, often as husband and wife.

They say:

"We challenge each other on many levels. Personality wise we are very different. Our relationship is both spiritual and based on our work, and that part of it is a piece of cake. The human part is the hardest part, and requires the most care and attention.

"We feel there is continual growth in the pattern and that we are doing what we are supposed to be doing, which is to honor that and through that, honor ourselves. Therefore, we are able to facilitate other people honoring themselves."

Both feel very strongly that people should, in Ian's terms, "walk their talk." To walk one's talk is to have mind and action in complete harmony and accord with each other and spirit. Many people say one thing (their talk) but actions (their walk) prove there was no reality or truth in their words. Only when actions and words are aligned and the same are people "walking their talk."

Both saw at a very early age that their multidimensional experiences were rare, and each came to terms with it in a different way. Carol first withdrew into solitude and books. Ian decided very early in life that he would keep his observations to himself until he mastered his unique capabilities.

Ian

"I was born in England, and up until the age of two, I had feelings of aloneness and separateness, crying all the time. As soon as my sister was born, I was fine. The crying stopped, mainly because we are from the same source and connected, like twins, on all levels. We are both very intuitive. It was a very happy time in a very loving environment with my parents.

"Once I asked my father what he wanted to do with his life and he said daydream. I had that role model. I would come into the house and he would be in his chair completely spaced out, daydreaming. He was living in another reality.

Knowing

"I had precognitive dreams and they were global. I might dream an aircraft crashed into a building and the next day I would read that an aircraft had crashed into a building, perhaps overseas.

"From my early childhood I would just know, though did not see, or feel. I just knew. It made life very easy in terms of knowing what was going to happen.

"Always in school I could be a member of any group I chose; I could be a friend to anyone.

"I chose at the age of four to not say things as they are, but to play on the same playing field as everyone around me. What that does, is make things work. When you tell things as they are, it doesn't work. Most people can't take that. What I chose to do was to be silent or to say the same thing in a different way. That is much more effective.

The Arts of Creating

"When I was seven and my sister five, one very hot day with not a cloud in the sky, we created a centerpiece in the garden. We put stuff together in a certain way, chanted and danced around it, and a cloud just came from nowhere, one cloud in the blue sky just rained and rained on us. It was really fun.

"My good friend Jake, a genius artist, and I would make up little creature games. A lot of creativity in terms of art work was expressed.

"I accepted everybody for who they were, and accepted myself for what I was, though I knew I was different. I knew when that difference was appropriate to express. I never projected it onto anyone, never would even think about reading other people's minds, because that just was not my awareness.

"My role, even at age nine, was teaching other kids. Give me a subject and I can know it very quickly without going through the process of learning it. If I can't know it, then I will engage my left brain so I can learn it, then I teach other people. My role has been to train for that.

Having Natural Fun

"When I was 14, a concept came to me one night when I was in bed. I developed this concept called Natural Fun—a state of being. This was just a state of being wherein it was OK for people to be with each other, and in which there was no judgment. It was a space of total acceptance. The concept changed my life.

"I had had no contact with anybody with cosmic ideas. I had an idea about it, but no way of knowing how to get there. It was kind of a tricky time because I had no idea what to do.

Life-Altering Events

"In my mid-teen years, my father had a very serious accident in which he almost died. His recovery took about nine months. Emotionally and physically this was a big trauma for the family.

"My relationship with him went from great to horrible, for at that time I assumed his role and felt responsible for everything and everyone. My mother turned to me to ask what she should do. It was a very challenging time.

"When he returned, my father had suffered a great change of personality and became very paranoid. He felt that I was a threat to him. Had I had no awareness nor compassion, I could have been really angry with him, but I knew this was something that came from another personality and it was not his fault. It was really difficult for me. It was incongruent, knowing how loving he could be and how angry he had become.

"There was no natural fun present in my life, so I turned to artificial fun, to alcohol, to sustain me.

"I honor that part of my life, for though it was very difficult, it taught me a lot. It was memorable but fun. My life seems to be on a very fast track, and perhaps I needed to get all these experiences in my teenage years instead of at a later time. I condensed. Because the consciousness was there, it wasn't difficult; it was enjoyable. In another type of consciousness, it could have been devastating and I do not recommend it.

"When I was 17 I went to Israel and stayed in a kibbutzim, and it was great. There I really got in touch with myself in many ways, in that sense of being I had intuited. It was wonderful, that space and energy was very, very clear.

"I have always been oriented toward community, so I could be with many groups of people and still be very much myself, for within that there was no pretense. Everybody accepted me.

The Fine Line Between Perception and Creation

"I am essentially a designer. I can look at anything and see how to do it better—energy, health, healing, seeing.

"Other designers may also have done that, the information is all from universal consciousness. I would have all these ideas, which I identified as my own, then someone would say, 'Plato did that'!

Nothing original here! That was really frustrating in my teenage years, until I understood that I'm not the creator but the channel.

"I began discovering the fine line between perception and creation. Was something already going to happen in the future or was I creating it? I didn't realize for a time that I was actually creating. I wasn't perceiving; I was creating. I would be creating energetically and things would come physically.

"What I was doing was perceiving my creation. Now that is my work. That is what I do and teach.

"I find that at least once a year I need to take training, to find what other people are doing, because truth overlaps. If my role is to bring everything together, then when I undertake that training, I know what is working and where it fits into the big picture.

Breakthroughs

"I went through a period when I wanted to do something 'creative,' to find my niche. I had no external guidance so I went into marketing as a market researcher. I would organize projects and know the answer beforehand, so I could write reports weeks in advance. I used all my skills in business consulting.

"It wasn't about reading how an individual was, but how the organization could best function. I worked with the organization, not the people. It was a great success.

"I started studying macrobiotics. In the space of one day I stopped eating junk food.

"One Christmas Eve, I had a big breakthrough. I experienced 'natural fun.' As soon as I experienced it, that was it. I had been waiting and waiting for this experience, but it just wasn't time when I was fourteen, now it was time.

"I realized all individuals wanted someone to be present for them, someone fully present, to trust. I was doing that and in that space there was acceptance. In order to be fully present there was no judgment. It was a very strong space of knowing

"I went to Findhorn and there experienced a major opening. I was lying down and my body started to move. I felt like someone spiraled in. It was freaky and physically painful.

"From that time on, I became a natural empath. When I walked into a room where there was anyone in pain, I felt it in my body. I had no control over it. I was a total sponge, I picked up any kind of pain. It was devastating. I couldn't continue; I couldn't function.

"I had to learn to deal with having become a sponge. It took me six to twelve weeks to figure out how to control this ability. When working with people, I had pulled their negative energies through me in a natural release flow. I had to learn to control that, learn what was happening and stop taking it all in.

"I went to a place in Greece, a healing center, and just lay on the beach for two weeks and healed myself. I found I could do things without touching people, straight .

"I was in a very peaceful energy space. I could see inside the body and work with that.

Developing a Philosophy

"I developed a philosophy where I could be totally multidimensional, still be in my body and be present right now. I could finally know that if information was relevant, it could come through right now and if it was not, it could come through later.

"My baseline intent is to live in the moment. It is important to me, that if I am going to be present with someone, I am going to be present. If I am not going to be fully present, then I am not going to be with them. Every individual I talk to, I recognize the Divine within them.

"I also have a baseline intent that I won't come into contact with those who are not ready for me. I know the possibilities of creating and that we can create Heaven on earth.

"Most of the people I met were talking and talking, it was all head stuff, things they had read. For me, if I haven't experienced something, I don't talk about it and I certainly do not teach it. I follow what is right, what is guided. If it is not guided, I don't do it.

Special People

"When I met Carol, I had just ended a relationship that was traumatic. I realized I could only be with people who knew what I was and could support me in being that.

"I was fasting at the time. I missed an introductory hypnotherapy class on Sunday that I had planned to go to, and went to another on Wednesday instead, only to learn that the same person was teaching both classes.

"There I met the second person who could actually see who I was, a reader who said, 'You are not supposed to be here on this plane. You don't need to be here anymore.'

"I already knew that. I am here by choice, not necessarily for me, but to help others. One thing I find difficult is to find people at a level that can support me in what I am and what I do.

"In meeting Carol, there was recognition. I heard church bells. It felt like playtime for me. I had been with people who were just talking about spirituality and the people around her were doing things. We connected. I felt guided to talk to Carol and called her a couple of times.

"It was soon clear to me that she was not in healing and had a greater purpose than she had yet manifested. I started teaching classes and took Carol with me, dragging her out of her safety net, so she could present her own experiences. I literally had to force her to lead meditations and to teach. She was so reticent initially, she had to be pushed.

Forms of Duality

After a long pause in deep thought, Ian continued.

"There are two forms of duality. The first is Western materialism, and in , western society particularly, that is how people can really botch things up. The second is the Eastern state of being out of body. There, also, people can get off their path by thinking things are out there and not here.

"If you look at each of these philosophies you can find a thread. It is nothing new. I see people who are dependent on others for their guidance; dependent, but do not follow it.

"They get a message to not do this on this date, or this will result in a negative learning experience. They are told they need to work on this issue, then it will not happen.

"But the person does not work on it, they do not follow through and, therefore, create a negative experience. Most of those experiences occur because people want to believe, but don't know how to follow through. They do not bring it into their daily lives.

"If we are to create a wonderful reality here, it must start with the individual taking responsibility.

Finding a Sense of Acceptance

"I do not know that I am so different. I do know that I am more of the same, more open. I am choosing to myself.

"For the many people that are incredibly sensitive, particularly those who are kinesthetic, whose feelings are deeper, the key is to find acceptance. It is critical for people who are developing their abilities, or are becoming themselves, to have that sense of acceptance. Without it, they can feel like a freak, or feel they are special, and then it can become an ego thing. The acceptance is the key.

"They are born into a world, or belief system, that says it is not OK to be themselves. It is not safe to be who and what they are, so the support is necessary for the individuals who come in that way, or who develop in that way, to be told it is OK to be."

The Ability to Perceive

Ian teaches different tools and techniques.

"I believe it is necessary to perceive effectively to be able to heal. If you can't perceive, and by that I mean feel, hear, know, you are more unlikely to heal completely.

"It is necessary to integrate the sub-personalities, make connection with the higher self. I teach perception and awareness techniques for releasing. My whole philosophy is getting the person's higher self into their body.

"There are techniques for releasing. When you release something you must put something in, because if you don't, what you are trying to release can come back in the same old place.

"Reconstruction is required, as well as protection, in terms of energy work. Essentially the whole process is to get a person aligned with the higher self."

Life is Integration

"When I came to the United States and sampled different lifestyles, I perceived people actually bringing joy into this way of thinking. Thinking that I am me, but with fun, too. The core for me has always been thinking that every individual I meet has that divine spark. You can choose to be within divinity at any point in time.

"Life is integration. I have a vision of what I am to be and do and I feel I am doing that.

"There was a point where I got stuck. When I was a business consultant, that wasn't really me, so I had to go back into that arena and reconcile being me. What I find is that until I move into each and every situation that I have created, any situation where I wasn't me, I have to go back into that and recreate it so that I am me in that situation. Once I have done that, I never have to not be me again."[6]

---

6. Ian Phillip White designs and facilitates energy empowerment training which provides tools to develop paranormal perception abilities, integrate sub personalities, find connections with the Higher Self, release blocks on all levels and to learn how to filter negativity out of life. He also provides a correspondence program, intuitive counseling and R.E.T. a form of Rapid Eye Movement coupled with neuralinguistic body movements. He gives workshops all over the U.S.

Chapter Two

More Than the Third Dimension

History relates that there has been an abundance of people who had the ability to access higher dimensions through their minds. These people have been called prophets, seers, diviners. Even science fiction writers, such as H.G. Wells and Jules Verne, have shown uncanny knowledge of the future in both their inventions and their writings.

The multidimensionally aware are truly a new breed of human, forerunners on the evolutionary path.

Although many more people with these super abilities will be born beginning in the 1990s, many born in the 1940s are now reaching their full potential.

Perhaps the most renowned multidimensionally aware person of this century was Albert Einstein. His ability to access regions beyond the third dimension brought in a new physics and opened the door to the development of much of today's technology.

Hyperspace

Hyperspace is defined as the spatial dimensions beyond time and the reality known as the three dimensional world, defined by height, width and depth of space. It is also referred to as the unified field, the second universe or multidimensionality. The third dimension, which humans experience, exists within hyperspace as a subset or one of many dimensions. This reality, according to theoretical physicists, may also be one of many, many parallel universes.

The existence of higher dimensions and hyperspace is well grounded in scientific hypotheses. In his book, *Hyperspace,* Dr. Michio Kaku states that a new geometry came into existence as early as 1854 when the theory of higher dimensions was introduced by Georg Bernhard Riemann. A rather quiet, small lecture was given before the faculty of the University of Gottingen in Germany.

> "In one masterful stroke, like opening up a musty, darkened room to the brilliance of a warm summer's sun, Riemann's lecture exposed the world to the dazzling properties of higher-dimensional space.
>
> "His profoundly important and exceptionally elegant essay, 'On the Hypotheses which Lie at the Foundation of Geometry,' toppled the pillars of classical Greek geometry, which had successfully weathered all assaults by skeptics for 2 millennia. The old geometry of Euclid, in which all geometric figures are two or three dimensional, came tumbling down as a new Riemannian geometry emerged from its ruins."

Dr. Kaku further states that the arts and sciences would be vastly influenced by the emergence of the concept of higher dimensions. Within 30 years, art, philosophy and the European literature reflected ideas of the mysterious fourth dimension.

Sixty years later Einstein utilized Riemann's four-dimensional geometry to explain the creation and evolution of the universe. Physicists, 130 years later, would expand from Riemann's four dimensions to a ten-dimensional geometry to attempt to unite all the laws of the physical universe.[1]

The Fourth Dimension

The brilliance of Albert Einstein formulated that time constituted the fourth dimension, a temporal rather than a spatial dimension. Quantum physics opened entirely new micro worlds, defining the smallest particles known to date. Einstein spent his later years working on a unified field theory in which higher dimensions formed the matrix in which to unite all of physics.

Today's theoretical physicists have clearly defined hyperspace, introduced the existence of "wormholes" or tunnels between dimensions, alternate universes, and theoretically, access to both the past and the future. Some of these physicists, such as Kip Thorne and Michael Morris of the California Institute of Technology and Ulvi Yurtsever of the University of Mich-

1. Kaku, 1994, pp. 30-31.

igan, are searching for ways to access hyperspace by a mechanical, third-dimensional "time machine."[2]

The Future of Interaction

There are other scientists who are, or have, incorporated the enormous potential of the human mind into their research of higher dimensions and the future of humankind.

Dr. James J. Hurtak, in *Negotiating With Other Worlds*, presents his views:

> "When you begin to work with your body as your island universe first, when you can begin to work with your body-mind as a laboratory of the Spirit, and when you can begin to see in your inner consciousness the naturalistic law of all evolutionary possibilities within the Cosmic Law regarding the other evolutions connected with you, then you will realize the profound notion that wherever you go, you will carry on the same love and recognition and compassion that you have started here.
>
> "It is, therefore, basic for us to prepare ourselves for space encounters on many levels of both the physical and mental, as well as the varied levels of meta-creation. Higher Intelligence seems to have brought us through some 30 years of 'consciousness conditioning' to accept their presence, and their concerns for our weapons of destruction. It may take another 30 years to complete that orientation, the end product being that we will have the ability to enter into a galactic family of nations. Indeed, we may encounter our brothers and sisters in space not simply in terms of the physical happenings, but in terms of the more important consciousness inner happenings already written within our soul and body. Humankind might discover that throughout the universe we are part of a Divine Creation and that creation inherently respects the divine road map of a space-time journey into the many branches of the tree of Life."[3]

A Multidimensionally Aware View of Life

Contributed By Blanche

> "I can see being born. I was in a calm fluid motion of peace and serenity, then all of a sudden there was a bright light and confusion and I was being bombarded with words and thoughts and images

2. Kaku, 1994, p. 245.
3. Hurtak, 1990, pp. 27-28.

that did not make sense. I tried to put it into focus and some kind of reality and my mind just would not do it. I felt like a seed in the ground that had suddenly begun to germinate. Changes took place, chemical reactions, a break through to the soil. That is birth—there you are."

Born multidimensionally aware, Blanche can remember arguing and saying in her mind, "Don't tell me that. That is not what I see, don't tell me that. It was as if I were not being heard." Some part of her knew that the problem was that her seeing was different.

"When I was small, my father would take me under his arm and hold me, protecting me from the chaos I created in that reality. I think my father always knew, was more aware of the reality I saw, for he, too, saw, but had conformed to societal dictations. Perhaps the transition for him was easier, less traumatic.

Always Analyzing

"I was very silent, always withdrawn into my own world, that dream world. To me it was more real than what my eyes saw. So I began, rather than fighting others, to accept, but to not let them interfere or take away from what was within me. I just let them be who they were, and I went off to be what I was. The someone I knew I was the day I was born.

"But rather than walk away, I incorporated understanding into my mind. Understanding of why people were as they were, who they were, and what they were. I was always analyzing what caused people to behave in the way they did. I did not let it change me or bend me. I think at that point I had realized that the power was within me, though I do not believe I verbalized it.

"It took me many years to perceive that I fought in a combat zone. I don't regret those years. I see them as a lot of energy going out, a lot of negative energy. I was running from the shadows and the dreams that came and repeatedly tried to show me myself. I would see myself in the physical reality running, competing, opposing. I was a fast runner. I could beat all the boys, I could beat everyone. That to me was proof that, inside, my strength was beyond anyone else's. Most of my life I always felt I was being pulled against the tide rather than flowing with it.

"I am now aware that I came into this world as a warrior. At the time I was not aware. Now I have put it into perspective; it is clear. The dream that went on for years, that ability for me to run. In my dreams I was running down a path that was dark with shadows. The light would only come through the tree leaves from the street lights. It was dark.

"I could see the light at the very end of the path and I would start running as fast as I could to get to the end. The shadows and darkness and evil would pass through my mind, and all of a sudden my legs wouldn't move. I would feel someone behind me, just ready to grab me and my legs would stop. I couldn't run. Though I could see the light at the end, I couldn't get there. I would awaken to this present reality again. When I was 27, I let go of the fear, and the dreams stopped.

"I just sort of evolved until then. One day my aunt said, 'You have been the ugly duckling all your life and now you have turned into a swan.' I looked at her and knew what she meant. I finally had it all together. I began to grow. But prior to that, it had been combatability rather than compatibility.

Negotiating Within the World

"I began to use the establishment instead of fighting it. I chose to turn and face my enemy. I developed compassion for those around me. I was so very much aware of that. I had always wanted to be involved in the medical profession, especially working with those that were ill. I wanted to give strength to them and to understand their diseases in a way that I knew I could perceive.

"I enrolled in medical training to become a Registered Nurse. I didn't agree with the courses, the educational aspect of it. It was difficult for me because I saw it in a different way. I didn't agree with the teachings, the principles of chemistry, biology.

"It was as if they did not have a full understanding of how the body worked. Many times I would argue that test questions were misleading. I understood it differently. The educational process, the part of putting pieces together to get there, was the hardest part for me.

"Once I got out of training, into the practical aspects of it, the hands on part was natural for me. I went into orthopedics and medical surgery preoperative and post-operative phases. I spent two years there, then two years in intensive coronary care.

"I took special courses, advanced courses in electrocardiograms and the different pharmacologies. Then I realized that, too, was the same old thing. I didn't believe in the treatment; I didn't believe in the drugs.

"I then went to work in the Emergency Room. It was always different. One minute there would not be one person in the ER and the next minute there would be 18. Accidents, gun shot wounds, immediate trauma, all demanding quick reaction.

"It was hands on, life and death situations where I knew something could be done. I had a feeling, a knowing. In the emergency room, with a full arrest case, I knew what to do next. I enjoyed those years, those were the best.

"With me, there was a knowing. I can remember listening to people and their complaints. Once a 70-year-old man walked in with a limp and told the doctor he had severe left hip pain. The doctor said to give him codeine for the pain; it was just arthritis. I walked back with him and when he got on the bed there was no pain.

"I thought this is not arthritis, this is something else. It was an aneurysm with referred pain into his hip. I checked his circulation, his pulse, and I went to the doctor and said he has an obstruction, probably in the abdominal aorta. Had the doctor not accepted my diagnosis, the man would have died of an abdominal aortic aneurysm.

"But the doctor listened to me, and I became known as an intuitive diagnostician. It was a natural thing, by feeling, by touching and knowing, more than anything else.

"For the first time I could apply all that I am without conflict. No fight, it just flowed. I finally felt such a smooth peaceful rhythm in my life; that was where I belonged.

"The doctors enjoyed the fact I was there, knowing that if they overlooked something, I would find it. I was very thorough in checking. They came to depend on me, trust me, honor my intuition. This was the first recognition that what I was, was a good, helpful thing. It was a natural thing.

I Began to Flow and Not Fight

"I began to let my senses feel and interpret the understanding of why things were the way they were, what was acceptable within the demands of civilizations and cultures.

"I began to see different cultures throughout the world, even throughout the United States, all the different levels and monstrosities in the patterns that we weave. I began to look and see people and to understand why they did what they did, and how it affected me.

"I began to flow with it and not fight anymore. Though I gave up the fight, I didn't give up my belief system. In a sense I made the decision to understand and fit into the environment I was in, while keeping inward integrity. I began to see that other people had emotions, rights and feelings. I wanted to understand them rather than just oppose.

"At age 27, I looked into the mirror, confronted myself and found who I was. I said I know who you are. Life changed, dramatically changed, at this point, an 180° turn. It was a pivotal point.

"I believe I took the right step and it began to manifest. Everyone that knew me commented on it. I think that is what it is all about, getting to the point of release and acceptance of self. It was as if, when I was born, I knew who I was and tried to grow in that way. But I found I was confronted by the opposition of this world and the demands and, I fought that all those years.

"Finally, when I let it go, I just slipped into place and realized and accepted myself for who I was. I stopped running, stopped fighting. It was a natural thing that was meant to be.

"I began to realize we were all one and the same and there is give and take. There was an acceptance with no judgment. If I accepted others for who they were as I accepted myself, and just kept the flow going, they became more accepting of me. They could sense, could feel there was no fight, no battle anymore. It was a give and take, a balance I had never felt before. There had always been a disequilibrium.

"It was a stage in my maturation. I look at life like a chemical reaction from where it started to where it gained enough momentum to turn itself around, with wisdom and knowledge. Those early years were one great cataclysmic spark of bombardment with reality. Others get it much earlier; it took me until I was 27.

My Soul Mate

"I met, at 29, the man of my dreams. I knew in that very moment from the sparkle in his eyes, that wherever he led me was where I was going. His recognition of me was instantaneous, too. When we looked into each other's eyes, we knew and we were never separated from that moment on. He looked at me and knew what I had longed for all my life.

"We came together like a flower with blooming petals and everything kept growing. He was a farmer, everything I had ever dreamed of. We had a very natural relationship being human, with romantic love, with children, with overcoming the little stresses of everyday life.

"I like to think we developed divine love, something that went much further than just this family romantic love. We understood each other beyond our inadequacies. We looked to the future, did a lot of dreaming, a lot of theorizing, hoping for a better life.

"Being a farmer and having the type of mind he did, he understood many things and enlightened me. Together we developed theories on how to correct the environment and correct the plant life. His love was the alfalfa plant. He would stand out in his fields and talk to the plants and their love and vibration would speak to him.

"We spent hours theorizing on how to correct the imbalance. Having been a nurse, I wanted to cure disease, and I felt we are one and the same—what is affecting the plants affects humans.

"If we could find a commonality, a simple thread that bonds and unifies the cause of disease, we could find a cure. We spent ten years theorizing. After the children would go to bed, we would have coffee and talk of dreams that he never shared with anyone else, nor did I.

I Was Dying

"We had moved into the house on the farm, where my husband had been a farmer all his life. I had been ill most of the 12 years we had been running the place. We couldn't figure out why. I was dying in agony—320 PO_2 (blood gas). The oxygenation, the exchange was 62 BP hypertensive."

In December of 1993, Blanche was ill to the point of dying. Her blood pressure dropped to 60/40 and she found herself up in the corner of the room. She had had many experiences of being out of her body during this period of time.

She saw her husband running frantically around the bed, from side to side, saying she looked like she was dying. At that point she immediately came back into her body, telling him she had never felt so well. Her blood pressure came back up.

She recalled having many visions unfold before her eyes. Later, she would share these visions with her husband, but for a year she kept them to herself. She knew she had been leaving her body, felt she had been up in the corner of her room looking through the walls. She thought that was all a part of dying. She wanted to get well, but did not know that she would.

> "I felt I knew I was dying. When I would close my eyes and lay down at night, I kept seeing geometrical patterns, spheres. I would watch them pass through my mind in different colors. I was seeing faces, like videos, that I didn't recognize, didn't understand."

The Exchange

Her husband made a pact with God, to please not let her die but to take him instead and, three months later he was gone and she was well.

> "Shortly before his death, my husband began telling me he would see visions of his grandmother, who had been dead since 1959. He was frightened.
>
> "He saw his grandmother pushing the upstairs water heater out of the house, telling him something criminal, something horrible, was going to happen in the house. Then she disappeared out the door. After his death I had the water heater upstairs checked and it was burning noxious fumes.
>
> "The TV had been coming on by itself in the middle of the night and my husband would find himself watching a program that was just exactly what he needed to hear about my symptoms. A doctor was discussing the neurotoxins and how toxic conditions manifest, how they affect the mind and body. All my symptoms were exactly what the doctor was stating on the program.
>
> "He began to realize something was terribly wrong. He called a laboratory analysis company and had the water in the house tested. He found a European technologist who would come out and survey the electromagnetic fields around the house and the chemical residues in the house and in the air.
>
> "When he died, I followed up on that and found over 38 different chemicals. There were low trace amounts, but the synergistic effect of one potentiating the other was probably lethal. There were high formaldehyde levels, two of which had been outlawed for 15 years. There were chlordane and PCP which are neurotoxins absorbed through the skin and affect the nervous system.
>
> "I, too, saw his grandmother and she told me that what killed her was killing us. I had to find it and stop it.

Death Is Not the End

"The morning of Friday, March 24, 1994, around 5:20 A.M., I got out of bed. Like any other day I had to get the kids off to school. When I woke the lights were on, and my husband wasn't in bed. I went into the living room, the TV was on, his slippers were at the foot of the chair. The footrest of the chair wasn't tucked in. His belt was on the floor. I called and he didn't answer. I thought he might be in the washroom off the kitchen, which was quite a distance from the library and the bedroom.

"I saw the dog. Usually he got up and jumped around, but he was just laying there, looking at me. It occurred to me my husband had gone to the office early. I opened the door to the garage and when I opened the door I walked into a pool of blood. There he lay, dead, a bloody baseball bat by his head. I saw murder. I called 911 and told them my husband had been murdered.

"At that point I stood there in a kind of light. It was 5:24 in the morning. It was dark, but there was light, and it seemed to permeate every cell in my body. His life was gone, I knew that. My life flashed before me. I saw myself looking out of a child's eyes into a world that had no meaning, no understanding. Words were just an apparent facade that we let overwhelm us.

"I saw where I was going, what I had to do, and where I was. I was well, I was healed. The whole purpose of what I had to do now unfolded before me. I have never lost sight of where I have to go. I maintained love inside of me. I felt the loss; I knew he was gone. I couldn't have him back, but I knew the purpose of why we had come together had yet to unfold. In realizing that my soul mate, my partner, was gone. I shifted from this reality and to a point, denied this reality. I shifted into a higher plane of understanding

"I got the children up and told them their father was gone and that they had to stay away from the garage area, because the coroner was there and the sheriff and the police. I got in the shower to freshen up. The calls had been made, family was on their way. I decided it was time I could cry.

"When I got in the shower, the shower walls began to vibrate. I became a part of them and they became a part of me. I shifted into another realm, another reality. I started talking to my husband and I begged him to please not leave me. I knew his spirit was still in me. I could see the white light piercing me and with every breath I could feel the air go in and come out and fill me and cleanse me. I asked him not to leave me. I begged God, please, to help me; what was I going to do? Words came out of my head into my thoughts and were not my words. They were 'Forgive them, for they know not what they do.'

"If it hadn't been for those thoughts in that moment, I would have lost the love inside me and been bitter and resentful. I would not have had the life I have had since his death. But I chose to hear and believe those words with all my heart. In spite of the reality of what had happened, that he had been murdered, I decided that death was not final. There is a spiritual world, and he would be with me and guide me.

Making Choices

"I chose to let go. I chose to follow the love in my heart and the forgiveness I was being reminded of constantly. I chose to follow through and find the answers on how to treat disease. It was our dream. It was how we had spent our time together. I knew I would rather do that than lay down and die with him.

"So I decided to stand tall, stand strong. From that day on I felt this intense love inside me, this intense vibration, and a flow with the atmosphere and the colors around me. I felt balanced and healed.

"This miraculous change was visible. The following morning my daughter said, 'Mom, you have lost 20 years and you are glowing. You are glowing like Dad was last night when I got up to talk to him, before he died. He was glowing and now you are glowing. What is going on? It is a miracle.'

"Comments like that came from others—my mother, my sister. Everybody that touched me seemed to be awakened and understood what I was saying. They were a little confused that I didn't cry more, for they knew how much I loved my husband, but they understood.

"I began speaking in a very simplistic way, yet in one which defined the complexities. I seemed to make the road clear for them, as well as myself, that we all had to live in this reality.

"The stresses of the day no longer bothered me. There was always the thought, 'We/he will always be with you. The fears of the day cannot harm you.'

"As I lived with that thought the stresses of the day that I had thought to be so incredible, getting up in the morning, taking care of the children's needs, getting them off to school, managing the house, managing the business, was part and parcel of all this information that I had been given. It was all one.

Continuing the Work

"His life and my life and our purpose in coming together was to lead to that. It was a lesson, an atonement for me, to prepare me for the future.

"I think he was warned by his grandmother's spirit, whom many have seen in that house, myself included. I think it was all part of the purpose, and I saw my future with a directive unlike any other time in my life

"From research, books and lectures, I began to document what we had theorized, a principle not previously applied. I began to put together the cause, the reason and the cures for all diseases.

"From that point on I realized the visions I had been seeing in my mind were manifested due to the things we had dreamed together all our life. Our love was now a divine love, not one to lay down and die, but to go on.

"I chose from that point on to live in this other dimension, this other reality of knowledge, seeing my thoughts in my mind and in my dreams, and making them come true. If I didn't dare to dream those dreams, they would never come true.

"The choice I made, then and there, changed my whole reality. I had an understanding that was profound. I could overcome anything that occurred, any reality I was confronted with in this dimension, in this world, because I could see my purpose unfolding. It had flashed before my mind like a video—the moment I found my husband dead.

"I knew it was his spirit guiding me, in addition to my own, telling me what I had to do. I had to go on. I had to do it with love and truth inside me, not with bitterness and resentment of his loss. Romantic love is something we put so much emphasis on, but I realized that from the moment we met, our love was one of divine love, and that would carry me throughout time.

Trusting the Guidance

"I realized that we had just touched the surface in our day dreaming. Those dreams in all our hours of driving tractors and nurturing the fields were what I was going to make come true, make a reality in this dimension. It was for him, as well as for myself and our children.

"I decided to become more introspective, to listen to my intuition and be guided by what my thoughts were telling me. I began to realize the visions I had been seeing in my mind were teaching me, guiding me.

"So I trusted those and I didn't trust the external reality that seemed to have pushed me all my life. It had pushed me in a way I felt was backward, pushed me in one direction when my mind told me to go the opposite way. My life now turned around and I was going with the flow to my ultimate destination, where I was to be something I had dreamed of all my life.

"I had found my love, dreamed with him for twelve years, but I had to go on. Death was not final. I had never really believed that anyway. My brother had died a year before and, from the moment he died, I understood.

"I really knew then that death was not final. It was not the end. We lived in a spiritual world, we just could not see it. We had been deluded by the veils that drape our reality and in that instant when I found my husband dead those veils had been lifted.

"After my husband died, I didn't have him to theorize with any longer. When I did not have him to bounce my thoughts off of and I didn't have his input, I think his spirit invited me to look inside myself and find the answers.

The Answers Came Rapidly and Synchronistically

"When I stopped only talking about it, the synchronicities of the day began to happen very rapidly. I would find myself in bookstores picking up books I would not ordinarily read. At home, I would open to a certain page and find the answer I needed. Simultaneously, I would turn on the TV and there would be another answer in my search.

"My dream to find a cure for disease, his dream to do the same, was something that was very clear now and I followed the visions. I relished my time alone with my thoughts and began to write, automatically, the things I was seeing and feeling and the synchronicities began to occur every day and every night.

"This influx of information had occurred for a year prior to his death, but I didn't acknowledge it because I didn't know how to tell anyone what I was seeing.

"With his spiritual guidance, it became more pronounced without him in this reality with me. I wouldn't even have to close my eyes and I would begin to see and the thoughts would filter in with an explanation of what I was seeing, or what I had been told on the TV, heard on the radio or read in an article in a magazine.

"In the library I found books on molecular physics. I began to look at the atomic structure and the principles of reversing electromagnetism. I talked with the heads of the Physics Departments and the Research Foundations at Berkeley and at Stanford.

"This has continued daily, moment by moment. I have not really had mood swings in this reality. I have had moments of grief and crying, which I equate with being normal, but the negative aspects of his loss, and the losses that have occurred since his death, have been compensated for because of the wonderful reality of that dimension.

"I go with the positive in all this learning. I get up at 2:00 or 3:00 A.M. and I read books and write 20 or 30 pages, mostly poetry. I then try to define very clearly what I have seen. Every night when I go to bed I am studying, researching. If I don't have a book open in this reality, there seems to be one every night in my mind and it is so tied in that the things I have studied previously begin to unfold the next day."

Chapter Three

Children of Tomorrow

Tomorrow's children will express themselves in wonderfully colorful and interesting ways.

Andrew Thomas Weaver, who lives in Raleigh, North Carolina, created and illustrated a book at the age of six-and-a-half that was so remarkable his parents reproduced it in 1994.

Titled *Freefall's Fantastic Journey,* it begins: "When Asteroid Andrew dreamed at night, he transformed into a photon-blue interplanetary explorer named Freefall. Freefall's aeroballistic hyperbolic navigation guided him to the planet Echo in the Galileo Galaxy."[1]

This is not exactly what the average first grader writes. Andrew also enjoys science, freeze-tag, roller-skating and planetariums.

Incredible Joy

Tomorrow's children have a bright look, a shine in their eyes, a twinkle that says, "I know something you don't know." Yet when a person looks them in the eye and mentally replies to them, "I do know," they respond, sometimes with surprise. These children have an incredible passion and joy that is obvious in everything they say, do and create.

They enjoy playing with mud, clay, finger paints, any artwork that involves touch and feel. They tend to draw swirls in outward spirals and often there is a two-finger track mark down through their drawings. There is usually a light source such as the sun in their art. Some of the very young ones put disproportionately large eyes on the stick figure drawings of humans.

---

1. Weaver, 1994.

Early Indicators

The multidimensionally aware children may talk at a very young age. David Henry Feldman, in *Nature's Gambit*, a study of child prodigies, tells of one family in his study group whose child spoke two and three word sentences at age three months, reported his dreams at age six months, saying they were TV in his head.[2]

When these special children start talking, it is sometimes evident that they have memories they cannot make others understand.

A multidimensionally aware child was born to parents who were aware of what he was to be. The mother loved deep sea chanteys and sang them often to the unborn child. He talked at age six months, and very early in his life, could relate his dreams.

He was only two years old when he told his mother that when he was still in the dark place, before he came out into the light, many times there was this awful booming sound which he could not get away from, no matter how hard he tried. His mother realized it was the booming sea chanteys she had sung to him.

Often they press their two forefingers together, indicative of a listening stance, but they do not process well auditorially. The person speaking is not being heard. Often saying, "Huh?" and "What?", it is apparent their attention is elsewhere, necessitating a repetition of the instruction or question. Though appearing to be listening, they are not.

Although they cling, the children tend to be hyperactive and wriggle, which makes it difficult for the parent to hold them. Told to sit down and be still, they are at a loss.

Highly tactile, the children will constantly touch everything. The parent's only safeguard is to teach them to touch very gently because there is no way to keep them from experiencing the world through their fingers.

Knowledge Beyond Their Years

Their outlook on the entire third dimension is different because they are connecting to other dimensions. When looking at a person or an object, they see beyond. It is like being able to view two television sets simultaneously in the mind, which was the description given by one 12-year-old.

They may have a grasp of very technical knowledge, especially energy to matter to energy technology and unique spatial relationships.

2. Feldman and Goldsmith, 1986, p .7.

Often multidimensionally aware children have a heightened interest in people of other cultures, the environment, nature and wildlife, space and the universe.

They have a precocious knowledge of how complex things work and the deeper natural order of things generally obtained only in higher education, if available there at all.

As they mature, they are filled with a knowledge that comes forth without any visible external source of input. Parents and peers may not understand the source of this information, and that is part of what sets them apart and makes them feel so strange.

In remembering her childhood, Posey related to us:

> "While floating in the bath tub, around age five or six, the room would become a brilliant golden color and watery, like liquid air. I would float and be free.
>
> "Visions would come, such as being able to see inside myself and recognize that I was made up of small pieces, so small I couldn't see them with plain vision, and that each one was shaped like a sun with planets moving around it. All of these planets with their suns were so small, yet packed close together, and formed my physical body.
>
> "The knowledge went further to describe our sun and planet as a place or cell of a much larger beingness. It was my secret and it stayed my secret, and no one taught me that it was bad or wrong because they did not know about it. It was easy to accept because it was the most real and loving thing I experienced in my childhood.

Bright Stars In a Dark World

Ingo Swann believes the human mind is so extraordinary that it is hard to see it as a product of evolution on Earth. The biodynamics are so ultra-extraordinary that it is completely impossible to explain them via Earth-based metaphors or frames of reference.

The human being—child, adult or aged—possesses an astonishing array of abilities, potential or developed. In his research Swann has found that no listing of human abilities exists.

He sees that children are mind-programmed only to fit some kind of social situation: religious, nonreligious, scientific, technological, philosophical, social. Abilities that do not fit in any of these categories are socially suppressed, which means that someone other than the child determines what they can, or should, become. A few, very few, talented ones arise above this social programming.[3]

The multidimensionally aware children are often born into families who do not, in any measure, understand nor appreciate their abilities, and as a result, the young are confused and often rebellious.

In his book, *The Omega Project*, Kenneth Ring pointed out how often child abuse is found in the children that show unusual talents.[4]

One theory holds that these children are so different from their parents that the familiar methods of parenting are totally ineffective. This leaves the parent with a feeling of helplessness, an inability to control, that often expresses itself in anger.

The children know they are different and do not fit in. There is always a wall between them and others. Even when popular among their peers, they feel they are never understood. There is a great need in them to be accepted, and acknowledged for what they are, for these children are aware that most people cannot understand the advanced information they access, or in what manner they access it.

One multidimensionally aware individual's story is typical of many:

> "I always felt different from other children. I didn't think I belonged to my parents. I didn't feel the way my brothers and sisters did. I felt like I knew more than everybody. Even at seven I was drawn into my parents arguments to referee them.
>
> "People used to comment that I was a very intense child. I was serious; I never felt like a child, always like an adult. I envied kids who were just kids. I didn't feel that way at all.
>
> "I had a lot of friends, didn't have any problem making friends, but I got bored easily and could never stay long with the play everybody else seemed so caught up in. I would go to another friend who was a different type of person. I have always cultivated people until I got bored. Like visiting different countries, that was the way I picked my friends.
>
> "Around age 16, I began having precognitive dreams about people. I knew if I wanted something in my life, I just had to dream about it and it would happen. I knew if I wanted a boy to like me, I would be so excited if I had the dream because then it was going to happen! It was almost like if I dreamt it, I could create it. It would be.

---

3. Swann, Ingo. Correspondence with the authors. April 4, 1993.
4. Ring, 1993.

"I did this in relationships, in dancing, in school work, in painting. Whatever I could dream, I could be. I started having psychic awareness about the same time. I would just know things, but I didn't talk about it. I felt no need to share these things with anyone.

Visions of Another World

Others rarely understand the source of these children's knowledge and can only relate to their own experiences of how they, themselves, learned things through asking questions, overhearing conversations, the media or through reading. Adults usually do not understand the concept of "just knowing from within" and look for an outside source of knowledge.

One such child remembers seeing and hearing things that were not real to anyone around her. She was taken out of kindergarten because she was so engrossed in watching the swirls of color and forms around her classmates, that she no longer responded to what was happening on this third-dimensional level. She remembered hearing people's thoughts and seeing the thoughts take form. She was taken by her worried parents for a psychiatric evaluation when she was six.

Many of these children are being misdiagnosed by the medical profession and put on strong medications in an attempt to reduce the "symptoms," such as the "inner voices" and the visions they speak of.

Highly psychically advanced, the children are usually very precognitive and often know in advance of events, sometimes accurately foretelling of a death or accident. This is often misunderstood by adults and the child usually suffers as a result.

General social conditioning states that "other realities" are only imagination, fantasies or make believe. Because those other realities are very real to the multidimensionally aware child, the child must learn to cope with a non-believing world.

An older child may be told there are no auras, no colors around people, and that there is no one there when they talk to spirits. The child who talks of having a spirit playmate is punished for telling lies, laughed at for inventing an imaginary companion, or is spoken of as having a vivid imagination. A child whose unseen friend is ignored by others learns to ignore the playmate too.

Typically, they cease vocalizing the knowledge they have. They may also painfully internalize their difference and this leaves them in a psychologically vulnerable position. Attempts may be made to "shut down" the internal experiences, to make them go away. Usually this is only partially effective, and so they hide their incredible talents from the world.

Ian recalls:

"I first remember multidimensional perceptions around age four. At that age, I made a decision based on the reality I perceived. I saw that most people were not truthful, weren't following their guidance from their inner truth, especially those in churches. As far as I could see, people's daily interactions were not based on love and respect for others.

"Even though I realized most people didn't 'walk their talk' (thinking one way and acting in another) and I couldn't trust what they were doing, I could still see that divine spark within everyone. But, I wasn't seeing any action in what was being preached, so at that time, I decided that I would keep any ability I had, anything that wasn't 'normal,' to myself."

Their Reality is Multidimensional

Lack of validation and understanding of these children's abilities can leave them very emotionally vulnerable. Because their reality is multidimensional, they can be very confused, not understanding why they are different, only knowing that they see what they see and know what they know.

Commonly, the children lack the language skills to coherently explain the multidimensional levels they experience. Like bilingual experts, they mix two languages. Unfortunately, this second language is not recognized as a language by the layman.

One such child, born in 1993, began speaking at a very early age. However, the language she used was not the language of her parents. Her unknown language had definite form, recognizable sound patterns, and it was very clear she understood that what she was saying had meaning. By age three she was still slow to form sentences in English, her mother's native tongue, and mixed in words from her early unknown language.

Profound Inner Experiences

These are the ones who may not make it, socially or psychologically, especially if misdiagnosed by the medical profession. Understanding of the phenomena expedites the integration of the child's world.

They can experience things internally in a very profound way. When surrounded by those who have no understanding of this, they often attempt to conform to what other people want them to be, rather than what they are.

Trying to conform puts immense emotional pressure on them because they lack the experience to trust their inner knowing.

Posey states:

> "I was a regular kid in a dysfunctional family. I had poor role models when it came to self-love, self-esteem and self-empowerment, save for my two great-grandmothers who were both healers."

Until they learn to trust their own inner knowing, they have no inner cohesion and often attempt to live by other's opinions. This often gives the multidimensionally aware the appearance of being indecisive, unable to stick to a decision, and emotionally unstable.

All children need a loving atmosphere in which they are truly nurtured and free to express themselves and their experiences, without ridicule or being told they are suffering from an overly active imagination. This, ideally, should start very early in life because the physical bonds are created at, or shortly after, the birth process.

Recognize, Nurture and Love Them

Sometimes the multidimensionally aware children have very difficult early years. One multidimensionally aware mother used her own inner knowing to nurture and protect her child, who was also born aware.

> "When I was pregnant with my son, in the fourth month, my placenta separated and I started hemorrhaging. The doctors told me that I was going to lose the child, but he hung in there with the placenta somewhat separated. He was due November 22, but the first week of October, I started labor.
>
> "I was in and out of the hospital three times, then, the third time an emergency C-section was performed, because the fetal heart beat had dropped dangerously low. Born weighing 4 lb. 2 oz. with the umbilical cord wrapped around his head four times, he was bruised and not expected to live.
>
> "Although he was rushed to a natal care center, they were not optimistic about his survival. His weight dropped to 3.5 lbs. In the hospital for two months with a blood clot on his brain, he defied all odds. Home for only a week, he was put back in again.
>
> "I would not allow them to do anything invasive to him, only monitor him. I was the pediatricians' worst nightmare. I brought chiropractors into the hospital. We would pull the curtains and do energy work on him. I would not allow certain tests, any injections, not allow him to be circumcised.

"It was inward guidance. I was just a student chiropractor, in over my head as to what was happening to him physiologically. I had no experience, just intuition. I was with him constantly, sleeping in the hospital.

"One time they put him out in a carriage in the hallway to be taken to X-ray later. They had just given him a barium bottle and we were waiting to be transported. I looked down at him and he was blue, totally blue and lifeless. I picked him up and he was so fragile and so frail. He was choking on the barium vomit.

"If I hadn't been there he would have been alone and suffocated in that hallway. There were many incidents like that. I knew I had to stay with my baby. His first year was tough. He had a lot of respiratory problems due to damage to his trachea from being on a respirator.

"However, I always knew he was going to be OK, despite his deathlike appearance at birth. He was late in developing motor coordination, but I knew from his eyes that he was bright and intelligent.

"I had him evaluated at an institute for premature babies and was told that he probably would have Cerebral Palsy due to an insult to the motor cord. They wanted me to do patterning. I said no, that was not what he needed. I continued taking him to chiropractors for adjustments. His pediatrician remarked that he did not know what I was doing, but just keep it up. He was improving.

"He started talking, learned the whole alphabet before he was two, had unbelievable listening skills and was ambidextrous. He also had an ear for music.

"As a toddler in diapers, he first connected words with objects by pointing. It was like the Helen Keller movie when she connected the word water to the feel of water. I held him in my arms and when he pointed to an object, named it for him. He started pointing all over the room; he wanted to know the names of everything. His language skill was amazing at such an early age.

"That is not uncommon with babies that are slow, motor wise. Now sports are his thing. He is restless in school, has a hard time paying attention, and is easily bored."

Connecting in the Dream World

Because of their advanced attunement, it is very common for these children to have conversations with other intelligences, often unseen by others.

Interaction with a vast array of beings is part of the hyperspace experience. Parents should not make automatic assumptions of who these beings are and why they are interacting with their child.

Parents need to be very attentive to the children who have night terrors or nightmares. They should be allowed and encouraged to talk out experiences, instead of being told the boogeyman does not exist. It is important that they not be told that parents will not let anything happen to them.

This is a very delicate situation, because, in actuality, parents do not have any control over many things and, as a result, a sense of betrayal can result. The child believes that the parent will protect them, yet things do happen. For the young ones, being told that their hands are magic wands that will make the bad things go away in the dream world will help greatly.

According to his grandmother, Terry, by the age of three, could read, carry on intelligent, adult conversations, and work puzzles designed for older children and adults. He was a gentle, loving child that never needed to be disciplined. He loved to draw and his artwork showed strong vivid colors of green, purple and pale yellow. Although, at times, he would draw only in pale blue.

At the age of three, he talked of the "blue aliens" that came to his crib, and played with him and sang to him. Queried, he always said he was not afraid of them, they were fun. Fortunately, Terry was born into an open-minded, receptive family, so was allowed to grow at his own pace with much parental support. These children are often far more aware of reality and what occurs in other dimensions than their parents are.

Coping In a Hostile World

An insidious kind of rebelliousness can exist in these children. It is possible that their empathic talents allow them to clearly see the blind spots, and the vulnerability of the adults around them.

When they strike out, they instinctively, like trained martial arts experts, catch their opponent off balance and use a person's weaknesses against them where it hurts the most. They know what to say to strike to the core.

Often, however, they are correct to rebel, and they sometimes use a Gandhi-like passive resistance. In a head-on confrontation, they know the adult world is stronger and can overpower them. This rebellion can be well hidden. The parent can be unaware of it. Perhaps on one level, the child, too, is unaware, but it is always there. It is as if the normal child's desire for independence is stronger in these children, yet, in a repressed way.

Most often the multidimensionally aware child will act from feelings or intuitions that are intense and deep and they will not necessarily share the same value system as their parents. Their strong adherence to their inner guidance regarding morality will not always be influenced by others' teachings.

> "Coming from a space of Gandhi-like love got me into a lot of trouble because I wouldn't defend myself." Ian remembers, "I had to be taught it was OK to protect myself. Around the age of nine, that was very challenging, to have to change that belief system and learn it was OK, because it just wasn't a part of me, to protect myself. When I was doing it, it just didn't feel right."

Seeking Escape

All these children must learn in one way or another to shield themselves from too much exposure of their knowledge and understanding. Some turn it off through alcohol and drugs, through retreating into permanent ill health, through escaping in out-of-body experiences.

Carol recalls:

> "It dismayed and upset me that I saw so many people with unreal facades. I would know who they were, what they were about, and what they were thinking, but what they were saying very rarely matched their thinking.
>
> "I remember almost nothing of the first five years of my life. I was always pretending I lived alone in a forest, for I felt separate, not a part of the family. I grew up in a rural area, so I could go out and play alone with my cats. I went to a country school, but never had any close connections with people. I read and I read.
>
> "As a child I was sick much of the time and as a consequence, spent a lot of time in my room. I had a rich inner life, knowing somehow that I had a place where I belonged, though it wasn't with my current family. My earliest memories are of feeling I had been dropped off here. I was always imagining I was in another land, another world, communicating with people that weren't here, on planet Earth.
>
> "By the time I was in the sixth grade, I had figured out that if I were to be popular and have friends, I must keep my real self in the background, covered up, not be honest about what I was seeing. A strong telepath, very clairvoyant, I was very precognitive in my

dreams even then, but I knew anything I shared would not be accepted. So, growing up was lonely on one level.

Posey said:

> "During my teenage years, I allowed myself to separate from this beingness—even though it never left me. I let alcohol, drugs, and the emotional roller coaster that naturally goes with them, take me to the bottom of the pit."

Another aware teenager just did not stay at home. "My parents were divorcing and it was a particularly hard time for me. It was the 1960s. and I got caught up with that movement. I spent very little time at home because my parents were so volatile. I would just leave—be gone days at a time."

A few who are strong and athletic and get along well with their contemporaries escape through physical activities, such as sports. Others are loners, not trusting anyone enough to share this incredible inner world of perception.

Rory states:

> "I was considered to be one of the most popular kids in school. In Jr. High School I received an award in athletics for the most sports ever played by any athlete in the history of the school. In eighth grade I was already in varsity high school."

"Fortunately," Ian says, "I was very good at sports from age eleven on, so there were no problems at school.

Little Ones Need Validation and Recognition

There are several ways to assist these special children, but they need and deserve better methods than are presently available. They are special for they are the forerunners of the evolutionary process. Helping all of these children helps all of humanity.

These children need validation, reassurance and appreciation. Not everyone will be able to understand them, and they need help to learn to accept this and cope with it. The understanding and awareness bonds are created when another individual validates the uniqueness and reality of the potential in a multidimensionally aware child.

A parent should think back to their individual experiences and remember the point in time when they realized that someone was extending validation or when they validated someone else.

Truth of their being is facilitated by looking into a child's eyes, accepting what is being said, conveying support, acknowledgment, being nonjudgmental. The child will smile in recognition; the bond is set.

Aware individuals who acknowledge these children may, or may not, meet that particular child again; it does not matter. That moment will never be forgotten.

It is that recognition of "kindred spirit" that can turn a young life around, just by another human having been very aware of their potential, thus forming a bond. This bond goes beyond simple validation. A person can validate someone without bonding, but cannot bond without validating. It is a fine line. Children sense the difference better than adults.

Learning to negotiate in a seemingly hostile world is a difficult task. These children need encouragement in expression in positive ways and to learn patience.

Art is one way of writing down, externalizing and objectifying their experiences. Even for adults, there is difficulty in finding words to express the inner visions. Art is a nonverbal way to allow a child to cope with things they cannot discuss. As with adults, they should not be forced to attempt to verbalize.

There are natural methods which enable the multidimensionally aware to focus themselves or ground, thus gaining self control. Focus (grounding) into third-dimensional reality is a vital tool for integration of the multiple realities. These children must learn to expand their hyperspace awareness to integrate physical awareness as well. They need to be taught to ground themselves, to become fully aware of the third dimension.

Belief and Trust

The lucky children receive validation and support from family and friends, learn how to control their journeys and turned their knowledge into successful contributions to society.

While visiting the Goddard Space Museum in Roswell, New Mexico, a six-year-old spent a very long time reading Goddard's private notes. When his mother, impatient to move on, tugged at his hand, he said to her, "I think I was him." Though amazed, his mother told him she believed him.

Goddard was considered the father of modern rocketry, holding dozens of patents used in World War II weapons.

Today this person is in college, majoring in audio visual communications. He is an extremely gifted artist with an incredible perception of spatial relationships.

Rory recalls:

"I had a very close relationship with my mother, I always had her trust, and she left me free to explore. At four, I was already riding a bicycle, and I would disappear early in the morning and come back in the late afternoon. I went to explore the world."

Ian remembers:

"My mother was very interested in my abilities. I could ask questions. There was never any judgment in my family in terms of my intuitive ability. Nothing about me was ever questioned, which was great.

"My parents were loving, allowing me to be whatever I wanted to be. When I was very young, my mother would ask me to rub her neck and shoulder muscles while she was watching TV and she mentioned often that I had very healing hands."

Allow Them To Be Who They Are

Children should always be encouraged to be themselves. Above all, they should be encouraged to explore, not suppress, the areas of themselves that are different. This is especially true regarding balance of the male/female energies within.

The natural tendency to formulate an internal balance is often suppressed, sometimes violently, by a parent demanding that stereotypical role modeling be followed.

The suppression of female gentleness in boys and insistence upon subservience in girls blocks the development of internal balance of male/female energy.

This is true for all children. Much of the violence being out-pictured by children today stems from having been denied their own identity and ability to express internal balance, to express, in a pure form and essence, the opposite sex energies they innately know exist.

Let What They See Become Their Reality

Blanche advises parents:

"I would say to mothers of multidimensionally aware children, in order that their struggle might not be so severe, try not to inflict your belief system so harshly on them. It might not be what they see at all. Let what they see become their reality.

"Parents have children and want the best for them. The babies need love, but more than love they need touch. They are tactile. The healthy love vibrations we feed them will help them to evolve into their rightful space and clear understanding.

"From a very early age children are being told no, no. With every no, don't, or you can't do that, we suppress the evolution that is within the DNA. We tell them they have to see what we see and the distortions begin to manifest. All the suppression of not letting them flow, creates the monsters in our society, creates the problems. If we have to manipulate with words, very few words are enough, not words to direct their thoughts. Let their thoughts flow; use words of courage, words of confidence.

"The adverse winds twist the trees and gnarl them. But if we obstruct the wind, then the tree does not grow to be strong. We have a tendency with children to block the wind and then they never gain the measure of strength needed.

"They need to be guided by the internal forces within them, then each would find its place because each is unique, one of a kind. They do as they see. It is very important to listen to what children say. As language evolves, and people become balanced, all people will be telepathic. The human race will evolve in that direction for that is the full potential.

"I think we are animals of love, generated by the love inside of us, the internal light, and we react too much to the external. I believe the balance, as far as emotion, mannerisms, all those needs 'to fit' so to speak, are an intrinsic part of what people have within them. My overall view is we are born with a potential inside us that we need to allow to evolve and not suppress."

Abilities in Conflict

Multidimensional children relate to the world from their inner selves and ideas. Blanche, for instance, always wrote her ideas in poetry first. The present educational system does not have guidelines or assistance available for teachers to productively guide these children. School curriculums are geared toward "normal," middle-of-the-road students.

Because multidimensional abilities often conflict with third-dimensional educational systems, failure sometimes results. The aware, gifted ones often have IQ's far above normal, but may not test at all well on standard tests. The multidimensionally aware children see far beyond the normal human ability and usually "read too much" into a simple question.

It was very difficult for Rory, as he recalls:

> "I was physically advanced, fully developed and I was tops in every sport I participated in, but school academics, I could not handle."

Most multidimensionally aware have difficulty accepting and learning from academia from the earliest grades on through the universities. They simply do not respond to sitting and being lectured to.

Rory continues:

> "In kindergarten, when I was four years old, I had trouble in school. The teacher told my mother I was not like the other children. She said that I would grow up to be a philosopher, but I would never fit in. I came up with things that adults could not understand.
>
> "In sixth grade I excelled in everything. I made all 100s on every test I took, because the teacher got me physically involved. My teacher said he had never seen anybody who could see things and understand things as I did. I'll never forget when he told me that. He put me in advanced classes for the next year and I flunked everything. I just sat there. In his classes I had been physically involved in everything.
>
> "The teachers couldn't understand. They called me lazy, said I couldn't function, so I was put in a low-function class with a teacher who again got me physically involved. Again, I got exceptional grades in everything.
>
> "I explained things to the class, told the teacher where to find certain books that I had never read, and what was in the books. I got 100s on every test and every extra credit. So, again, they put me in advanced classes the next year and I flunked everything because I just sat there. I graduated second from the bottom in my class."

From a different perspective, Ian worked hard to conform.

> "At school I had a reading level of age 18 when I was only seven, so I was pushed ahead two years. Generally I had very loving connections with people. I came in with a kind of Gandhi attitude ."

Special Teachers For Special Children

Fortunately, there are multidimensionally aware people who initiate unconventional teaching methods which can be of great service to these children. One such former school teacher writes:

> "During my many years of teaching, tutoring and doing therapy work, mainly youngsters with reading problems, I have found quite a number of unusually bright, creative children. Some of those have been multidimensionally aware.
>
> "During the decade of the mini-school I worked with small groups of from five to six children, from 8:00 A.M. to 12:00 noon, their whole school day. I initiated several experiments in Extended Sensory Perception, quite successfully.
>
> "Telepathy, by way of colors and geometric forms as used in the Duke University experiments, were highly successful. In addition, I used a game which I called Pretend, so the kids would not feel afraid that they had to try to do something."
>
> "I had them relax in their chairs and pretend they were about five feet behind where they were seated. Since space tends to collapse on very upset people, and all in my group had had severe problems adjusting before coming into my program, I had to get them to a happy, relaxed condition before starting the games/play.
>
> "Once they were [relaxed] with eyes shut, perceiving the world from their 'ingrained' position, I asked them to report what they could see from there. It was not long before they were genuinely perceiving from the new viewpoint.
>
> "Results were out of this world and back in again. One lad, for example, mentally hopped up on the roof of the house and looked about, and suddenly said, 'Hey! You know that badminton bird we lost last week is on the roof? It must have blown across to this side, because it is stuck in the leaves of the pear tree, only a little bit is showing.'
>
> "Then he opened his eyes and asked, 'May I climb up and get it?' Of course, I got him a ladder. The roof was a very shallow pitch and up he went with all the other kids waiting below to catch the badminton bird. He walked straight to it, tossed it down. One of the kids caught it and everyone rejoiced.
>
> "They then went back to work. I think those kids will never again become totally jammed into their physical/chemical bodies and hopefully will never again be 'identified' with them because

they learned, without being told, that they are people operating bodies, but free as beings."

Special Beyond Your Imagining

In *On Wings of Light,* Ronna Herman writes:

"Of late, many people, especially parents and grandparents, are becoming concerned and disturbed about the children of the world. They know something is wrong and radically amiss, but they cannot identify what has changed or is happening. The little ones born since around the year 1970 are unique, different, special beyond your imagining. Many are prototypes of the new humanity."

"The children of today require different rules and standards—different care and handling. They are more sensitive and closer to Spirit. The veil between dimensions is thinner and they are bringing with them operative abilities and skills that have lain dormant for thousands of years in most of you. Abilities that you have had to work to perfect and refine. Attributes that will come naturally to them and will seem normal. Do not stifle their sensitivities, their creativity, their spiritual awareness. Teach, or just allow them to be the androgynous beings they wish to be—a perfect balance of masculine and feminine energies. Many of these beautiful ones will be ambidextrous, multifaceted in their abilities, talented beyond your imagination, if you will only nurture them and allow their spirits to soar. Notice how the heads of many of the babies being born are a little larger than the norm, also slightly elongated as well. Their brains are larger.

"It is time for a complete revamping and restructuring of your educational system. Many of you have been protesting and advocating this for a long time, but time is running out. The schools no longer serve the children, but are constructed to support the bureaucracy and an antiquated system that has completely broken down. There are many extremely qualified workers who so desperately want to teach and bring life and truth into the school system, but they are either afraid to challenge the system or have been turned away for being too radical, or nonconformists. This will also be changing…and soon."[5]

5. Herman, 1997.

Formula For Success

Ian followed a deep inner journey to find his place in the overall scheme of things. Rory began to find his place in life as he observed healing taking place when he worked with people, mentally seeing their trauma and silently creating a form of healing energy. Posey chose to seek higher spirituality and developed a deep awareness and interaction with the Christ Consciousness. Carol opened up to her beingness and, like Ian, began to teach others how to find themselves and be comfortable with that beingness. Blanche consults with experts around the world, lending her special vision to assist with inventions and ideas to make the world a better place.

These are the successful ones. All have developed stamina and staying power against incredible odds in a society that neither understands nor appreciates their tremendous capacities. Very few feel that they are totally understood by any one person. All feel they have a higher purpose in life to fulfill. Special understanding and loving kindness is needed for those who are not succeeding, not conforming sufficiently to find their place of service in society.

Society's Grace

Tomorrow's children will need more public awareness of who they are and what their purpose will be, for there will be many more of these extraordinary individuals coming into the world. Tomorrow's children will need society's understanding and support of their very special gifts and talents.

According to author Barbara Marciniak, more of these children will be born into the Earth plane beginning in 1994. She states that these children will carry a very high vibration, the vibration of love and the ability to effortlessly create. They are a new race of beings, who will be born very gifted and will need to be very nurtured and protected. Sound will be very important to these children, for they will create with light and sound. They will find each other and every community will have a few of them because they will act as a focal point.

They will have a ridiculous sense of humor, clowning and playful, but are, at the same time, very gifted. They will have a larger head and may be born as much as two months premature in order to be able to pass through the birth canal. They will be born telepathic and many will be born with the ability to speak.[6]

---

6. Marciniak, 1992.

Chapter Four

We Are Never Understood

A Multidimensionally Aware View of Life

Contributed By Rory

"When I was a very little kid I was physically way ahead, walking and doing everything before I was a year old. I was always a trouble maker and nothing ever fazed me. My brother would beat up on me, and I would giggle through the whole thing. I never had to fight back. Violence was never a part of me.

"When I was in the army, I wouldn't hold any kind of a gun. I never could, never would, so, I was discharged in 31 days. I can't destroy; I get nauseous at the thought of death. I can't handle it. I can handle dying, passing on, but not the taking of life.

"When I was little, I smeared things, I stepped on things, nothing ever bothered me. I had all the confidence in the world from infancy on and no one could shake it.

"I loved to explore. I remember as a two year old I would throw things up in the sky and watch them separate. I would always find another way of drawing pictures. Now try it this way, try it that way. I just 'knew' things.

"I was a loner, but never alone. I always felt as if there were a lot of people around, not play people, mental people always with me, constantly, even today. I don't know if that is my higher self, for I have no concept of what it is. I never, in my entire life, had a best friend, never ever wanted one. I can't get close to people because I am always gone, exploring.

School, I Just Could Not Do

"In school, I don't know if they socially passed me or I just barely got by, but I never really passed anything. I kept flunking out.

"Maybe I just knew enough so they felt I knew it. I had a learning processing difficulty. I cannot process auditorially. I am highly visual, highly visceral, highly tactile. I have to touch and feel.

"Even now, my visualizations, metaphysically, are touch. I want to see things. If you describe it to me auditorially, I'm lost. I go places and do things by touch. If you talk to me on the phone, I physically touch something to make it real.

"My major was in psychology. In an English class, they wanted me to read and analyze a poem. I didn't know how to analyze a poem. I didn't have the patience to read a poem, so I created one, on the spot, and signed it 'Author unknown.' Then I wrote an analysis.

"Since it was mine, the analysis had to be correct, but I got an F on it for an incorrect, completely erroneous interpretation. When I told the teacher I had written it and it was not from an unknown, she was furious. Once again I was in trouble with the Dean. How can a teacher tell you that you have failed on your interpretation when you created it?

A Rebel

"Was I a rebel? I guess I was. I couldn't fit in, but my mind was always participating. I was rebelling in that I was playing with them. With pompous people who play games with me, who say this is the only way to do it, I will play their game a level above them."

Rory rebelled by pulling a spoof on college professors who told him to do something more normal.

"I told them I was going to teach an earthworm to do what a student couldn't do, go through a maze.

"I did it and received all kinds of awards, but it was really a spoof on the professors because I used a water gradient and not a teaching method.

"At the awards ceremony, I made the announcement that it was a spoof on statistics and scientific experimentation. They tried to throw me out of school for that.

"I went to the Dean and told him that instead of throwing me out of college, he should give me all kinds of awards and praise, and write articles about it, because it showed the scientific community how easily they are duped. How easily deceived they can be, the directions they can take that can subvert other people. I said, 'I have shown you how to check things out.' They let me back in and I got an A and the professor was fired.

"I never got my doctorate. I finished everything, but never sat in front of my committee.

"In graduate school a person on my committee for the doctorate said, 'You have no idea how far beyond you are. You write articles and you write papers and you never read the books.'

"I dropped out of the profession because I didn't go that last step, I don't have that piece of paper.

"I studied neuropathology—rehabilitative medicine. I have a Masters Degree in speech pathology and I have worked in neuropathology. I have gone through three Masters programs.

The Healing Gift

"I have worked in rehabilitative medicine—strokes, cranial nerve damage, spinal cord injuries. A tremendous amount of healing was being affected, but the problem was that I didn't know about reciprocation then. I tended to absorb everything the patient had.

"Can you imagine being in a hospital and working with 100 to 150 patients or just overseeing a particular wing and being in the rooms on a daily basis, absorbing everything from it and never releasing it? My body absorbed it. It just wore me down, completely wore me down. But the patients got better!

"Since I have learned about reciprocation, I have never had a problem. I still absorb things, but I don't keep them.

"I had to leave neurology because I developed pseudo-narcolepsy—self- inflicted narcolepsy. Because I don't escape by drinking or taking drugs, I developed sleeping sickness to avoid working with patients.

"I kept deteriorating; they kept getting better. Stroke patients were walking out of the hospital. There was a lot of success, but I never told anybody what I was doing.

"It is not difficult to focus on two levels. I can be focusing deep on something, give myself a message, focus that my body will receive a message. I will send out what I am working on and I am still focusing on what is going on around me. My full attention is on one subject, but I can continue sending.

"How do I do it? It is an enigma. I have no theory. I don't even have an hypothesis. I honestly do not know. I know I have been given gifts of knowledge, of seeing things. I see things in such incredible detail and it is always helping. I go places. I don't know where I go, and I don't feel myself going, but I always come back with knowledge.

Don't Tell Me You Understand

When asked how he would help people that were confused, upset and turning to drugs and alcohol to get away from this inner knowledge, he said, "Drinking is a way out. I won't drink because I don't want to be controlled. I know I'm vulnerable. I know of only one answer—don't.

"The multidimensionally aware need acceptance, not understanding. They pick up immediately such condescending statements as, 'I know what you are talking about, I recommend....' I won't listen to that.

"If the average person says 'I understand,' I just say horse ____. We need acceptance, not understanding. 'I hear what you are saying and its OK.' Not 'I understand.' We don't want to hear, 'I accept you for what you are,' that is too typical.

"I reach such a level of complete frustration that I don't have patience with people, no patience with BS.

"We have the ability to play such incredible games with people. Like the TV program *MASH,* laughter is our defense mechanism. When we don't understand our own situation and we, symbolically, get knocked around and beaten up, we become facetious and have no patience with people at all.

"We go out of our way to try to please people, and no matter what we do, we are always wrong; we always get in trouble.

"The moment someone says, 'I understand what you are going through or what you are going through is OK, don't worry about it,' crude statements go through my head. I just think, 'Shut up.' That's how I think. 'Just go away, you have no idea.' It is easier to be alone, but I am never alone! I always 'know.'

Assisting the Multidimensionally Aware

"Multidimensionally aware people need to be able to call a center of some type. They need someone to talk to, someone to interact with. A center that could offer stories about others who have gone through it would be the best thing the multidimensionally aware could have.

"Do you want to talk to somebody? Give us a call, write us a letter. We have other people who will be happy to talk to you.

"Start with one, end up with many. They tell you, and that opens doors to others. People who don't have these gifts can now understand hyperspace, because they hear the things multidimensionally aware individuals go through and they say, 'Look at what these people are contributing.'

"Have physical things for us to do—releases. The only way to find out what physical things are needed is by sitting down with some people who have been through it. Physical activities such as jogging and weight lifting are critical. Without those we fall apart. We need other physical things, for we are constantly going at rapid speeds, our bodies change temperature.

"There are three bodies that we have simultaneously and we need to change the bodies. One is the physical body, another is the adult which is the analytical left side of it, another is a metaphysical body that travels and receives.

"We have got to mentally separate the three parts of the body. If we are too analytical, we will self-destruct.

"We have to do silly things, play on swings, tell stupid jokes, laugh, go swimming, sweat, be angry, make mud pies, cook, have fun, be frivolous, crazy. This is necessary for no other reason than to not analyze what we are doing. Invite us over to just say hey, hang out with me.

"The multidimensionally aware are so beyond what can be imagined thought-wise that if there is condescension or analysis, it will destroy us. We cannot be analyzed.

"Why in the world would anyone analyze happiness—so it can be duplicated? Just do it. Why in the world would anyone want to analyze this talent? Why not feed it, nurture it, love it, let it grow and nurture everything in its sight.

"If someone found a material, a product that could make plants flourish and grow, give off an incredible amount of oxygen, incredible electricity, that no matter what was wrong it could heal and bring joy, what would they do? Would they analyze it or would they just give it away to the world?

"Why are people so busy analyzing and dissecting instead of nourishing and developing it and bringing it out? How does anyone bring out a child's happiness and education? Is it brought out by analyzing and ripping it apart? No, it is brought out by going out there and getting on the ground and playing with it and experiencing it, caring.

"That is what they tried to do to me, analyze me and make me fit into a curriculum at school. They tried to make me fit and I don't fit. I can fit in, but I had to stop dissecting and start experiencing.

"How are aware individuals helped? The same way all people are helped, by being nurtured.

"We will teach you. Stop dissecting us or we will die. People think that by analyzing they understand, but understanding comes by not analyzing. Understanding comes by experiencing.

"That is misconstrued in the field of education. If a person goes into a lab and takes what is analyzed and studies it from a book, the learning comes from the experience, not from the dissecting. Dissecting only tells the cold hard facts about the dissection. It does not tell anyone anything about life.

"Life is electricity, its energy. It is so much more than just what we can see and feel. To help us, give us a place to grow where we can just be. We need not only to be nurtured, but to be accepted in a way of just being. When people say, 'I understand and I accept you for what you are,' that just means, 'I'm different, aren't I—so you accept me!' So what!

"Experience is a greater analysis than cutting something up. For example, cut up a dead person and analyze every part of the body and medically learn the complete function, but miss out on what life is about.

"People who have the higher function, have it because of the part that is not in the body. Why dissect it? Experience it, because that is what life is.

Acceptance in Action

"I don't understand most of it, but I certainly know that I need an environment of acceptance in action, not of verbal acceptance. I haven't had acceptance all my life. I have had such rejection that I have literally talked about taking a scalpel to my soul, just removing it, hating who I was for having so much knowledge.

"I briefly found acceptance with one special friend. I didn't have to always be there. I could disappear and it did not bother her; she just knew and that was a unique quality.

"When she heard the things I was doing, she would say, 'So?' Not, 'I accept you for what you are,' it was just, 'So?' Big deal, that is you! It was like me going up to you and saying, you have two eyes and you say, 'So?' When I suddenly had visualizations, it was just 'So?' She was matter-of-fact, like, 'Are you going to cook lunch now or work on the mathematical problem?'

"A Downs Syndrome child is always happy. Why? Because they don't analyze anything. They just experience. What is there to analyze? They can't comprehend it.

"Look at all us brilliant people who spend all our time analyzing and how happy are we? We have totally lost sight of the gifts that we have. These people already have the ability to communicate here mentally, but not physically. It is lost through analysis. Do it and it will be destroyed.

It Can Be Taught

"Can it be taught to someone else? The idea that it is there can be taught, especially through anecdotes which help people. Stories that people want to hear and the things we learn from them are from emotion, not analysis.

"Say to us, 'I'm Ok, You're OK' because these are our gifts, not because we are different. Empathy is condescending, but interaction is not.

"My son is a highly gifted child with an IQ of 164. In the second grade he did a diagnosis of a mitral valve disorder of the heart.

"He was asked to be in the highly, highly gifted program and I said no. I want him in the high achievement program with the regular kids, because he is a regular kid. He just comprehends at a different level. So what? He plays baseball, basketball, falls off his bike, gets dirty, gets in trouble, asks questions.

"He is what I want him to be, a regular kid. Today he is a sensitive, regular kid who has comprehension."

Fitting In

Because so little is known about hyperspace or the human ability to access it, both the multidimensionally aware and the people they interact with face incredible challenges. Learning to cope with hyperspace experiences can be a most confusing and difficult time, but doing so brings incalculable rewards.

The understanding that there are many multidimensionally aware individuals in the world and that this is a human capability, is vital. Society has been very reluctant to validate the existence of "paranormal" abilities on any level.

Until the world accepted his theories of highly advanced physics, Einstein was considered "mentally deranged" by his scientific peers.

Ingo Swann writes:

> "My many researches and testing regarding these matters have confirmed that enormous super-capabilities of all kinds naturally dwell in the human species, that many of the capabilities haven't even been identified, that the human-capability spectrum is enormous."

However, Swann explains that the research has also confirmed that knowledge of and participation in the spectrum is reduced and sometimes functionally obliterated, not by individuals themselves, but by participation in various on-going social processes which have formatted their consciousness.

All have entered into these social processes by the circumstances of their birth and subsequent experiencing within their cognitive confines. Consciousness patterns are formatted accordingly, and people become unwilling carriers of the social processes that act as barriers to their own self-developmental powers.

Most people believe, and social conditioning teaches, that they first and foremost are a physical biological entity. This serves as a basic core reality, and many subsequent phenomena encountered are filtered through that core—with the result that phenomena which fit the conditioning are accepted while those that don't are rejected. "In fact," Swann points out, "each human being must be a life-unit before being a biological entity, largely because bio-bodies themselves are not carriers of life."[1]

---

1. Swann, 1993, General Introduction.

Broadening the "Normalization" Band

There are few organizations specifically designed for assistance and education of the multidimensionally aware, although there are groups, individuals and some educational institutions currently working toward this goal.

Hopefully, in the future an acceptance of multidimensionality will be established and much progress will be made toward normalization of these experiences.

Ideally, the primary objectives would be to help people understand multidimensionality and how this ability affects not only the individual, but family, friends and peers as well. As with all extraordinary experiences, the uniqueness, as well as the commonality, must be explored and understood.

Often just an explanation of multidimensional capabilities is very helpful for the person, as well as parents, siblings, significant others and peers.

Any educational structure designed for the multidimensionally aware needs to be a multidisciplinary team effort incorporating the widest possible knowledge base. Those competent in nontraditional areas are now working toward establishing the badly needed basics, as many educational systems have fallen far short of even rudimentary comprehension of the needs of gifted children of any caliber.

Often multidimensionally aware individuals enter the helping professions in order to give their gifts to others like themselves who might come into their lives.

Those teachers who currently recognize and value highly gifted children often have wonderful results, as was shown in Chapter Three.

A major problem for the multidimensionally aware is one of focus, for they are often fascinated with what is being perceived in hyperspace. They are still aware of their body, immediate surroundings and of bodily functions, but the body and the third dimension are not the focus of attention.

There are many methods from which the multidimensionally aware and parents may choose to integrate the experiences with third-dimensional awareness. However, each individual must find the path that is best for them or their child.

The art of grounding is one essential tool. The term grounding means the ability to be fully and completely aware of *all conscious processes and the third dimension* at the same time. When balanced and focused, people are functional, without balance and focus; they become dysfunctional.

Not only people who access hyperspace, but other people as well, do not ground themselves often enough and will appear "spacey," adrift, preoccupied and distracted because their focus is elsewhere. Lack of grounding causes many problems in everyday life, varying from constantly losing things to serious physical ailments.

Focus of attention also defines the focal point of "life force" sometimes referred to as the etheric body.

When conscious awareness (the etheric body) is not fully integrated or grounded into the physical body, disease, pain and discomfort arise because the body has a built-in mechanism which tells it that, when conscious awareness or the etheric no longer inhabits it, it must die. When people habitually fail to concentrate completely on the body for long periods of time, the body starts its death process.

Grounding completely is analogous to sending oil through an engine, greasing all the component parts so that they will work properly. This is especially true for the multidimensionally aware because they spend so much time in mental activities.

Grounding is most easily accomplished by sitting still, breathing slowly and deeply from the solar plexus area and concentrating fully on the body, feeling every part. After a few minutes of breathing, each body part is tensed and released, beginning with the toes, then the feet, legs, torso, arms, on up through the face and scalp area.

Sitting on the ground, bodily connecting with the earth is very grounding, as is working with any earth material such as dirt, mud, clay, sand or stone.

Visualizations may also be used for grounding. Sinking the feet deeply into the earth, picturing the color black, or mentally visiting a very restful place in the sun with water—a lake, river or the ocean—work well, as long as bodily sensations are incorporated and it is not just a mental exercise.

Any technique that combines complete physical awareness and a peaceful state of focused mind will ground a person.

The Body Chemistry

The correlation between mental activity and the physical body is strongly exemplified by the multidimensionally aware. The high levels of mental input actually cause chemical changes in the body. *People who naturally access hyperspace do not always take the necessary steps to stabilize the body for these experiences.*

It is very common for the multidimensionally aware to lack energy, be depressed or have prolonged, sometimes severe, periods of ill health. Many times there is Kundalini activation which may also cause physical sensations and symptoms.[2]

Social Difficulties and Cultural Dynamics

Because some of the aware individuals view themselves as so different from the majority of humanity, many will turn to the self medication of alcohol in order to numb the sensations, both mental and physical.

Others utilize drugs to justify or "normalize" the experience. If others are experiencing something of the same thing, then the feeling of being different or abnormal is lessened, i.e. everyone "trips" on drugs.

Speaking of his teen years when Ian utilized alcohol, he says, "It was a totally conscious decision. I never became an alcoholic, because I made the decision that I wanted this altered state of reality. I did not know how else to get it, did not know anyone who could show me. It was a choice, a different way of managing things." It was a life experience for Ian, and once he had the experience, he went on to other things.

Unfortunately, not all of the multidimensionally aware share Ian's strength of self-knowledge, for many fall into the drug/alcohol trap and do not get out.

There is also often misdiagnosis by the mental health profession. This is especially true of multidimensionally aware children whose parents, teachers and peers do not understand them at all.

Because of the strangeness encountered in the multiple dimensionality experience, some may choose to consult a mental health professional. It is most advisable that the therapist's concepts of extraordinary experiences be explored prior to entering into a professional relationship.

To be mistakenly diagnosed and labeled as mentally ill brings immense stress which only confuses an already overloaded system. People experiencing multidimensional perceptions are not afflicted with mental illness; they are simply people experiencing hyperspace.

Unfortunately, for many professionals, the state of the art is far behind the times. The American Psychiatric Association's *Diagnostic and Statistical Manual III* (DSM)[3] still lists psychic phenomenon as an aberration. However, DSM IV radically changed positions in some areas due to updated research.

---

2. For a comprehensive examination of Kundalini activation and subsequent symptoms, see: Grenwell, 1995. pp. 31-34.
3. American Psychiatric Association, 1980.

Historically those persons who have had extraordinary experiences, *i.e.*, mystical visions, UFO experiences, near-death experiences, etc., have been subjected to psychiatric and lay labeling regarding their sanity.

It is vital that the experience not be confused with mental/emotional disorders. The following is a broad-based overview of the most commonly diagnosed disorders and a brief summation of the most important differentiation between those disorders and multidimensionality experiences.

This discussion offers guidelines only and is intended to be utilized and evaluated as such.

General Overview

Multidimensional awareness has many aspects which, taken individually or collectively, could reasonably be mistaken for symptoms of a specific mental health disorder. The key points, then, become those very distinct areas which indicate that multidimensional experiences are not those of a primary disorder.

Generally, multidimensionally aware people have had a relatively trauma-free childhood. Many describe their childhood as "wonderful." They are able to sustain a good to high degree of interpersonal relationships with family and peers, although they often state that no one really understands them.

Epilepsy

Very often multidimensionally aware individuals will have a high increase in their personal electromagnetic fields, which may register as excessive electrical impulses to the brain.

Epilepsy is also caused by excessive electrical impulses in the brain, therefore, the multidimensionally aware may be mistakenly viewed as a borderline epileptic.

However, a correlation with verbal accounts of entering another dimension would not be present in epileptics.

Highs and Lows

Accessing hyperspace gives the multidimensionally aware a natural "high" and the ability to obtain incredible information.

Returning to third dimension can precipitate a balancing "low" and can be very similar to coming down off of drugs. Subsequent depression may follow.

Journeys in hyperspace may be accompanied by chemical changes within the body. These chemical shifts may affect the person very much like jet lag.

Bipolar Disorder

Correlation with verbal reports is again a key to rule out Bipolar Disorder (Manic-Depressive).

The Bipolar person has no hyperspace experience while in the euphoric phase of mania. As with depression, mania stems from a pathological reaction to object loss, characterized by very deep denial.[4]

Mood swings can be a side effect of multidimensional awareness, especially in the beginning of the experiences and until the person has come to understand the phenomena.

Confusion, fear, self-destructive thoughts, severe depression, internal conflicts, stress and indecision may also be experienced in varying degrees if the multidimensional ability onsets later in life, because there may be little or no understanding of what is being experienced.

The multidimensionality experience may be fatiguing if it is not brought under conscious control. These symptoms are caused by sleep deprivation and/or grossly interrupted sleep patterns.

Perhaps the major indicator of multidimensional experiencing is the person's ability to return to third dimension awareness and normal functioning because of outside stimulus. They will be aware of others entering a room, a ringing telephone or doorbell and respond accordingly.

They have a solid "reality" orientation to third dimension when attention is focused here.

The multidimensionally aware are not restricted by the third-dimensional linear time frame. They may be aware that they are traveling through time, and this awareness may induce culture shock since this is still an age and culture where time travel is relegated to science fiction.

Additionally, aware individuals are often involved in being healers, often give verbal reports and information to others based on their hyperspace information, show great psychic ability and have supernormal cognition.

---

4. Pfeiffer, 1968, p. 17.

Schizophrenia

In contrast to multidimensional awareness, schizophrenics suffer from disturbance in all areas of life—thinking, feeling and acting, which disrupt all normal forms of relating to and interacting with their environment.

The most striking characteristics of schizophrenia are:

- gross disordering of the thought process;
- dissociation, ideas do not follow a logical sequence;
- blocking—ideas do not follow through to a conclusion, but suddenly change to an entirely different topic;
- anxiety, often escalating close to panic;
- neologisms in using made-up or "new" words or
- condensation, combining familiar words which may have meaning only to the individual;
- hallucinations, usually auditory command voices; and
- paranoid delusions, feelings of being pursued, watched, cornered, attacked.

Subcategories of Schizophrenia

Schizophrenia is broken down into several subcategories dependent upon the major affect of the individual. This break down includes Acute Undifferentiated, Hebephrenic Type, Catatonic Type, Paranoid Type, Pseudo-Neurotic Type and Chronic Undifferentiated Type. Schizophrenic symptoms may vary from mild to severe, with severe cases seldom, if ever, returning to pre-onset normality. [5]

Multidimensionally aware individuals do not suffer from gross disordering of the thought process, but rather have a tremendous influx of additional data added to their normal awareness.

The confusion lies, not always with the multidimensionally aware individual, but in the fact that others around them are unaware of what the person is seeing or experiencing. Their descriptions may sound, at first, chaotic, but with time, the person accessing hyperspace will have the ability to logically and sequentially describe the feelings, events, and visuals they experience.

---

5. Pfeiffer, 1968, pp. 35-61.

Anxiety may arise from a lack of understanding of the multidimensional experience, but can be pin-pointed to this specific cause and is a realistic, reasonable fear, alleviated by understanding of the phenomena.

Communication often becomes a barrier for multidimensionally aware people because of the lack of equivalents within language itself.

New language must be developed to bridge the gaps between known third-dimensional reality and the reality of hyperspace.

This is much like the language which has grown around computers in the last twenty years. Words which are coined to accommodate the new experiences of hyperspace can be given an appropriate and applicable meaning, with clear definition.

Auditory Hallucinations

The auditory hallucinations experienced by schizophrenic voices usually "command," seeming to overpower the schizophrenic person. The commands are usually very hostile, concrete and literal, often suggesting some form of damage be done to self, others or property.

The multidimensionally aware can hear while in hyperspace and can carry on conversations with other beings there. The content is directly associated with the content of the hyperspace experience and is not dissociative.

Rarely, a voice carries an urgent tone, indicative of the necessity of attending to or completing some action, such as returning to third dimension awareness.

Paranoia

Due to the unusual and unexplored phenomena of hyperspace, the multidimensionally aware might experience some degree of paranoia. This is both understandable and justified in view of social conditioning to both mental health issues and extraordinary events.

Multiple Personality Disorder (MPD)

Multiple Personality Disorder (MPD) could be a common misdiagnosis for those experiencing multidimensionality.

The criteria for diagnosis of MPD is that the individual is perceived as having two or more distinct personalities, with dissociation being the primary defense mechanism of the "A" or alter (dominant controlling) personality.

The primary personality sometimes experiences "black outs" or periods of lost memory when alternate personalities evidence themselves.

Alternate and subsequent personalities may be aware of the primary personality, but the primary personality is usually not aware of the alternate personality, hence dissociation, or "losing time"—having no recollection of certain time frames.

Depending upon the personality traits of the alternates (and/or subsequent) personalities, the primary personality may present a wide variety of symptoms. These symptoms include:

- depression,
- mood swings,
- self-destructive or suicidal behaviors,
- headaches,
- sleep disorders or recurrent nightmares, including night terror and sleep walking,
- panic attacks,
- phobias,
- anorexia,
- unexplained pain or somatic complaints such as gastrointestinal or cardiac disorders,
- auditory hallucinations with the voices often being hostile or critical and coming from within the head,
- visual hallucinations or other disturbances of the vision and seizure like episodes.

While usually not diagnosed until adulthood, 89% of MPD sufferers have been misdiagnosed at least once. Common misdiagnosis include: depression, borderline and sociopathic personality disorder, schizophrenia, epilepsy and Bipolar Disorder. Statistics indicate that as many as 98% of MPDs have had severe, life-threatening childhood trauma.[6]

For many MPDs, appropriate treatment can result in improvement in the quality of life. Improvements commonly result in reduction or elimination of confusion, feelings of fear, panic, self-destructive thoughts and behavior, internal conflict, and stressful periods of indecision.

---

6. Cohen, et al, 1991, Introduction.

Multidimensionally aware people do not have changes in personality facets for there is no primary, secondary or subsequent personality struggle for dominance.

In contrast to the MPD primary personality blackouts, or lost time, multidimensionally aware people do not have blackouts. They remember their experiences. In fact, the multidimensionally aware have an extremely accurate, almost encyclopedic memory for detail.

They are fully aware that they are experiencing two dimensions simultaneously. There may be disagreement with the content and knowledge of linear thinking, but the multidimensionally aware are knowledgeable of these differences and do not lose their ego integrity.

Those Who Dare To Go Beyond

The challenges of both defining the experience of multidimensionality and separating it from the cultural pathos by which such experiences are surrounded is incredibly challenging. Much exploration lies ahead in the yet unknown realms available within the human mind. Those professionals who choose to give guidance and assistance to the pioneers of hyperspace exploration fulfill an invaluable role in the evolution of humankind.

Chapter Five

Helping To Find The Way

Andrija Puharich, M.D.

One of the first people to recognize and scientifically research individuals who could mentally access other time/space continua was Andrija Puharich, M.D. He first became interested in parapsychology when he was 30 years old, in 1948. He worked with such notables in the field as Eileen Garrett, Peter Hurkos, Arigo, the Brazilian healer, and Uri Geller.

From the late 1960s, after his experience with Arigo,[1] until his death in February of 1995, the noted inventor, scientist and physician devoted the rest of his life investigating the paranormal. Puharich pioneered in the development of electronic systems for enhancing ESP.

Arigo's death caused Puharich to do great soul searching and re-evaluation of his life goals. He gave up his work with the company where he had developed over 50 patents for inventions to aid hearing problems. He freed himself of all ties and began a new way of life.

"I had two goals in mind: one to develop a theoretical base for all of my mind researches, and the other was to find human beings with great psychic talents who would cooperate as research subjects."[2]

Many of his manuscripts remain unpublished, including a monograph on his Faraday cage experiments. Among his published works were, *The Sacred Mushroom* (1959) and *Beyond Telepathy* (1962), later released in paperback in 1973. Perhaps his best known work was *Uri*, the story of the Israeli psychic, Uri Geller, whom he traveled with worldwide, demonstrating the powers of the mind.

1. Fuller, 1974.
2. Puharich, 1974, p. 35.

Correlating With Science

Puharich spent years interacting with the multidimensionally aware, helping them to understand their complex talents in terms of known science, human physiology, psychology and philosophy. He was profoundly instrumental in assisting many multidimensionally aware grow into their full potential.

In discussing his work with the multidimensionally aware, Puharich cautioned, "When the mind becomes uncertain of what it finds, or thinks it knows, then it turns to the outer world and utilizes observations and experiment as a check upon itself. And this is a necessary precaution because a mind unchecked by facts can get out of control and fantasies can become injurious to one's existence, or to others."[3]

Although Puharich worked with and studied many of the multidimensionally aware, he was most widely known for his association with Uri Geller, whose metal bending feats attracted world wide attention.

Uri, however, is a multidimensionally aware individual with many more talents than bending metal. One of Uri's gifts is that he can literally write blackboards full of equations.

The Nine

Both Uri and Puharich were able to hold conversations with other dimensional beings. Puharich's watch would stop or things would materialize or dematerialize, indicating communication with the Nine, a collegium of voices reaching man on earth.

He stated, "The controllers of the universe operate under the direction of the Nine. Between the controllers and the untold numbers of planetary civilizations in the universe are the messengers. It is the messengers who help to fulfill the destiny of creation by gentle accentuation where and when they are needed. Some of these messengers take the form of spacecraft, which in modern parlance are called unidentified flying objects, or UFOs."[4]

Puharich saw the Nine as a somewhat computerized, large group mind. They would give assignments because Puharich and Geller had a commitment with the Nine through which they sought and were given guidance. He saw this group as highly evolved beings, closely aligned with God.[5]

---

3. Puharich, 1962, Foreword.
4. Puharich, 1974, p. 10.
5. Puharich, 1974, p. 155.

Materialization and Dematerialization

Some of the abilities of the multidimensionally aware are to dematerialize and/or materialize and levitate objects. Objects tended to appear and disappear constantly in Uri Geller's presence.

The multidimensionally aware go beyond the boundary area in modern physics, which means they can cause physical objects to suddenly disappear and reappear somewhere else.

Another characteristic, kinetic ability, is electromagnetic energy emanating from an individual which can affect other electromagnetic and electrical systems.

There are thousands of people who can distort and transform metal objects, affect electronic devices, etc.

Many children learned from watching Uri on TV that they, too, could bend spoons.

The tapes Dr. Puharich received from the Nine would always self destruct, literally disappearing from the tape cassettes.

Uri

Uri Geller does not know how he does what he does. Having only a high school education, he was reluctant to discuss his ideas.

> "I believe that in telepathy, I am passing the light speed. I feel that telepathic waves travel at a speed of light or faster. Every object gives off radiation, which moves out into the universe. When we pass the light barrier, we can see into the past or into the future, and we can transmute materials one into the other. Everything is based on the light speed, and once beyond that there is no end to what can be done. But, as yet, we cannot find the particles beyond the light speed because they are too small. I also believe that there is no limit to the smallness of particles.[6]
>
> "If we go out of the route, and we leave the third or fourth dimension, we go on into another dimension and another form of life. I believe there is life everywhere in the universe. There are advanced beings who can pass the light barrier, who can travel millions of light-years in an instant. They can transfer themselves to different dimensions; they can change themselves into any form they wish, and appear as ants, birds, people or even UFOs. These space people now know that earth people are finally advanced enough so

6. Puharich, 1974, pp. 69-70.

that they can show newer forms than they used to take in Biblical times. That is, they take different forms now."[7]

Life's Journey

Renée, one of the people who worked briefly with Puharich, said,:

"He very definitely identified me as one who could access hyperspace and said, 'I would like to help you find your way to your true purpose for being here.'

"That was when he shared with me that he felt his soul's purpose for being here was to discover that entities were here for a different purpose than just to be a human. They were here on a mission for humankind, but many of them had gotten confused. He felt they needed some kind of a support system, some kind of assistance in realizing who they were. He felt that his life journey was to find those children and help them awaken."

Recognizing the Unusual

Puharich found Renée unusual in that she had the ability, under hypnosis, to travel and explore with both parts of her brain, each bringing in a different kind of knowledge from hyperspace. He was able to talk to her on two different levels at one time.

He was also fascinated with the fact that she could read libraries of information at night in her sleep. She still is able to put a book under her pillow at night and know the contents the next morning. Sometimes she even reads paragraphs out loud in her sleep.

An unusual incident occurred during her time in Puharich's home. In his office one day she found a picture of him as a young man. From the picture, Puharich and her second husband could have been twin brothers.

A shiver came over her, for inside her soul something said she was to have met Puharich, that she came in looking for him. Instead, she met and married a man in the medical profession who looked like he could have come from the same mold.

It answered how she could have married someone who was so incompatible. She told Puharich she had slipped a cog, that there was some part of her that had always been looking for him.

---

7. Puharich, 1974, p. 71.

Easy to Work With

She found that Puharich as a researcher was very comfortable to work with:

"He helped me see that I was not just having crazy dreams. I felt he was a voice from God talking to me in a place I could touch and feel and be OK with. I was not to be considered somebody that needed to be put off in a zoo.

"This was the first time, also, that I had touched a real person in my life that I could talk to about the kind of things happening to me, and it was OK. It didn't rattle him at all. I realized it didn't have to be a religious experience, or connected to the church, or demons or be judged. I was just accepted. That was a beautiful comfort and I will always cherish it.

"His questions gave freedom, so that a person didn't have to try to match what they thought he wanted. His openness was one of the keys to his getting the multitudes of variables he got, and why people were so comfortable with him.

"Part of my wanting to work with Andrija was that I didn't know anyone else to experiment with—I had been hiding all that time. I didn't want anyone to be estranged by me and he really was not. He just made me be OK. Whatever I did or said, however far out, was fine with him, although he never voiced that. He just indicated his acceptance."

Chapter Six

When You Know Who You Are

A Multidimensionally Aware View of Life

Contributed By Renée

Renée, born in the Southwest in the mid 1940s, is a petite blonde with huge sparkling blue eyes. When she was four, she had a mystic experience, feeling the presence of Jesus Christ. She awoke in the night and saw Jesus in a moonbeam. Though He spoke to her, she does not remember what He said. She went in and woke her parents and told them she had seen Jesus and wanted to be baptized. Her father, a minister, baptized her the following Sunday.

She spent her early years in Cody, Wyoming, much of her time communing with nature. Her orthodox parents constantly reminded her that her behavior reflected on them, so she was not allowed to participate in the usual teen activities, not even the sports events.

She was taught piano from an early age and loved to sing. At age 11 she was entered in a state voice contest, and was asked to sing at a funeral the day before the contest. She was absolutely terrified at the funeral and swore that she would never sing again, anywhere, ever.

Semi-hysterical with fear, she cried until she could cry no longer. Then a calm came over her, she saw a light and heard a voice that said, 'You do not sing for yourself. You sing for me and you sing of me.' She was never again terrified to sing before an audience.

In her first 27 years, she married, had a daughter, divorced, married again, and had two more children. The second child, a boy born prematurely, was accidentally oxygen deprived while being transported to a larger hospital and, as a result, suffered cerebral palsy. When he was three years old, she was told that he would be a vegetable, never speak, or be able to care for himself. The doctor told her that the kindest thing she could do would be to institutionalize him and get on with her life.

Angry Desperation

The shock of this drove her into a form of angry desperation. She refused to accept the verdict, determined to gain a normal life for her son. She studied herbs, massage therapy, cranial therapy, any and everything that she felt would help him. The long, agonizing struggle, with two steps forward and three back, paid off. Her constant prayer each night, "God, I don't know how to do this. Show me a way," was answered. Her son healed, later attended college, developed a strong musical talent, and is today self sufficient.

Another personal crisis arose in her mid-thirties. She was working at a mortuary, assisting in embalming. One night she dreamed she dressed her long blonde hair, put on her make-up, went into the mortuary, lay down on a prep table and embalmed herself. Upon waking, she realized she was in serious danger of a mental breakdown.

Desperate, she left for Texas to enroll in a school for morticians. One afternoon, she stopped by a mortuary to pick up supplies and decided to observe an embalming in process. As she left, the inner Voice again spoke to her, saying, "You are not here to administer to the dead, but to the living." She never went back to mortuary work.

Kundalini Awakening

A series of coincidences led her to begin to read in metaphysics. She learned that under light hypnosis she could travel out into the universe and obtain information.

Then one day, in a workshop utilizing pressure points for energy, she experienced a Kundalini awakening.

She describes it as:

> "There was an intense experience of cellular explosion and I felt that every cell in my body disappeared. My cells became a part of the integrated universe. It was an explosion, but not forceful nor painful. I was expanded, floating, aware that every cell of my being was part of the universe and was touching every other cell that was of universal essence, a consciousness beyond our galaxy.

"That experience is hard to describe in words. For instance, if I were to think about my liver, it became a whole universe. I could tell and feel the energetics of this particular space, yet it was all a cell. There were billions of cells and only one cell.

"That experience inside of me was such an immense, intense integration, I felt that I took the entire universe within myself. The Kundalini energy went through my whole body. My kidneys actually set off a nearby Geiger counter. They were on fire, as well as my whole spinal column.

"Now, looking back, I know that Chinese medicine says the kidneys are the generator of the chi. I felt I was gifted with the experience of that expansion, and at the same time, was given the experience of creation itself. As if that was the creation process of the human form.

"It was one of those peaceful places, that expanded awareness. I wanted to stay. It was like being one cell in the universe and you were part of the whole and yet, you were the only one there.

"It was oneness at its extreme. Everything that is, is in one space, and you are totally aware of all of the molecules that it takes to make up that one space. That one space was bigger than 25 galaxies. It was infinity. It was an experience of infinity. I didn't choose to come back. It just happened. I couldn't verbalize anything at that point.

"I backed up to my mediator during a break and when I put my spine against his arm, it burned him, creating a redness like a sunburn. Coming back in was so excruciatingly painful, I screamed and made shrill noises.

"I had cried for so long, it no longer was a release. I started toning. It just happened. I didn't consciously think, if I tone, it will go away and be easier. I didn't have any conscious thoughts. But, when I started this tonal sound I found the pain was breaking up.

"To come back into human form from that expanded awareness was not only very confining, but the necessity of the extreme compression to bring it all back in was painful. It's as if you had this material that was your skin laying underneath your cellular experience and somebody said now zip it back together. Only when you do that, zip up, you are only going to be one trillionth of the size you were. That was just like, ooooh! I can't fit! I can't fit all this into one space, into one container! The pain came when I came back into my body.

"The awareness of coming back in was like sucking every thing up with a straw. OK, kidney here, slurp, that's a kidney. Here is your liver. Every organ is individual. In the energies that they are, each organ has a core, a rhythm. Each has a sun, moon, stars, that just floats around and makes up this one whole unit.

"Every part of me came back in, one piece at a time. Every piece of my anatomy came back to my consciousness of a body laying there on a table, one element, one system, one piece at a time.

"The lady that was holding the pressure points on specific parts of my body had a calcified spine that was causing the nerves to her heart to shut down, and she had just had a heart attack. During my experience, her calcification all broke apart, all went away. The energy that brought about this expansion affected the people around me."

The Power Within

Some time later, attending a lecture by a well-known UFO authority, she realized that the behavior symptoms he described of contactees fit her exactly. The lecturer described the fear of the unknown that caused experiencers to either consider themselves "special," or to withdraw, and remain silent. But the only contact she was aware of, was of the Christ when she was small, and the 'Voice,' and the presence that had come again and again in her life.

She had a gift, she knew that. It had, in fact, been a great puzzlement to her as to why everybody else went seeking answers outwardly, through research in libraries, or by asking questions of other people, when she didn't have to do that. All she had to do was go within and ask. She thought it was weird, and strange, to have somebody within give answers, but she had to be in crisis in order to do it. She didn't utilize it well until there was a crisis.

Since every day with her cerebral palsied son had been a crisis of sorts, she must have begun to draw on the power then, but not in a conscious, deliberate way.

Cerebral palsy at that time was being treated the same as polio paralysis. There were no answers to be found, so she began to use her inner sensing as to what to do, for in working with him there were no guidelines. The physicians at Crippled Children's Hospital in Dallas kept asking her who was doing the therapy on the child. No professionals were helping her. She alone was working with him.

Utilizing her knowledge of herbs, she opened a health food store. Her clientele was comprised of people seeking help for health problems from other than the medical profession. This led her to begin workshops utilizing pressure points, group therapy and other methods. She became very successful.

Strange Writings

One night Renée was awakened and told mentally to go into her office and write. On a little pad, at a speed she would normally be incapable of, she wrote about seven pages, writing backwards, from right to left. When finished with the pages, the writing was in columns, down the page. She could never again duplicate the strokes, nor the speed in which the writing was done.

The experience of compulsive writing never happened again, although she was wakened a couple of times and told to go and write. She never did, because it just did not seem to be purposeful to her. Unfortunately, the writing was later lost.

Renée knew of Dr. Andrija Puharich and she was impressed by his work. She planned to attend one of his lectures in Houston, Texas. She had not shown the mysterious writing to anyone, so she took the pages with her to Houston, hoping to have an opportunity to show them to him. After the lecture, she showed the strange writing to him backstage. Fortunately, mutual friends arranged for her to drive him to Dallas, where he was to lecture again.

He told her that in his trips around the world he had found ten women, she being the eleventh, who did this type of writing in a language he termed to be equations and a star language. He believed it to be a musical language of another planet.

In Dallas the next day, she lunched with Puharich and two ladies. He had her show the writing to them. Both the ladies recognized the language in it and both were writing it. One lady had reams of the writing. She was an artist and had written on big sheets of sketching paper.

No one had succeeded in decoding it. He told Renée that he believed that, under hypnosis, she would be the one who could decode it. Puharich indicated that he would arrange a weekend at his place in Raleigh, North Carolina, where they would get together and do that. However, the hypnosis decoding never took place.

Exploring the Human Experience

While in Dallas with Puharich, Renée took him to a Beverly Sills concert, which he enjoyed immensely. They agreed to keep in touch, and began a correspondence which led to her assisting him with his diabetic condition.

She was invited to his home for a weekend and she and her husband drove up to see him. Her husband had taken his work along with him, so she spent her time with Puharich.

He regaled her with stories of his life, told her about finding Uri Geller, and some of the interesting escapades they had been involved in. She told him of her life, her near death from polio at age four, and other episodes. He repeatedly told her, "You are not supposed to be here."

She did one hypnosis session with him at that time. She remembers very little of the session. She does remember that when he asked her how long she had been on this planet, she said something about the first time she had come was 38,000 years ago. After the session he told her, "You have lived multiple experiences in this present body to do the work that you came here to do. You called forth an immense amount of human experience in this one lifetime to catch up, because you haven't been here before, in body, only as an observer. You don't remember; you haven't had enough human experience to know what it is like to be a human being. You have only been in body five or six times.

> "So, what has happened is, the program was to compound the human experience, make many lifetimes happen in one lifetime. That is what I believe has happened to you, because of the immense amount of experiences, the impact they have had, and, also, the fact you were given the strength to do it. You are not of the Earth plane, you are of another galaxy. Home to you is not this galaxy. This is not your homeland."

When he told her that she was not from this planet, it did not particularly surprise her, for she had a memory of, as an already defined fetus, floating down a tube and landing in her mother's body. The tube had not been her present father's penis tube, but some other tube from some other place. Her mother's and father's blood type is different from hers.

When Puharich, however, told her husband that she was not from the Earth plane it shook him up so much, it caused problems.

Past Lives

Puharich arranged for her to begin research work with him, but one of the great tragedies of her life intervened. Her oldest daughter was killed in a car accident. Renée was devastated and unable to work for a year and, thus, lost the opportunity to work further with Puharich. However, she corresponded with him until just shortly before his death in 1995.

> "After that, I made attempts to access past lives. Anytime I have succeeded, I have never seen myself as being in a body. I have been able to describe things that happen on the Earth plane from the position of an observer. I can give layouts of a city, clothing, times, buildings, things happening at certain times. I have never been in a body while doing it. I have looked for attitudes, rather than persons; I have looked for how we, as a humanity, come to a belief system. I would be shown a part of the process that built a particular cell memory."

It was only about ten years ago that she began to speak out about some of her experiences, other than to give witness in a church setting.

Merging With the Higher Self

She states:

> "We are not, in traditional religion, taught how to listen to God or how to listen to a higher consciousness. In Western culture we are taught to verbalize, but not how to listen. Now I'd say there is a marriage of what I would call my higher self that allows me to make a consciousness shift. I can do that now on somebody's question and know I have made that shift.
>
> "What I picture is like a cord or thread that could be to a master computer. It is like a shaft of light, an energy, or more of a vibration or frequency than I would describe as a light, because there is a tonality to it.
>
> "Sometimes there is a ringing in my ear. It is like somebody hits me on the head when I am not listening. Then there is a shift that takes place. That is the only physical thing I get, the ringing in the left ear once in a while, like somebody is going, 'Zzzt! You are not listening!' Then there will be an opening.
>
> "When I first was introduced to channeling, I knew I could channel, but I resisted the word altogether. Then one day, I heard a man talking, saying that he could channel multiple entities, but he was

bothered by that at one point in time, until he realized God was going to use him as a human telephone. I thought OK! I can do that!

"It took a shift in consciousness to get used to this. I feel that people get invested too strongly in one thing. They would travel hundreds of miles to go see one entity channel, when they would not sit still and listen to their own higher consciousness.

"That irked me, people taking classes on channeling, when there wasn't a purpose behind it. I think that made me more grounded. I kept looking for purpose. Where was the betterment? If it was harmful, I didn't consider it Godly.

"My definition from those early spaces was that if it didn't say love, if it said hurt, harm, fear, anger—I was not going to entertain it. Even my own anger grieved me for a long while. I did not consider that Godly.

"I now understand the energy behind that anger was for me to open up higher and higher to my God, however that is defined. I see it as multiples, as a honeycomb, a matrix above the top of the head. There are little beams of light and channels of information that come out of this matrix.

"Any of us, really, according to desire or necessity, have the ability to shift into that. Geniuses can get clear, patterned information, out of one channel of light, very much like Andrija Puharich did. Some of us, according to our own inner desire, are more available to this.

"If we are readily available to this and invested in what is true, then we start throwing out the unnecessary parts of our lives. I was never afraid of the power. I was afraid of what I would do with it. Afraid of how people would see me, if I were to do anything with it.

Defining Purpose

"I would guide people to not be invested in the outcome, to not be invested just because they have been given a piece of information. People get invested in the romance, the flirtation, of being a person who can do this, can get these messages! So what! Everybody can! Everybody does, to a certain degree. That does not make them special.

"That is where everything gets distorted. The importance lies in the usability of the material, or the availability of the material to be helpful, that it have purpose.

"My pattern has been to be on purpose, to be consciously on purpose. If there is no purpose, I am not charmed by it. I can't just sit down and read a lot of the material on the market now just because it is channeled information. Much of it is too elementary, or there is no need for it, or it doesn't serve.

"I want what brings me closer to my God, and that relationship, and knowing that I can maintain that relationship in this body. I believe that if it is serviceable to you, then go for it. If it is not, then it is yesterday's news, and may not even be the truth.

"Desire of the heart brings it in. I think you are given discernment. The methodologies are unique to everybody and not unique at all. You have to ask the question. If you really want to know if something is 'real,' is the truth; you pray that God gives the availability to know if it is so.

"When things come in then, always, go back and check with your highest authority. I am not invested in not being a failure. If I'm wrong, I am wrong. It is OK for me to be wrong. Its OK for me to not know. I don't have to give anyone an answer. But, when you check with your higher power, you get affirmations, confirmations.

"God is not the author of confusion. My God is not a confused God.

Truth is Truth and Can Be Known

"I am kinetic, most of my information comes through my feelings, though at times it is auditory. I do not usually see images, except when I was a child. It comes as an impression and has been proven through many incidents. What is true is true, and there is a knowingness. I feel a place, almost like a rod, a clear straw, in front of me. This place is like looking down the center of a straw, looking at the light.

"There is a centered space inside of me, not overwhelming, very subtle. A resonance fills me with what I call a knowing that is this *hummmm*. When it is there, when I have that feeling, there is no straying from what has been presented to me. I know very clearly to listen to what is there, whatever information is being accessed is the truth.

"I do not channel. With me, there is a resonance, an inner knowing, whereas a channeler is more or less repeating information. They do not have the inner knowing of whether it is right or not. That is my definition of what others do, what they say is channeling, and I do not equate myself with that. It is another place of integrity, for if I attach myself to that particular definition or statement, there is a lot of trash out there that I do not choose to line up with.

"At times, there is a third party in the conversation that I can hear and another person can't. There is a sense of discrimination, because I don't have to tell the other person what is being said.

"The deep mediums allow another entity to come over them, and they do not remember. I can do that. I have, but I resist it. I do not like for people to seek me out to channel for them.

"The expansion of that awareness, whatever energetics your higher consciousness or your source is, once you have touched that, then the 'you' that you have known on a pure personality human experience is almost like another being. It is like a split personality, yet, you know inside of you, that it is all one and the same.

"When mine first happened, I wondered what was the difference between me being like this and being a split personality. Am I clinically now a multi-phased personality? To me, the only thing that makes the difference is the usability of it and the integrated availability of being a productive, functioning human being versus being dysfunctional.

"When you experience a higher realm of consciousness—and higher isn't even the word, source consciousness is—when an experience begins to be real to a person, for a little while, you are going to feel really special. Then the experience is of oneness—wholeness without arrogance.

The Love

"If a source is of the higher realm, you are going to feel love like you never felt it before, or like you have never imagined it to be, because there it is everything and nothing at all. There is no judgment, there is no predisposition, no expectation. Just this awesome energetic that holds you, and the consciousness of your being, in a place that you want to stay forever. Wherever that place is, you want to stay there forever.

"At the same time there is this trickling, twinkling, little consciousness that says, 'And there is more,' and there is more.

"It is, I think, the attachment to the physical experience that holds you back. So that personality, the human experience, creates personality as we know it, ego, etc. In order to integrate, there almost has to be a separation, so that you know the difference between the one versus the other. Then to bring that into integration would be to feel I Am, or higher source consciousness, is becoming a part of me.

"When that happens, there is a very dynamic shift to the human personality. The ego moves in an entirely different way, to a different drum beat. When it merges, love becomes a part of the integrated whole, healing the human beingness that is other than the virgin consciousness. In other words, the Christed Consciousness comes in giving the opportunity to dissect and reject the song of the cells that are of the lesser thought forms.

"'This will always be this way' from science and all of the learned experience in human form, becomes not important. One begins to prove beliefs as not important anymore, because that is not what is. What is, is the realm of spirit. You cannot *not* serve it; you cannot *not* prove it. The parts of the personality begin to play in it and that dance becomes an integrated process. But, until you have experienced one versus the other, one doesn't have an availability in the human experience to make a definition of it. You need a definition of one experience versus the other.

"To me, the super conscious is a realm that is often not tangible in human form, so that we see it as something other than us. It is other than us when we live in fear of death. When we live in a consciousness of death, it is separate.

"That is one of the keys of my integration because I view death in a completely different manner than most human beings. I do not believe there is such a thing.

"The world of the physical and the spiritual are two different places, yet they are one and the same. At the point of death, the world of spirit is much more alive than the physical world. It is a shift of focus—which is alive, the physical form or the spiritual form?

"The spirit goes with the spiritual form into a spiritual world. The realm of spirit is very much like the human realm, depending on your acceptance of who you are and what your fears are."

Chapter Seven

We Have Yet To Discover

There are certain phenomena associated with hyperspace which science has yet to explain. For the most part, these phenomena are either ignored or ridiculed because they create paradoxes. Most phenomena of exceptional human experiencing lies within this paradoxical world outside of physicality.

It is, by necessity, virtually impossible to incorporate these phenomena into third-dimensional physicality without at least a working understanding of the incredible complexity of hyperspace.

One such phenomenon much ignored by modern scientists, and one in which many of the multidimensionally aware show outstanding abilities, is that of healing by methods other than those acknowledged by modern medicine.

Arigo

Puharich believed one of the miracle workers in healing was Arigo, from Brazil. He personally visited Arigo in the years between 1963 and 1968 to find out how the human mind has access to these powers, and what the human mind can do to release them to aid conditions on Earth.

He stood right by Arigo's side when Arigo operated, so he had to believe the evidence of his eyes. He believed Arigo was actually doing the things credited to him, but he had no explanation as to how these miracles were achieved.

On August 22, 1963, Arigo removed a lipoma tumor from Puharich's elbow. Puharich then took pictures of the removed tumor and the knife. He felt that if the wound did not become infected in spite of the unsterile conditions, it would provide a real test. He used no antibiotics or antiseptics. The wound healed in three days.[1]

In September of 1967, Arigo, without being asked, healed a chronic ear drainage that Puharich had suffered from for years.[2]

Although Arigo operated on several mind levels at once, he was never in trance.

Puharich stayed out in the country when he was visiting Arigo and saw many lights zooming across the sky. He often sat up all night, taking pictures of the UFOs and collected stories about them from the local people. When he asked Arigo point blank about the UFOs, Arigo denied any intervention from that source.[3]

However, Puharich believed Arigo was an entity on an exploration mission on this planet, to see what was happening, and that he then returned to his home world. Arigo had stated that his mission was to take the temperature of the human race, medically, to see where they were in their minds and hearts. He knew he was here for a very definite period and, two weeks before he died in a car accident, Arigo told some of his closest friends that his work was finished and he was leaving.[4]

Finding the Hidden Gifts

Renée had been attending a workshop and for some reason began to feel very strange. She relates:

> "My energy level was just gone. I felt like I had a huge magnet on my body and feet, and I didn't have the energy to move. The longer I sat through the next to last day of the workshop, the worse it got. By the evening, when my friend and I got to our room, I told her, 'I'm going to bed and I don't care if I ever wake up. I quit. I'm going home and sell my equipment, the store. I am getting out from under all this stuff. I totally quit! I mean it! This is it! I'm done, over!'
>
> "My friend, a midwife, said, 'You don't mean it. Go to sleep.' I did mean it. I cried myself to sleep, something I almost never did at that time.
>
> "The next morning the conversation in the workshop turned to AIDs and somebody said it was God's curse. I knew he was way off

1. Puharich, 1974, p. 28.
2. Puharich, 1974, p. 29.
3. Puharich, 1974, p. 32.
4. Puharich, 1974, p. 34.

base, but I didn't even get angry. I didn't say a word. I just sat there. I also realized that by just sitting there, not saying anything, how far down I was. I felt nothing made any difference. I thought well, I guess I've made it—I have quit.

"When we went to the airport, the airline personnel had mixed up our seat assignments. We were separated and the plane was full. We had had our seat assignments for two months, and we were upset about it, but they assured us we would get to sit together on the plane. I wasn't saying anything. To me, it was just one more thing. I had quit and I couldn't even get home. Just leave me alone.

"We got on the plane and where we were to sit, two seats together, was a girl with a baby. There were baby things everywhere. There was a carry-on and a diaper bag and some other thing. We had to hustle around putting all the stuff out of the way. We were going to be really crowded, because we were on the wall that divides first class from coach and there was no place to put our things. I had to sit in the middle and I hate sitting in the middle seat. My friend, a midwife, leaned across me and tried to play with the baby.

"I tried to get her to trade seats with me because she wanted to talk to the woman. I didn't care about the woman or the kid. You could tell it was her first baby; she was very protective of it. My friend finally understood that the woman wasn't going to let her hold the baby and she settled down. She turned to me and said something about one of the mineral formulas I designed. She wanted to use them in her practice. I explained it to her.

"The girl with the baby said, 'I don't mean to be eavesdropping, but are you doctors?'

"No ma'am, we are not. She is a nurse, a midwife and a Rolfer, and I am a nothing."

"'I didn't mean to get in on your conversation. I just got on the plane having waited for the doctor to call me, but he didn't. I am going to see my parents and my baby is really quite sick. She hasn't had a bowel movement since we got out of the hospital, two weeks ago. I don't know what to do. I can't even nurse her because her mouth is all broken out.'

"She turned the baby around and showed us that its mouth was completely broken out with thrush.

"I learned she had been on antibiotics for four days when they were in the hospital. They had the baby, a two-week-old baby, on 250 milligrams of a drug that will do liver damage to an adult. I was furious.

"I said, 'I don't normally do this, but in my carry-on bag, there are some herbs that will help your baby.' I don't usually carry tinctures of anything around with me, but I had these tinctures!

"I said, 'I don't have to give it to her, but if you will rub some of this particular tincture on her belly, she will have a bowel movement pretty quickly. Between my friend and I, if you will let us do some adjustments, she will be a lot better. I even have something that will help her to nurse. Is that all right with you?'

"We soon had this baby pooping and cooing with a smile on her face. She had not cried yet. We stretched her and released the sacrum, and released two sutures on the top of her head that were locked in. All of a sudden, you could watch the thrush in her mouth start to disappear, and she nursed.

"When we got off the plane, the woman's family was not there as yet, so we helped her with her things. She stood there with big tears in her eyes and said to me, 'Ashley will never know you, but I will never forget you.'

"My friend turned around to me and said, 'You know you are an angel. You can't quit.'

"I can't. I got it loud and clear that, for whatever reason, I had chosen to be here. I was here on assignment, so to speak. If I did get to a place where I thought I could quit, somebody, something, would happen and I couldn't."

Renée had begun her healing with trial and error. When her three-year-old son was diagnosed with cerebral palsy, she was told he would never walk, never talk. She spent the next 15 years using every possible aid within, and outside of, the medical profession to help him.

Working with her son, she developed a unique therapeutic program of nutritional foods, herbs, vitamins and physical therapy. As a result, he is now fully functional. Her main purpose in life became assisting people in transforming traumas into blessings. Renée has developed many formulas for use in healing for animals, as well as people.

The Healing Band

Another healer learned of her abilities to channel healing after studying the Alpha/Theta levels of mind. At first she was very skeptical, for she was trained as a Licensed Practical Nurse. Finally, she realized that the excuses she had for not believing that healing comes through energy exchange were ludicrous, and she accepted the actuality of it.

She envisioned healing as a broad band in hyperspace. When the command was given in that frequency, healing occurred. Within that band, however, was a narrow ribbon of perfection, and when the command was given by the mind within that space, healing was instantaneous.

When doing long-distance healing, she spoke with the soul of the person, explained they had a choice, to go or to stay, and if they wanted to stay she would send the energy to help the body heal.

Robert O. Becker and Gary Seldon write in their book, *The Body Electric: Electromagnetism and the Foundation of Life*:

"...If some people can detect fields from other organisms, why shouldn't some people be able to affect other beings by means of their linked fields? Since the cellular functions of our bodies are controlled by our own DC [direct currents] fields, there's reason to believe that gifted healers generate supportive electromagnetic effects, which they convey to their patients or manipulate to change the sufferer's internal currents directly, without limiting themselves to the placebo effect of trust and hope."[5]

Seeing With a Different Perspective

Healing information comes in different ways to each multidimensionally aware person. Blanche sees the cells within the body.

> "The brain is a transducer and interpreter of what our body feels within this third-dimensional reality. We need to let our bodies teach us how to heal ourselves.
>
> "I developed a mass in my abdomen, which obstructed the blood flow into my lower extremities, causing abdominal discomfort and difficulty in breathing. I had an MRI at the local hospital and they diagnosed a tumor which was putting pressure on the abdomen and the lung.
>
> "During the MRI, while I was lying on the table, I was thinking about the process, what they were seeing, how they were seeing it. I envisioned in my mind the oscilloscope aligning atoms by electromagnetic bombardment.
>
> "The electrons would fire and they would all migrate back to their position. Then the light on the oscilloscope would light up and

5. Becker and Selden 1985, p. 269.

in the area of the tumor there would be no electrons firing. There would be a dead space and that would make the diagnosis.

"They looked like soldiers standing at attention when the Sergeant came into the room. I thought that was not normal; they should not be doing that. The atom is a sphere; they should continue in that circular momentum with that spin. They should not stop and align after the Sergeant dismissed them or the electrical bombardment of the atoms stopped.

"I thought that is totally wrong. We have to reverse the principles in this machine and realign that cellular structure and wake it up at the atomic level.

"Then in my mind I saw a hand at a plug in a wall and I didn't know whether it was pulling the plug out or putting it in. I realized it is already plugged in, so how could they be putting it in again? I realized we had to reverse the principle of magnetism, that magnetism in the light would realign the cellular structure and interfere at the atomic level.

"If a ferric condition at the atomic level was inducing subferric compromise, which is the balance and the basis for molecular and cellular formation there, I realized that magnetism and light would fracture the ferric domain and realign the cellular structure. I knew then the hand I saw at the electrical plug was unplugging it. That inferred to me I had to reverse the principles of the machine.

"I began to visualize a machine that literally would induce the same sort of reaction. I saw a machine affecting the blood by utilizing the principles of magnetism to fracture the ferric domain. I saw an IV utilized intravenously, not by infusion, but like a dialysis, running the blood through a magnetic chamber and fracturing the condition with the DNA and realigning it.

"When people were bombarded with the magnetic influence of the machine, the atoms would align in dipolar formation. All aligned, the magnetic polarity would be released, and they would realign to their proper positions of normalcy.

"Then I began to see that Dr. David Damadian's magnetic resonance imaging (MRI) machine, using electrical principles to diagnose different conditions in the body, was basically just an image of an area without light, without stimulus or vibration in the cells. I called Dr. Damadian's office and spoke at great length to his secretary. She wanted me to send some documentation on what I surmised in treatment of the condition as diagnosed by the machine."

The Color of Health

Utilizing color in healing is an ancient art and there are many different formats for this energy transfer. Many gifted people read the auric field colors to determine the state of health of a person. "Off" colors in the aura are indicative of ill health in most instances, whether it be physical, mental or spiritual.

Some multidimensionally aware can access the energy of the off color, follow it to its source, enter the cells and determine what condition is present. Often they are able to realign the cells, induce a balancing color energy and affect healing in this manner. This is the same methodology, only more advanced, utilized by healers with healing energy.

The ancients were very knowledgeable in the utilization of light for healing purposes. Light is information; color is refinement of the information contained within light.

Roland Hunt writes in *The Seven Keys To Color Healing*:

> "Color Healing is a Divine Science.
>
> "It is not a cult, or fad, recently invented or discovered. It was used effectively in the Golden Age of Greece, and in the Healing Temples of Light and Color at Heliopolis in ancient Egypt, and again, it was revered in the ancient civilizations of India and China. Throughout the ages there has always been the employment of the Color Wisdom to establish poise and harmony; to soothe and sustain, to heal and restore, and to create anew. They were all expressions of the urge in the One Divine Creative principle in Light-waves.
>
> "Color is, therefore, a Divine Force—nothing less!
>
> "...In Color Healing the White sunlight is used, in all its spectrum of Color wavelengths, to run the motor organs of the human machine efficiently, not alone to restore the physical body, but to tone and refreshen the Mind and nourish the Spirit...."

The sun is the focal point in our galaxy, as well as our human systems. Energy-waves from the sun create, sustain and renew life upon Earth and the other planets. These planets and Earth, in turn, reflect their vibratory energies to each other.

> "The self-same principles that sustain Life in the cosmic system naturally sustain Man in his lesser, micro-cosmic system—in the working of the major glandular organs, or centers, of his body.

> "If through some failure in Cosmic Law and Order, the Earth were to be plunged into complete and continued darkness for but a few weeks, and then restored to Light, all vegetation would be found to have lost its colorful vitality, to have become anemic, and would finally wither and disappear. There would correspondingly have been a similar effect on the health and vitality of humanity. We all depend on Light more than is yet fully realized, for, as we see above, even our foods are densified chemical Light-waves...."

Through their faculty of reasoning and the power to employ will, humankind has used creativity to utilize various forms of cosmic energy. Electricity has eliminated darkness and extended daily hours of usefulness.

That same creativity and free will has, however, often ignored the value of light. Humans have immured themselves in insufficiently lighted, cramped houses in congested cities and towns.

> "Worse still, he has, all too often, drawn the black-out curtains of ignorance and prejudice over his mental, emotional and spiritual understanding.
>
> "Through this negation of light we find many people suffering from a large variety of physical and nervous ailments—many of which originate in either mental or emotional perversion or inversion. Such people are plagued with all manner of inhibitions.
>
> "Broadly speaking there are two classifications for disease:
>
> That which is infectious, or induced by wrong environment, i.e. through faulty working, living or climatic conditions, or in other words, having physical origin;
>
> that which originates in the consciousness of the individual, i.e. in our emotional behavior, mental attitudes, and spiritual outlook—or metaphysical in origin.
>
> "Color has the beautiful and purposeful mission of alleviating both classes of dis-ease, not with the patchwork substitutes of drugs, but with the pristine power of Light, which works on all levels of our being. Truly, it is very largely due to our general inability to illumine our lives emotionally, mentally and spiritually, that we have loss of tone or disease physically."[6]

6. Hunt, 1971, pp. 17-18.

Seeing the Disease

In speaking of his healing abilities, Rory says:

"At will, I can increase my body temperature and make it go extremely high, and this helps people. From childhood, my hand always got hot. If you have nothing wrong, my hand stays cool. If there is a problem, my hand burns.

"My greatest thrill is helping people when they have no idea I am doing it. I do it on a daily basis.

"I was always interested in healing, that was a known. I see things; I see colors; I see angles of light that do not make any sense. I do not see halos or auras. I see many different types of things. I have been told by a psychic that it is a level above seeing auras, where very few people could see.

"For example, working with a horse with a damaged leg, I saw a triangle from the back through the hip area, through the right leg, going down, with circles at the top and at the bottom of the triangle. There was puffy flesh around the circles, with three different shades of colors, green, light blue, off white.

"When I am focusing my healing energy, as the healing takes place, the colors change, turn a different color and it is done. I have never associated a particular disease with a particular shape, because there never was any exactness.

"You have a broken bone, another person has a broken bone, I would see two completely different shapes, colors. Never any similarity. Never exactly the same shape and color.

"I get people to talk to me when I am working on them. It is not a matter of what they say, although that is important, what the sound of their voice does is serve as a catalyst. It gives me the inward resonance—their vibration—that I can resonate to, and it allows me to better provide healing energies for their pain or disease. Basically, it is the vibration, not the verbalization."

Swimming With the Dolphins

Children, not having been conditioned to believe only in modern medical practices, are especially open to receiving healing through unusual ways.

A national TV program, *Sightings*, presented in November of 1994, an incredible case of a child with Downs Syndrome being helped by working with dolphins. These were dolphins that were allowed to swim free, yet sought out the company of humans in need. There is a very noticeable effect in the uniqueness of the bond that exists between dolphins and humans.

A psychologist, who has found that dolphin-assisted therapy is a powerful tool for teaching neurologically impaired children, states he has found that the children are interested in three things: animals, music and water. Being in water, plus the fact the dolphins are so intelligent and sensitive, creates the optimal situation for healing.

Sammy (pseudonym), diagnosed as Downs Syndrome when he was born, was the third child in the family. A congenital disorder, Downs Syndrome resulted from an extra chromosome in the cells of the body that limits the growth of the brain. He was not like a normal baby. When he cried, he did not make any noise; he just lay there. His retardation was severe, and the doctors said he would be a vegetable; he would not have thought processes. At the most, he eventually would walk, be able to dress himself, and maybe, learn to feed himself.

His mother refused to accept that, but, even after two and a half years of intense struggle, it seemed the toddler would never speak. The miracle came on a visit to the zoo. When they got into the dolphin show, his eyes flew open and his mouth gaped. To her amazement, he did not take his eyes off the dolphins. He had never paid that much attention, for that long a period of time, to anything.

After the show, when they were feeding the dolphins, although there were a lot of kids there, and he just stood and stared. The dolphins came right to him. They did not go to their food or to the other kids. They wanted to play with him. They were talking to him and splashing him, and he smiled.

It was a breakthrough moment that would eventually lead his parents to a dolphin project in Miami, Florida. There were two problems: he was withdrawn, and his language was severely delayed. Sammy loved the water, and he loved working with the dolphins. He was not allowed to interact as much as he wanted to unless he tried very hard, so he was highly motivated. He paid attention and as a result, his language started to improve, and his confidence improved. He was allowed to go in the water more and more and this was very important to him.

In the months that followed, the dolphin therapy succeeded. The inability of the child to talk, run, or swim disappeared.

The theory is that animals can reach children when people cannot, due to a kind of unconditional love and interest in the child. This bond went even deeper with one special dolphin named Bea. She and Sammy bonded immediately, to the point he could not even do the therapy exercises. She would just take him away, to the middle of the pool, and stay there.

Then Bea became very ill. She would only come to the front of the pool when he was there, and then, one day, she did not come. Two nights later, his mother was awakened in the middle of the night. Sammy had been sound asleep. He sat up in bed and said, "Oh, my Bea," and climbed out of bed and raced to the front door, calling, "Bea, Bea!" Bea had died in the night, at that very moment.

The dolphin-assisted therapy resulted, after three years, in Sammy developing near normal skills in awareness and muscular control. He progressed past the mold Downs Syndrome children are put in, but a natural disaster brought his therapy to an abrupt end when a hurricane forced the family to move.

Sightings wanted to know if his amazing success could be documented scientifically, so they arranged for the family to accompany members of the Aquathought Foundation on a trip to Cancun, Mexico. The Aquathought Foundation is a research foundation located in Southern California which studies the effects of dolphin interaction on humans. *Sightings* sent a camera crew to "document any unusual effects on the child when he met these new, unfamiliar, dolphins."

Before he even saw the dolphins, a detailed recording was made of his brain waves. This information would be compared later, after his dolphin swim, to information received during the swim, while he was taped on sixteen points on his scalp for an electroencephalogram.

His brain activity, before he entered the water with the dolphins, demonstrated high-speed brain waves, a state of consciousness not conducive to efficient learning. After swimming with dolphins, the electroencephalogram showed a state definitely indicative of a more conducive state for healing and learning. The scientists in the *Sightings* document concluded that "Dolphins use a complicated sonar system to help them maneuver through the water, a natural form of radar. Dolphins are able to send out sound waves that travel through the water and bounce off objects in their path. The returning sound waves allow the dolphins to create a mental picture of the object. Remarkably, because the human body is mostly water, a dolphin echo locator is able to pick up the images of the person's internal organs, their bones, and their brain. The dolphin echo locator energy, which can be quite intense, is strong enough to make changes in the body, actually at the level of the cells. For some reason, those physiological changes push the organism, in this case, a human being, to a state of better health."

Sammy's comprehension and retention skills in school have dramatically increased. Now, he cannot be told apart from other kids on the playground.[7]

Angelic Energies

Often children are still close to and very comfortable with the multi-levels. The fortunate ones have adults around them that understand and assist them in distinguishing between the realities.

Janet was one of the lucky ones in that her nanny was trained in Mari-el healing, which is an offshoot of Reiki. Janet's father in fits of rage had abused her physically. As a result she had a high level of anxiety and only felt safe when with her mother.

The nanny worked with Janet, heart to heart, explaining about the Light, how to hold the power, helping her to understand she was not helpless. The nanny remarked that it was like talking to an adult, so great was the little girl's understanding. She also helped Janet express herself with her artwork, especially using the play dough children love.

Janet saw entities, recalled past lives, and knew how to shield herself from energies she did not like. When she played at the Burger King playground with kids she had never seen before, she would tell her nanny who they were in other lifetimes. Sometimes she would just sit by her nanny and refuse to play with certain children due to what she believed they had done to her in the past.

One day she shut her bedroom door and told her nanny not to go in there, as "ET" was scaring her. Her nanny explained that if the entity was not friendly, it should be asked to leave, and so began an exorcism in each room of the house. When she got to Janet's bedroom, Janet said, "Its standing right by you!", although the nanny could see nothing unusual. After the exorcism Janet was fine, agreeing that the ET was gone.

There is a very unusual picture of Janet and her little brother, taken when they were sick in bed. On the left hand side of the picture, a very plain figure of an angelic being in white with widespread wings is visible.

---

7. *Sightings*, November, 1994.

Guardian Angels

Guardian Angels often appear to people in life-threatening situations, and the multidimensionally aware seem to have many interactions with them.

One older multidimensionally aware individual relates how he was saved from certain death by an angel when, as a small boy, he had gone to look at a rock slide where one of his friends had suffered a fatal accident. Though he was forbidden to go in the steep canyon country alone, he brazenly decided that he needed to go because he was afraid. He even decided to cross the unstable area of rock himself.

After carefully testing the stability for three yards or so, he felt it was solid enough, so he proceeded until he reached the middle. Then, the entire area gave way and began a slow but steady descent down the steep slope toward a canyon.

Being quick witted, he surveyed the situation, knew he could never reach the edge and so, as he had been taught, lay face down, distributing his weight as far as he could by spreading his arms and legs.

This attempt, however, did not stop the steady descent of the falling rocks. He buried his face in the rocks, absolutely terrified, knowing he was going to die. So great was his terror that he did not at first realize that although his eyes were tightly closed, he could "see" the rocks beneath his buried face, not only that, but he could see the cliffs above as well. He barely had time to wonder at this phenomenon when he distinctly heard a voice telling him not to be afraid.

The voice continued to instruct him to dig his left hand into the slide and he would find a solid rock which would hold his weight and stop his slide. He did as he was told and found the solid rock, grabbed hold with all his might and stopped sliding.

Gratefully, he turned his head expectantly toward the sound of the voice, but instead of the hiker he anticipated, he saw only intense yellow, golden light. The light illuminated the cliffs above, as well as the still sliding rocks on each side of him.

Then he saw a very white light with the head and shoulder outline of a figure. There were no facial features. Much to his surprise, the figure appeared to hover over the abyss. At the same time, he saw that his feet were a mere few inches from that abrupt edge.

The figure continued to speak to him, telling him to be calm and rest for a few minutes until the rocks stopped sliding. After what seemed to be a very long time, the rocks did indeed stop. He was then told to dig with his right hand and find more solid rocks until he could, very slowly, work his way to the solid bank.

Slowly, one handhold at a time, he worked his way across the remaining slide area. Digging, finding a solid rock, sliding across, then carefully digging and finding another. Eventually, he reached the bank, and once safe, curled up and sobbed and cried, relieving his terror.

When he at last opened his eyes, he saw three deer watching him. To his amazement, the deer ran lightly across the shale without causing a slide. As he watched, he slowly became aware that his perceptions were extended far beyond his body. He could, in fact, sense the essence of the water droplets spraying upward from the water falls, feel the essence of the spruce and aspens on the far bank.

With his extended senses he felt the entirety of beingness of the surroundings, the cliffs, the moss, the rocks, the rainbow droplets of water, the animals. So intense was his awareness that he literally became one with all things. He mentally hovered over the abyss, feeling the great depth below and was not afraid.

His perceptually altered state lasted until he reached home. When the incredible feeling left him, he had the sickening knowledge that he had foolishly risked his life, but he never forgot the extraordinary experience of oneness.

The feeling of at-one-ness is often the gift of an angelic presence, but few ever receive such specific instructions, even in life-saving events. Eastern philosophy is much more specific than Western in describing transcendent events.

The Angel of the Dark

The Angel of the Dark has appeared to Alice on more than one occasion. The Angel is almost three stories tall and covered from the shoulders to the floor in large, matte-dark feathers with iridescent tips. It is as if she folds her wings close to her like a cape to shelter and cover her. She wears a wooden bird mask with a very large, sharply defined beak. Her message:

> "I am the Angel of the Dark. It is my task to show the contrast of dark and light that you may more clearly observe the golden light. I am not dark in the sense of 'evil.' I am dark to blend into your shadows, to take your shadow thoughts and evaporate them, evanesce them.

"Give to me all that is less than, all that you wish to be free of. I am of your past. I am an Angel of the Divine Plan. I am here to remove all that holds you back, all that deters your spiritual progress. I wear the bird mask for I am related to the vulture, the condor, those that serve by removing carrion.

"I am the prophecy spoken of in Peru, 'When the Condor flies with the Eagle, there will be peace in the land.' I make the circle complete. I am the balance, the yin and yang of the bright angels such as Michael and Gabriel. The eagle soars toward the golden light, I cleanse the shadow side into perfection."

She spoke with gentleness and love.

Angels come in many guises. They are not always snowy white and do not always shine brightly. It is best to remember the admonition, "You may be entertaining angels unaware."

Chapter Eight

Connecting To the Earth

A Multidimensionally Aware View of Life

Contributed By Posey

At a very young age, Posey knew of a "beingness of golden light" with whom she interacted until her teenage years, when she allowed herself to separate from the inner knowing. Even then the beingness never left her.

"I never feared death because I had an instinctual knowing that it would take me home to my real family. Now I can see that I chose the difficult route to self knowledge, through trial and error, and by blocking my inner guidance.

> "I quit hard drugs at age 16. Three years of hard drug abuse was all my soul was willing to bear. It gave me the warning bell, twice, and there would be no third ring. But, I just replaced drugs with liquor. I still did not know how to use my power appropriately.
>
> "On my 19th birthday I was given an inner warning that I did not overlook. I stopped liquor, tobacco and red meats on that day. Since I did not change my friends then, also, it was difficult to maintain discipline in their presence. I became preachy at times and received humbling in measures equal to my arrogance.
>
> *Ease and Grace, Love and Truth*
>
> "I believe that the Guardian of the Golden Ray, who watches over me, saw that I was serious, and began directing me back to learning through ease and grace, love and truth. Even during my rebellion stage I had visions, premonitions and a knowingness that there was more.

"I could not yet explain in clear terms my devotion to this life within. I was regularly ridiculed when I tried to explain what I knew inside. I believe this happened because I was trying to live or experience the Light being of myself in a dark life-style where my uncertainties were reflected back to me multifold.

"For each drug or drinking friend that disappeared from my world, an empowered one slipped in, mysteriously or coincidentally. The universe drew God-empowered women into my world, one after another. Each has mastered a different portion of female mastery, and they are role models of truth, love and devotion to the Creator's will. These empowered women nurtured me through a most difficult rebirth. I met my husband-to-be, my soul mate, a short time after.

"I received infrequent visions of myself in the future, brief glimpses of me at different stages on my path, as a breatharian here on Earth, as an Ascended Female Master on a mother-ship, as a healer.

"However, having just begun my path, I did not mentally accept any of these. I thought them grandiose illusions of ego. Contradictorily, at the same time, in my heart, I knew them to be real and that no one could change those realities. I also kept silent about these thoughts, as in my childhood, and one by one, the ones easier to believe came into physicality.

Flying Surgeons

"As for the ships, I am no stranger to them. They were a part of my childhood, and, later in my twenties, I was taught the energy signature, shape and species of everyone who had business with Earth. I was never abducted, due to being highly guarded as a child, then educated as an adult.

"Those who find themselves in the company of flying surgeons will need to verbally affirm that they wish to disconnect all ties to them, to break all previous contracts made with them. Most importantly, to affirm and follow through with the choice to evolve without any experimentation of implants to speed up vibrational frequencies in the physical and psychic bodies.

"Once the consciousness is able to soar above the psychic field and into the lucid astral state or higher, then the flying physicians have no power. They cannot transcend into the next level of consciousness with their abductees and keep them from becoming lucid.

For all of the work they do, we must remember that nothing happens to us that is not part of our choosing, be it conscious or subconscious.

Assisting on the Ships

"During dreamtime, I began assisting those on the more evolved ships with evacuation procedures during earthquakes and other disasters. I did not fully understand whether these were drills or the real thing, but because they felt real, I took my job seriously and only questioned it in my mental spare time.

"This job called me to help those caught in devastation's path onto the smaller class ships, and then scout the area with a sonar tape consciousness to check for anyone left behind.

"I was always the last to board the ship and this tested my sense of security and trust, nervousness and fear. It seems that I did OK because this remained my job for years. I would be activated into remembering by someone saying a key word or sentence, seeing a picture of a space ship, or hearing about a natural disaster somewhere in the world.

"Intellectually, I did not believe that it could have been a real incident, yet my heart knew that this part of my life was valid and important, and that I would be called back and could choose to serve again.

"When I programmed into my mind the energy imprint of what I was scanning for, I began to be able to scan great distances through physical structures.

"The ship's area for all those caught in the disaster was like a cargo bay. We were allotted use of that area of the ship and that was all. Its vibrational frequency was tolerated by humans at any level of evolution, yet the piloting section above this chamber was of a higher vibrational frequency.

"I came to learn later that a higher level of mental maturity was required to step into the upper level. Stray thoughts caused stray piloting.

"These rescue missions were to evacuate individuals who chose to change their destiny at the last moment. They chose to wake up through ease and grace, and to awaken to their part of the Creator's plan to enlighten the whole. In that instant, they would light up like beacons in the smoke and call with all of their will to be saved, body intact.

"Have you ever been in an accident situation where it looked hopeless, yet you called to the Creator, with all of your will to be spared, that you would change, wake up to life's call? It is the same here.

"Only 20 to 25 fit snugly per small vessel, and I found myself helping a lot of children on, who in their innocence, could not move out of devastation's path when their parents chose to end their time.

Self Awareness

"At the same time, gifts bled through to this life where I was able to use that same sonar consciousness to warn animals that my car was coming down the highway. That is important in this country and I am happy to have them in the forest where they belong, not on my bumper. I learned the preciousness of each life and to cherish my own.

"After I had completed this group of services, I began escorting people and animals to the Light, as I had in my childhood.

"It took a lot of repair work, years, to get my lower bodies patched up and able to come so near to the Light again. The drugs and alcohol had eaten gaping holes in my energy field and I was opened up to be taken advantage of by the lower consciousness forces. So I had assumed the 'escort during natural disasters' job as part of my healing process.

"I gave birth to two beautiful baby girls in that period of my life and knew the preciousness of their entire being, body and soul. Also, in daily physical life, I found myself working on mental disciplines and controlling the amount of time and energy I gave to stray thoughts. I began wrapping my children in blue light and entrusting them to the Creator, rather than over-mothering them with concern and negative programming.

"Watching what I created with my thoughts was the daily and nightly homework, and still is. Relying on the Creator to guide me and watching the synchronicities, led me to more evolved beings living here who also kept a hand in the sky and a foot on the ground.

Protocol

"As I evolved mentally and spiritually, my maturity brought me to serve on the more evolved sections of the smaller ships, then onto the larger ones. It was at this time that protocol and etiquette lessons became extremely important.

"All of me needed to be assessed, and my life on all levels became filled with intense lessons in self-awareness and a deeper dedication to self-mastery. At times I was impatient, since I could see an expanded sense of myself as ascended already.

"On one journeying occasion I was on a small ship receiving what felt like reminders on how to operate a smaller class, disk-shaped shuttle. I could see outside of it and caught sight of a huge mother ship docked in space, right next to us. 'Well,' I thought, 'that's where I belong. I already know that stuff from before.'

"I extended my consciousness through the small ship and into the mother ship's hull. I met the most brilliant of golden Light and two perfect males, who turned to me and with thought, spoke one word that filled my entire being and resonates through me to this day, '*protocol*.'

"As if someone rang a wakeup alarm, I apologized in complete humbleness and retreated to the position I was placed in, back on the shuttle to resume my flight training.

The Ascended Masters

"On the physical realm, I became more psychic, my tarot reading turned into automatic writing and I learned the essence and feel of Ascended Masters. First I gave allowance for Sananda to transmit love and guidance through me, then he would bring one friend at a time: St. Germaine, Archangel Michael, El Morya.

"After some time, I allowed the female Ascended Masters to come through. My personal rule was only ascended energies, that is seventh dimension or higher, and that's all.

"While my channels were opening, I received many over amperages and learned to ground better, using my golden cord down to the center of the Earth. It all felt quite unique, because in those days, not everyone was channeling and having flight training.

Recognizing and Trusting

"I trusted my knowledge to only a few close friends, who were also moving through dimensional doors, and met with ridicule everywhere else.

"My sister recommended that I go to a doctor and get some medication, because it sounded like I was slipping off the rail. She came to see the validity of it only after she stepped off the liquor/drug path herself, and opened her eyes to the possibilities of the infinite universe. She now channels, and we journey to the same place to do group work. She has taken the Native path, and is moving to self-mastery with deep devotion.

"I came to recognize that I can convince no one as to the true reality of interdimensional journeying, except to allow them to experience it for themselves. As my guidance and guides have shared their love and helpful suggestions with me, I can only do the same for others.

"By this time, I was able to lie down at any time and draw myself, through meditation, into the presence of the Ascended Masters, and complete my job in their presence. I would complete my journey by coming back to physical consciousness and lying still for an hour or more, usually to fall into a deep sleep, only to wake up famished. This journeying took a lot of energy and focused attention, to keep the memory and feel the vision of everything that happened and fend off sleep trying to take hold.

"A subtle depression would overtake me for several days after each journey to the ascended realms. It was much different than merely channeling their energy and maintaining the amount of energy allowed in. After returning to physical reality, I would be sleepy for a few days and cry for no apparent reason.

"I ate almost nothing, and had very little ability to focus on the physical needs around me, which was not easy on the children, who by now were one, two and eight. I extend deep love and appreciation to my husband for taking over my household job, while I tried to get my emotional and psychic bodies aligned to what the mental and etheric bodies were experiencing.

"How did I deal with it? It lasted for a few months, two or three days adjustment after every journey. Then I called for Supreme guidance. Why didn't I think of that sooner? Guidance help came, as always, through the play of life.

Festival of Honor

"I was asked to align and stabilize the Ascended Master's energy here in our area with a festival to honor the masters, angels, archangels, divas, fairies, elementals and other kingdoms that we take for granted.

"This site was to remain as a permanent holy ground where people from anywhere could come to heal themselves, the planet and the universe. In accepting this job and getting deeply involved in the etheric portion of it, journey after journey, brought me to deeper understanding of what was involved in establishing an etheric retreat.

"Falling asleep after each journey continued, and so did the short depression that followed. I did not understand it at all, and felt confused as to how I could balance three very different parts of myself to be whole and one being here in this body. After all, this depression did not follow my journeys in the early days. I could experience the beauty and come home honored to have touched such Godliness or of having completed a healing to the Earth that I could be proud of.

"I focused on my responsibilities during the festival and allotted everyone else the power to do theirs. I already knew that this very land was used by the aboriginal Indians for a peace treaty between many tribes and their energy imprint and the imprint of the peace treaties' success was a part of this land's cellular memories.

"There were many of these same natives still there—disembodied and aware of our presence—open to assist in any way, as though they had waited for hundreds of years for our arrival.

"During the weekend festival, my nightly journeys took me to a stack of twelve space ships docked over the grounds and I was escorted through each one until I reached the top one.

"Twelve very different types of beings sat at a round conference table. My job, as the thirteenth being, was to represent Earth, as an ambassador from our people. The memory of it was suppressed because my mind could not handle the presence of such different looking, and feeling, beings. Those highly evolved do not always look like Ken and Barbie.

"Earlier that morning, I had automatically sketched a picture of a stack of space ships with the festival grounds under it, the heads of twelve beings in one continuous circle, and a dove, that anchored the line at the northwest corner.

"I had wondered to myself where that sketch came from. I was putting my book away when I heard my son's muffled voice downstairs, and a word jumped out of his conversation. This word brought back the memory of that night's journey, superimposed over what I was seeing with my already open physical eyes.

"I saw a hand laying on a round table. I instantly asked whose hand it was, and I knew by the energy imprint that it belonged to someone wise. The hand pressed into the table, and the table took its shape down to the creased end spaces in between each finger. It was the color of sand and marble, yet warm and alive.

"I knew this material instantly, and flashed upon other times I had been in contact with it, all superimposed upon this hand on the table scene and the view outside through the loft window. A plethora of information bombarded me, in perfect synchronicity, all in a few seconds. As the hand drew out of the table, the table resumed its original flat surface, and the words, 'When you hear a certain word you will remember,' flashed into my consciousness in my own voice.

"I lay down and brought the rest of that evening's work back to consciousness, and reviewed my other interactions with this space ship, or others like it.

"I came to recognize that the masters upon the ship meld their life force into the ship, embodying it, and allow it to be an extension of their consciousness mixed with matter. We had used this same method during Atlantis, and other evolved moments of history.

"I came out of the vision sleepy and a feeling of depression set in. I called with all of my will power to have it stop and never return. That held it back somewhat, but I knew that I had not yet healed it.

"Later that day, as some of our guests were leaving, I wished them well and as I closed the door, the tears came. In that instant, I knew what the problem was. It was part of my plan to be of both worlds, but I had to leave the ship and close the door when my job was done and watch those beautiful loving souls leave without me. My awareness had to come back to the 'now'—to washing dishes, tending to the children's needs, and the regular duties of a mother and housewife.

Awakening

"I had received an awakening, the gifts of both worlds, yet I now knew that it was my responsibility to open and close those doors myself. I was neither abandoned, nor yet deserving to stay in the ascended realms. It was my job to remain in both and merge the two, fusing them within myself and the Earth plane, and the universes simultaneously.

"More clarity came in my vision work. I knew that I had earned my right to be welcomed back at any time. I had earned it with self-love, self-healing and evolving my consciousness to draw close to the ascended realms.

"Pivotal points in my life had occurred when God's grace drew me into the presence of Earth's Masters, and my soul family here began popping out of the woodwork. Some of my deepest changes occurred with the Buddhist teachings, and a master here who channeled the Ascended Masters.

"A true awakening experience occurred in 1993 when a friend and I studied a certain text for the prescribed three months, journeying daily to Bimini by higher self, then going physically. Returning to Atlantis and encountering my mission was one of the most awakening encounters I had.

"My journey into the past did not make its full impact until I began using the gifts I had previously abandoned. I had locked them away, within my own cellular sands and painful oceans of emotion, just as Atlantis herself had hidden her power beneath the sand and sea. To cut it short—I had abandoned my post!

Atlantis

"My service in Atlantis had been to climb upon a temple, large and golden, that had an especially fitted throne at the top and an archway that tunneled through from the front to the back. From the temple throne, I melded my consciousness into the temple and it came to life, just as had the round table in the conference room aboard the ship.

"My emanation was a golden white, and I was completely focused upon lighting every cell of my body and the temple on fire with the God presence. Before me, a river flowed—a river of souls that needed little attention on most occasions—but now it ran thick and dark with confusion and chaos. The souls went through me, as I became the entire temple.

"As they flowed through this tunnel and emerged like a river of life on the other side, I could hear their life song become pure again. All darkness was banished by the golden Light.

"My task became more and more challenging as the river began to build up and push against me. The darkness threatened to overtake my position as transmuter, and I feared that it would overtake me, carry me away. The vision ended as the temple began to crumble and I pulled my energy back and took it to Venus, where I could reexperience pure unconditional love again. I had abandoned my post.

"After seeing that past life, I recognized how fear had stopped my growth here on Earth. So, I humbled myself and called for guidance to take me back to my post that I might reexperience it.

"I humbly asked for assistance because I desperately wanted to experience that love here on this planet, in this cellular body. To go beyond the fear of being overwhelmed by darkness and despair, and regain my self love and not turn to an outside source for it, was my goal.

Raise the Amperage of the Light

"As I went back, I found that my first lesson was to see that guidance was always there with me. I had not been humble enough to call for higher level assistance. So now I had passed this old test, in this lifetime, by requesting to go back, and I had asked for assistance when I needed it.

"During the revision I learned how to raise the Light and put equal conscious focus on grounding it into the center of the Earth, because up until then I had assumed only enough grounding to get the smaller jobs done.

"I was unprepared for the unexpected. It is best to have the entire grounding potential for when it is required, rather than scramble for it in mid-mission. I also learned to emanate my light ahead of myself, up the stream, as well as to focus on the temple and to assure that all is purified on the other side of the temple.

"An inner eye, a frontal eye, and an eye on the back of the head, were all working simultaneously. The heart, working in the same way, emanating to the front or into the future, the center or the now state, and the back or the past, all simultaneously, like the harmony within a melody.

"Beyond that, I recognized, with true heart knowing, to raise the amperage of the Light and the Light will always prevail. If in doubt, ask for higher guidance, that is what it is there for.

"I knew to apply present knowings or new insights found here in the now, because that is why they are resurfacing—to be used to serve the Creative force of our universe and beyond.

"These may be only a child's lessons in the big cosmic picture, yet I have come to recognize that if I put off today's homework because I am eager to get to art class, in the long run, art class will not be an option next semester. I will still have to do that homework along with the present day homework.

The Support Team

"Shortly after this marvelous adventure, the friend who had sent us a certain text asked our meditation group of six to assist on the etheric level during a mission.

"The trip took three groups of dedicated individuals to three portions of the world and one group to three activation sites. Our new friend was on the Easter Island team, and I knew by her level of mastery that this would be an eventful mission for everyone involved, including those who took their 'support team' job seriously.

"As support team, our objective was to anchor our friends in love and light, and through heart connections and seeing them in our third eye, send them all of the love, light, ease and grace we could allow to flow through us. No wonder my grounding needed an overhaul in Bimini.

"A teacher had received clear and concise instructions that she had shared with the ground crew. These were messages from the Ascended Master Kuthumi, to help the planet and her inhabitants into the golden age.

"In my guidance the Ascended Masters asked me to study certain books with references to the pyramids again.

"My journeying during meditation time took me to Egypt over and over, and to a pyramid and time I could not place. At times, I almost felt I would come home with sand in my pockets. The occurrences were so true to life, it felt as though I were there with my full attention and consciousness.

"A team of us, both males and females, stood and concentrated on a blueprint of a pyramid to form in thin air. It was a large merkaba, formed etherically, and hovered just to touch the desert sand. We each had a portion of the keys and codes to bring this amazing structure together in its perfection.

"It was also our job to maintain its integrity, until the physical matched it exactly, to form its duplicate in the sand. My job was twofold, to maintain focus on the merkaba, and to 'call up the sands' to meet the etheric pyramid's specifications.

"With the language of Light as symbols in the third eye, and a specific tone to coincide with it—with specific intent, clear motive and divine power from the source and Earth—the sand rose up like a wind storm and by suction, the merkaba pulled it into this precise form. The merkaba pulled and we pushed with such precision that there was no room for any degree of error.

"Imagine, to have possessed focus so immense in that time and space, and then to return to this one where the mind is so slack. I was unable to even balance a checkbook. I felt I had much catching up to do. It was a major humbling.

"As the gifts had awakened after the Bimini trip, here also, the Ascended Masters had me work with others in the etheric to construct and hold an immense merkaba over the entirety of a certain island in the Pacific Ocean. While the ground team worked on that island, they would be safe and able to concentrate on the immense job they had to complete.

"This merkaba was to remain for some time to stabilize the energy the ground crew had just anchored and activated. This journeying took place as I meditated and supported my friends each day during their mission in progress.

"The Ascended Masters were teaching me to make use of the gifts in the etheric and allow them to gear down to the physical realm. I have found that the supportive role on major Earth missions can be very rewarding, if we take these responsibilities seriously and ask for guidance, to know how we can be of the most assistance to the team effort.

"There are no 'glamour' jobs in a true team effort. I have found that working with those who are truly connected to the ascended realms know that they are part of a combined effort, where each piece of the puzzle must be strong and aligned to the final outcome, the perfection of the plan.

The Sacred Trust

"My sincere desire in sharing my life experiences is to strengthen other's connections to the Source. In acknowledging that we are all built equally, I do hope that we all awaken to our hidden potential as easily and gracefully as possible, and walk into the Golden Age with pride, rather than regretting our lack of insight and failure to follow our higher guidance.

"After this journey in the etheric, the symbols and tones began coming back to me. They were to be used in conjunction with other gifts that had awakened previously.

"Releasing the heavier, darker energies from the cellular structure, cellular memory of homes and estates came naturally. I felt extremely confident with the level of guidance I was receiving and the gifts I had at my disposal.

"Nature responded and the rain fell when deep clearing of the soil, trees, or others really needed it. Connecting with the divas to make it happen was not difficult, and they were more than happy to assist in a clearing of the area they were responsible for. In fact they began welcoming me and encouraging me to provide more Light grounding and purification.

"I found that as I connected even more deeply to the Christ energies within, little birds would be attracted to my area. I decided to test this 'bird attraction,' and purposely called several small birds over to where I sat on the veranda. At the same time, I focused deeply upon the Christ Consciousness because I knew that they would not respond to a regular human energy, but needed to recognize the Christ's energy imprint of purity, innocence, humbleness and compassion.

"It took some releasing of ego and allowance to be Christed, but, within a minute or so, several little birds landed in the trees, and one hopped onto the railing that I was leaning against. He hopped around, only a couple of feet away, then I thanked them all and asked him to leave and be free.

"This was a most remarkable experience for me, even though it may seem to be a trivial occurrence. It confirmed to me the reality of our powers here as humans, and that it is a sacred trust, to be kept clear and clean, and only used that the planet, and all of her inhabitants, seen and unseen, evolve.

Gifts From Time and Space

"I used three parts of the language of Light, one to release the dense, painful, suffering type energy, and another set of symbols and tones to infuse the liquid Light, packed full of the keys and codes of Creation, back into the cellular structure of the land and home.

"I have found this process to be gradual with many places because the owners try to hold onto the old patterning and change at a gradual pace.

"With unclaimed land the effect is much faster. Therefore, I have been guided to call the soil, home and people to surrender back into the hands of the Christ and the Christed assembly, and allow the marriage of the Father/Mother source to be, once again. In perfect union the Christed energies are reborn within the cellular structure of anything.

"To become Christed we know that we must become balanced within, the yin/yang and female/male energies.

"When I hear a yes from all parties involved, only then do I continue with the diffusion of misaligned power and infusion of Creation in a wave. As with all things, free choice must reign supreme, no matter how it may seem to be best to go ahead.

"When we are willing to draw our gifts and hidden powers back into this time and space, the entire world and its reality will benefit from it, especially if we are brave enough to use these gifts, once we have reawakened to them.

"That is why the Ascended Masters are here, to diffuse down the Light for us, as we do for the Earth and her other inhabitants. I have accepted guidance from the seventh dimension frequency and higher, because it is beyond duality and that is my goal.

Concentrating on the Light

"In between awake and asleep is a lucid alive consciousness that takes us to the depths of our cellular memories and beyond, into the universe. The powers and pure love we left behind, buried by the sands of time, await our conscious effort to unveil the dusty film of neglect and allow those gifts to glisten forth.

"In test upon test we prove our pure motives and good intentions to use those gifts for Creation alone. Our tendencies to destroy, separate, take away free choice are all eradicated. We allow our power to be one with our self love, and we ascend another step on the stairway to perfection here on Earth.

"Ascended Guidance has taught me to begin journeying only through portals that are guarded by an angelic presence, a kind of seal of approval, you might say. I begin by asking for the highest wisdom to unfold and guide my journey, and I give thankful prayer when I am complete.

"In concentrating on the Light, I do not concern myself with the shadow realm, yet I do not fear it. In my Light body, nothing can harm me. As the darkness is illuminated by the light when you turn the light bulb on, so is ignorance illuminated by knowledge and the proper use of it—wisdom.

"Stray fears and loose thoughts can get us into trouble here, but it is less obvious because of the time lapse between the fear projection or stray thought and its manifestation.

"In the Master's world (as is becoming here) all thought is projected as language and they would not only hear your thoughts, but see them as you were creating them in your imagination. In my experience the ascended realms do not procreate or share intimate imaginings with us. They love us unconditionally, yet leave us to figure out our physical needs with each other here.

New Gifts Unfold, Then Spread Out To Others

"I will continue with what is unfolding and if all works in the same flow of ease and grace, I will reunite with more of my soul's family and develop deeper bonds of support and service with the ones I am already in connection with.

"The electromagnetic grid line is part of my being now, and I will continue to work with it and to support it with liquid golden Light from the Creator and anchor it wherever I am called to do so.

"My communion with the Ascended Masters will never change. They have taught me a Who's Who in my universe and helped me realize my hidden potential, or a fraction of it. I look forward to more growth and guidance in the years to come.

"My adjusting seems to be a gradual process where a new gift reawakens and I adjust, then I release more personal baggage or ego hold, and another gift surfaces, and there is more adjusting.

"In general though, being in touch with my soul family has given me more purpose to move forward here. Now I know there is unconditional love for me here and it is surfacing more and more. God bless my soul family. They have awakened in me the potential to love everyone dearly, starting with here, with myself, and fanning it out from there."

Chapter Nine

The Corn Farmer Who Walks Between the Worlds

A Multidimensionally Aware View of Life

Contributed By D. B. Valdez[1]

D. B. Valdez, The Corn Farmer Who Walks Between The Worlds, is Native American and Hidalgo Spanish by heritage.

Married, with two children, a Vietnam veteran, he has dedicated his life to working in the barrios of a large Western city.

He perceives himself as a person from the future who has returned to this time for a specific reason. Through self-hypnosis he has viewed the moment of his birth. According to him, he was born with a caul, and taken from the delivery room to a space ship, examined and possibly "treated" in some manner.

He has also seen the time and manner of his death. The authors have known him for over 15 years and see him as one of the most service-to-others persons they have ever met.

On Multidimensionality

D. B. states:

> "The ancients brought the essence of consciousness in the DNA of man across the islands of the sky to the Earth. Much understanding was left by them, for they left, so to speak, imprints, the knowledge of different places for those whose consciousness would

1. Correspondence for D. B. Valdez addressed to the publisher will be forwarded.

awaken at a future time. It didn't have to be a large number of people who would awaken and spread the knowledge.

"My symbol is a circle with a square in it. When a square is superimposed on a circle so that the corners of the square barely come outside of it, a useful diagram results. It consists of the perimeter of the great pyramid of Cheops and the circumference of the circle represents most pyramids, no matter whether they are off planet or on. They are designed, for all practical purposes, to accomplish the squaring of the circle.

"In essence, we are squaring the circle and cubing the sphere. That is one of the things that has to be understood about multidimensionality in order to be able to find a place of coordinates.

"They left those coordinates for people to find or to find people who have passed through the understanding. There is a golden number that was left by the ancients for us to enable us to find the keys to certain things.

"When the studies were done in the pyramids, the genetic memory was to have passed on through the crystal consciousness of the Christian Christ. He was to have taught about the patterns where the dimensional doorways are located.

"Man cannot travel to any other place in the universe in the physical sense. The physical body cannot break the laws of the physics of the universe, even though man would like to think it possible. Man is still trying to use technology to get to dimensionality. Technology has to adhere to the laws of the universe.

Approaching the Dimensions

"In the Hopi legends, the sacred stone tablet has one piece missing. The missing piece refers to the fact that, while they seem to have kept some understanding of how to work the dimensionalities, not many people can figure out how to get to the dimensions.

"There are two different approaches. One is the psycho-chemical approach that alters the pathways to the brain through the ingestion of chemicals indigenous to where the person lives, i.e. mushrooms, peyote, any of the things that alter the chemical way the synapses fire in the brain. Those are psycho-chemical keys to open some of the doors, but it does not do any good to open those doors, if, when the person crosses through, they do not know what they are doing. That is where people go off the deep end and come back coo-coo.

"That is why it is so important to start with the basic teachings about the Light, which is the second approach.

"To teach about Light, the spectrographic analysis of light itself must be taught. The best way to reawaken the understanding from inside the consciousness is to take a triangular prism and shoot pure light through it, so the separation of light itself can be seen at the level where light is constructed—the photon level.

"The knowledge comes from the Rainbow Society of the ancients. The Two Horn society of the Hopi are the people in charge of the metaphysics. They were the ones who were to teach the people about the true essence of the rainbow.

"The Christians have said the rainbow is a promise from God. They have it right, but it is more than a promise. It is, for lack of a better word, the key. It is the turning point of the dimensions. Out of the primary colors, the 360° of arc of each one is assigned a color, from the lightest to the darkest.

"The center of chaos must be entered. That which we think is the most mixed up, is the thing that has the most balance. That is chaos. Chaotic activity is the birthing place of everything. It is the doorway.

"The Mobius strip[2] is actually the ancient Egyptian sign of the figure for eternity, infinity in a multidimensional field. In this level, it only has one side all the time, but if put into the fifth dimension, where all eight sides are accounted for, it then has depth, space and an endless field.

"In a multidimensional field, it then becomes infinity. The pivotal point (the heart of the Mobius strip) is the connection to the All, the Creation. This cannot be gazed upon with any kind of eyes, metaphysical or other.

"These perceptions cannot be seen by an ordinary human eye because of viewing a flat- or two-dimensional point. One of the best ways to explain this is the new little dot things that have the hidden pattern in them. If a person cannot see that pattern, then they have all the right ideas and the right equipment, but are missing the signs. They have to alter their perception of light, which means they cannot believe what they are seeing with their eye unless they see into the dimensionality of it.

---

2. According to *Random House Dictionary of the English Language,* unabridged, a Mobius strip is a continuous one sided surface formed by twisting one end of a rectangular strip through 180° about the longitudinal axis of the strip and attaching this end to the other.

"When they look at those pictures, they see chaos. When they see into the dimensionality, out of chaos comes understanding, if rightly perceived.

Facilitators

"The multidimensionally aware may have a sense perception that seems chaotic. That is one of the things that can drive hyperspace people mad sometimes. They have an answer, have something inside themselves they just cannot get out, cannot verbalize, cannot explain to anyone. Consequently, a facilitator is needed.

"A facilitator is able to show them the inner pathways, show them themselves, so that when they walk away, they become a different person altogether, because they have learned to perceive.

"Facilitators show people that they have to be taken to a different perception. They have to be taken to an altered state of consciousness and shown what is true about reality and what is not true about it. Most facilitators have worked in this so long, they tend not to show themselves, they won't come forward. Students have to find the way to them.

Teaching A Different Perception

"We have a race of people living on this planet who live in an altered state of consciousness 90 percent of the time—the Aborigines. They are the ones called the spiritual keepers of the gateway. Not every Aborigine, not every Native American, has the answer, as some people think, but some do.

"In order to teach people these things, I have to take them to a different perception, to an altered state of consciousness and say, now look, this is what is true about reality, and this is what is *not* true about it.

"One thing I do is set people down and make them study things that they think do not mean anything to them at all, but they do.

"Once the way is found, then comes the ability to do other things. Down in the deep Rapid Eye Movement (REM) sleep point of the body, it is as if the consciousness was walking into a huge building with a ring of keys, one floor has this, one floor has that. As they knock on each door, in this big building, eventually there is a door that one of the keys opens.

"They have to first be able to get to the person who is in charge of the room, the moderator, and communicate with them. They have to talk to the moderator of each room before they can get into a room. That moderator is the one who perceives them to either have understanding or not.

"Then they can walk in and have an interchange of ideas with the people who are there, even though the people cannot be seen, or felt, or heard. Still, there can be an interchange. The consciousness is online and able to approach from a different perspective. Not through the telephone, or the computer, or through TV, but the parallels are the same.

"That is basically what happens in multidimensionality. That is putting it very simplistically.

Traveling Through the Dimensional Gates

"What most religions call the spirit is what we would call that part of the person that is able to travel those planes. The astral plane is like the membrane inside an eggshell. They can travel along wherever they want to, but they never get outside of the eggshell itself. They are still connected to it, in one of the many levels of consciousness.

"They discover a whole new thing about living in dimensionality. They learn that they do not have to go any place in the universe to be any place in the universe, for they are already there. That is a concept most people find difficult to understand.

"I would call them the rainbow warriors. They are the ones that will end this dream and begin the new dream and a new reality.

"That concept explains one reason why we are dealing with the cousins, or the brothers, that come from other places. They are greatly interested in the same kind of concept and understanding that we are putting forth now. Except that a lot of them went over to the technology millions of years ago, and, because of this, have been blinded to the inner understanding of dimensionality.

"They are forced to travel the universe in a physical sense, and even though they have pushed the limitations of physics itself to where they can do some of the things they do, they may not, as yet, understand that the way to travel in the universe has nothing to do with solid form. It has nothing to do with going anywhere.

"It is finding the point in all the degrees of arc that match one another up to the eighth degree. When they match one another up to the eighth degree, then they have brought that part of the universe to where they are. Not actually brought it, it exists there, but just have found the pathway to it—through the maze.

"When they can walk the maze, then they can walk the pattern. Learning to walk the pattern is one of the reasons why, in Native American physics, the patterns are more important than what they teach. The pattern itself is sometimes the path they have to learn to use.

"The multidimensionally aware cannot break the laws of the universe in order to travel. In these perceptions, they have to travel through the dimensional gates. When traveling through the dimensional gates, they are not using any kind of perceived energy because they are not going anywhere.

"The macrocosm is within in the microcosm, and that is where they have to go to perceive it. It is not shifting anywhere. They must go within to perceive.

"Some of the Native American's most sacred ceremonies are the going within, to the intellect of the holographic consciousness. Within, everything is already there. It is one of the hardest perceptions to teach people: that everything that is known within the universe exists within themselves. Everything!

The Corn Lecture

"One of my lectures is the corn lecture. It begins by telling that when the universe was in total harmony, and every subatomic particle was in its perfectly aligned place, everything that existed in reality, existed in something smaller than a grain of corn.

"When the thought of consciousness, the thought of the Creator, passed through this, it was very much like applying heat to a popcorn kernel. When that water inside changed, that steam was the big bang. When that thought of Creation passed through that inner thought of consciousness, the universe was born. Everything and everybody was born in that universe at that time.

"People say I am talking the Big Bang, the expanded theory of the universe. No! I am not talking the expanded theory of the universe. That is a scientific perception.

"Look at the universe, it took form and grew, but it is not expanding in all places at the same time. In some places it is expanding, and in some places it is contracting.

"If we look at the universe as a giant heart that is beating, that is the life of the universe. That is where all perceptions of the universe come, in the heart of the universe, in that one sacred beat. That is why we use drums and different sounds to tune the people to the beating of the universe. When put in rhythm with the beating of the universe, then they are in tune with the other perceptions and may cross over into each one of them.

Getting In and Getting Stuck

"In that understanding is why, even though the universe is as endless as it is, there are some of us who are grounded and have our butts sticking out in that other place, wherever that other place is. We have no name for it, we only know of its existence. That gets pretty interesting because we are almost at odds with each other.

"If the universe is everything there is, why are we saying there is something outside of it? The universe is a word we use for what we can perceive. That's our eggshell.

"The thing about dimensionality, the whole concept of dimensionality, is to learn about light. Light penetrates through everything.

"A quantum physicist from San Diego has gone from quantum physics to shamanism, and understands they are the one and same thing. Physicists, using the observer effect, realize that a photon changes from one place to another when they pay attention to it. The observer has an effect on the observed.

"So they have to be very careful about how they observe, to not look directly at something. Just perceive it to be there, instead of directly observing it, because if they do, they change it, and once they have changed it, then, of course, everything else is changed up the ladder one way or changed up the ladder another way.

"That is where people get lost in their thought perceptions of multidimensionality. They get into a place they can't get out of. I call it the squirrel trap, where the gates are open, very inviting, and there the jewel or the food, or whatever, sits, inviting them to come in. The minute they do, they spring the trap, the door closes and that part of their mental understanding is trapped in a dimensionality that maybe they can't get out of.

"What happens is, they lose a lot of the perception from within the consciousness, and without that perception in its proper place, they are lost until they find the key again.

"Those perceptions are needed in order to be able to understand the dimensionalities and how to cross into them. That is why the dimensionalities shift from one place to another.

Learn It But Don't Use It

"One of the things that is totally hidden from humankind on this plane is psychokinesis, because within psychokinesis is the ability to move things in the dreamtime with thought. If that is done here, however, in another dimensionality, when that ability is needed, it is not going to be there.

"It is like taking a car, filling it full of gas and getting out in the desert and taking all the gas out to start a big fire. Then there is no gas in the car and it is impossible to go anywhere. In other words, its not good to use that type of energy in the dreamtime.

"A medicine person of great understanding is tempted to do certain things, heal people, help people by using the power. What is supposed to be learned, is to help them and heal them without using the power. In essence, a power is being used, but not 'The Power.' Semantics are not sufficient to define 'The Power.'

"If I say, yes, I'll teach you how to levitate things, but you can never use it. How would you know you had learned it?

"Right! That is the power of faith. Look at it this way, if a guy is standing in the middle of Hong Kong without his five physical senses, how would he know where he was?

"Say we switch a person dimensionally and that person says, 'OK, I understand everything about the way light works'; they can start from that point.

"People are going to need to be able to figure it out when they cross into dimensionality. Do not waste the resources here in the outback—they are going to be needed out there. It is a hard perception to get people to understand. Learn it and try to not use it. It is wasted energy manipulating third-dimensional reality, which is just an illusion.

"The laws of the universe state that energy cannot be made or destroyed, only altered. But, if someone alters it all the time they are here—again this is a hard phase dimensionally—there is substance to it. Molecular action is put together into substance. The only thing that goes through everything is light. It is the old thing about reaching into the rock and feeling the heart of the rock and not damaging it or damaging yourself at all.

Perceptions Must Be Altered

"Holograms and virtual reality teach us that we can't trust our eyes. Like the dots on the cardboard, it cannot be seen using normal perception.

"Perception must be altered. The dimensional brothers who are helping us evolve put out a lot of things to see who will see and who won't. Like the crop circles, I tried to send a message to everybody who knew me to see if anybody would call back. Nobody did, which was disappointing to me. I thought I had put it out strongly enough for a lot of people, but I hadn't.

"When the dimensional brothers asked me which crop circle to make, so that I could call the people who understood, I told them to make a certain symbol, and they did a good job, but nobody called to say they had recognized the crop circle as my symbol.

"For the longest time I didn't want to do any of it, for there just wasn't anybody who could understand what I had to say. So I put certain things out and hope somebody will nibble.

"The Aborigines tell me that now, I am starting to learn that the more you cross over into the dimensionalities, the more this one is erasable.

"I see what they really mean by the dreamtime. Their dreamtime is where reality has substance. What we live in now is the dreamtime. It has substance.

"I am not frustrated any more, though I used to be. Now I understand. I have gone everywhere I can and listened to everybody for 30 years. I feel lonely again, perhaps because my consciousness has gone beyond all of this.

"This happens in the universe. Every now and then, there is a throwback, and a throwback is one whose consciousness comes from the future, is stuck here in the past and aware of it. It is so lonely, there are things I have to give that I can't give.

"There are others here, for lack of a better word, called Creatures of the Light. Nothing can hide in the Light. Everything is revealed and once a person starts to live in that Light, it is not the absence of color, it is the total mixing of color.

"In that total mixing of color, nothing can hide from the scrutiny. Everything is revealed in the Light. When a person sees that, they understand. When people cross, they go to the Light. Light is the best name it can be given, but it is not light; it is not dark. It just is.

The Whirling Rainbow

"Colors are important. They are what the ancients wrote with—not writing—certain things were given because of the light spectrum. Those that 'steal the color of the light, that sit alone deep at night, the wisdom of those that fly at night, the Six Point Cloud People are our plight.'

"The Six Point Cloud people gave the wisdom and understanding that color actually has to do with energy. There is a relationship in direct proportion to the chakras, the colors and how they used light for healing.

"Today argon lasers manipulate energy at the photon level, the same level as sunspot activity. Photons are so small that they pass through everything—solid matter—because of the polarity field switch in magnetic fields.

"The four directions are identified with colors. Yellow to the East where the sun comes up and light comes from. Black and brown in the West, where the sun goes down. White to the North. Green and red, Earth part, to the South. The Plains people chose red to the South and the Pueblo people green to the South.

"There is a direct relationship to where a person was born on the medicine wheel to color. The colors that most affect them in the light spectrum can work better with them than for someone born across the wheel.

"Different things are painted certain colors because the colors affect human beings psychologically. People favor colors that are more healing to them.

"The power is given to the people in the whirling rainbow. In the whirling rainbow are the three primary colors—red, blue, yellow. Any one of them placed over any of the others is part of what we call the three-dimensional light point.

"When mixed together, they form the grounding brown. Once people learn to ground into that, in order to go to the next step, they take the next secondary color and mix it with the next primary color, continuing until finally they get to the indigos, the deep dark purple.

> "The reason purple is so important, and always has been in the mythology of humans, Earth people, is that it has always been the royal color. It was called the royal color for a reason, from the time the Egyptians were taught to activate the pyramids.

Emanating Understanding

D. B. Valdez has spent his life using his multidimensional abilities to increase humankind's understanding of reality beyond the third dimension.

A close personal friend tells of an unforgettable experience she once had with D. B. :

> "We went to a large party, one I had been invited to attend. We walked in the door of a massive room and, within one minute, everyone in the room seemed to be coming to greet us.
>
> "The vibrations in the room changed dramatically from nonchalant to joyously festive. I have never seen such a change in so many people, in so short a period of time.
>
> "Later I said to him, 'I didn't know you knew so many people.' He looked at me and said, solemnly, 'I never met any of those people before tonight. Spirit is all one.'"

Your Belief System Formulates Your Perception

D. B. Valdez explains his views on Spirit. "Your belief system absolutely formulates your perception. In my Native American way, I keep it in perspective by understanding that spirit is often associated with those who have passed on.

> "Those you are connected to are the ones who do not pass judgment on you, on any of us. At times, it is hard to talk about the things you regret. It doesn't matter. Where we are is not the true reality.
>
> "Remember when someone was a teenager, how they laughed when you tried to discipline them? That wasn't important. Think about the times you laughed until you almost cried. That is what is important. Those are the things to remember. Those are the things that are truer than the misinterpretations of one another's feelings. They perceived [that] you did this or did that, but those perceptions are all wrong. You are laboring under misapprehensions of what the spirit world is about.
>
> "The reason they never come back, is they have no need to. Its hard for us—remember the magnetic fields, like attracts like—that is the reason why we can't seem to reach the ones we are the closest to.

Call this reality the positive, the next negative—no connotations—just fields.

"No matter how hard they try to approach, they can't because of the fields, so the intermediary becomes important. This is what spiritual shamanism is. The shaman is the one who is able to understand you can't approach the one you want to approach, because of the ways of the universal laws.

"In praying and asking, you take the energy from yourself, asking for the sign. You should understand that when there is no answer, if there is no response, that there is no answer.

"Even the little brief glimmers of understanding that you sometimes get, come because you are putting so much power into it. Use the power to pray to say you understand. The more you understand, the more you take away that negativity, the more it balances itself out. In other words, we have to let Spirit work itself.

"Let them be at ease, because every time you call them back, you pull them back from whatever they are doing. That is why time eventually takes grief away, because your intellectual brain starts to forget. If you give your grief power, you are keeping them here.

"In working with terminally ill people, the difficulty is not with them, because when they understand, they are ready to cross. It is the people around them that are keeping them here as long as they still have physical cognizance.

"I laugh at death; I spit in the face of death. The reason I do, is that you have to make that constant effort to say death is nothing. It is one of these shadowy dimensional figures we have let overcome us and put fear into us. There is no such thing as death; there is no such thing.

Walkabout In the Big Picture of Consciousness

"When I am 'out there,' I try to teach people to go on the walkabout, but it is a different kind of walkabout now.

"One thing is amazing to me. I have to begin with the foundation of Native American spirituality, because in it is found the grounding for others.

"I call it being mud heads, the mud people. These are the ones that have more understanding about dimensionalities. They haven't been tainted by the steel, the copper, the wire and electricity and everything else. The more that you are Earth grounded, the more you understand.

"It is turning a page in understanding. People get stuck in the micro-perception. In order to really expand, you have to let your consciousness flow over the entire universe and see the big picture. That is a good title: 'The Big Picture of Consciousness.'

"I know the time has come now to go ahead and say the things I have to say. I can show ways to do this, and there are ways, the little shavings, the adjustments to make the door fit, but people have to be grounded in the Earth colors.

"That is the reason that we have ceremony, not just to have it, but to understand the use of the tools. I teach it through the Native American philosophy and perception. I teach the first-grade level. If I do not pass them to the second-grade level, they do not get the next level after that.

The Four-Worlds Perception

"I teach what I call the four worlds perception. The fifth world perception is understanding how the four, in combination with one another, bring the fifth one about. When you graduate from that fifth one, then we take you out in the dimensionalities. The dimensionalities are the doorways to all these other places.

"We are right now in a part of the 360 degree dimensionalities that is not real. It is finite.

"When the children of the stars start to understand who they really are, where they are really from, it opens up from within.

"Attempts have been made by Christ, Buddha, and Mohammed to teach this, but nobody gets it. They look for God without understanding what they are looking for. They want things to happen out of their desire, instead of putting themselves into it.

"The power of faith is only motivated by the power of understanding. In order to be able to see these things, that power of faith must be there. Faith is when the intellect, or the consciousness of the intellect, applies what it understands to the dimensionalities.

"When someone blows against a feather and sees it move, a simplistic way to say it, is that they didn't touch it with anything but the air. Multidimensionality is not touched with anything but thought.

"The length of your eternity is the power of your love. Give love, and I don't care how bad you have been or what you have done, none of that matters. We are one in more of a sense than anybody understands.

"You have to look at every person like you were looking at your own child or your lover. Treat everybody the same way. If you have no love; you have no eternity. To not have eternity is the scariest thought. You are there, however, you just don't know you are.

"Everybody wants to go to heaven, but nobody wants to die. The reason you are still alive, and the reason you are going to die, is through the graciousness of the Creator that has given you the chance to be able to perceive what is true."

Manifesting Through Your Own Power of Love

"The opportunity has been given to manifest your own destiny through the light of truth and love. Creator has given you the power and the will to be able to look at death and not be afraid of it. Accept it and go gloriously into that light.

"When you turn yourself over to Creation and that energy that is the universe that you are and will always be a part of, then you understand why the rainbow and the colors were placed there.

"Once you understand the power of the light, you understand what makes life work. What makes energy work is not anything in the physical world, but the manifestation of love, or caring, for everything that exists. Glorify everything that exists, because everything that exists is a part of the Earth. We shape it, we manufacture it, but everything that exists first existed in thought.

"The Creator has put forth the understanding that we are not to hold ourselves up as anything special, but to hold ourselves up as the minority of people who know the only way to change things is to change ourselves and teach the people around us. The rest of it will take care of itself, in that thing which humanity has manufactured called time. It starts within yourself. There is a path.

"Our old understanding that is ancient within us from the beginning of the universe and the understanding that goes into the future that we are a part of, and will always be, makes it obvious that the Creator has taught us one imperative thing.

"The most important part is living what you are doing today. It does not matter what it is. Do it with a joy and do it with an understanding. We are only here for a little while, so do as much as you can, however you can. What you learn now is going to serve you in the other 360 dimensions of creation.

"Our flesh is of the Mother, but our spirit is of the Father. The Mother is anything that has firmament in the universe. The Father resides in between the spaces of firmament. Our existence is between and always has been. Endless and forever means exactly that, endless and forever."

Chapter Ten

Children of the Belonging

A Multidimensionally Aware View of Life

Contributed By Asda

Asda, a cheerful, charming young man in his mid-twenties, although more adamant than most that he remain anonymous, nevertheless spoke freely of his origins, his life struggles.

Born into a family of experiencers, Asda was the middle of three children. He was three when the youngest was born and remembers holding the baby and knowing they were kindred souls.

As they grew older, they played mental games:

> "We would play psychic poker. We called it telepathic poker. Instead of money, we would use chips and guess what the other had in their hand and that way we could increase our ability to understand each other.
>
> "We could pick up on certain vibes from the earth. When we came upon an object, we would study it—how it was, where it came from, where it had been.
>
> "We could pick up on electrical fields around wires. Our hair would stand on end.
>
> "When we needed something, it would turn up in a few weeks, say something for the car or the house we really wanted. We would find it for next to nothing."

Sibling Rivalry

The siblings were very telepathic, but they were also always very competitive.

One would often say to the other, "Shut up! You are thinking too loud and it's bothering me." They had a strong sense of intuition about others, and were very intuitive about dishonesty and anger which they hated. It was a shock to their nervous system. Apart, they could always psychically "tune in" to each other, even to the point of seeing places and people the other was seeing.

> "Sometimes we would slow each other down, to get even. As children we had animosities, one-upmanship. We both knew we had something special, but there was constant competition."

They had playmates, whom they called the "cloud monsters" and thought they were just mischievous children who could come and go freely about the house, pulling pranks.

Visitors From Home

Asda remembers, even when very young, staring at the stars, wondering where home was and the people he loved and missed so much. It was only in their teenage years, when they saw a computerized drawing of an ET, that they realized who their companions had been.

> "At first, we didn't really want to believe, but we were excited at the idea that we were being visited. It was a verification. There are instances where these people [ETs] have walked up and shown us things—have shown us that we were not alone.
>
> "At the time I didn't understand what was going on, but both of us would have dreams of different places we had been to and seen. We didn't put the pieces of the puzzle together until we were older.
>
> "One instance, that I haven't mentioned to many people, was aboard a vessel. I don't know if it was a physical ship or an energy structure. They said, 'You are one of the chosen ones. You have a job and you are to do this.'"

Extraterrestrials were around all the time when the children were young, and Asda could not understand why they had to leave. He said, "I felt this over-presence of love, nothing like I have ever felt since. And awe, but sometimes some of the stuff they did to me was not agreeable, such as medical exams.[1]

1. After Asda was grown, they once inserted a glass tube in his penis past where the seminal fluid is mixed to collect the undeveloped sperm. This will keep, but not if it is mixed with sugar and protein of the seminal fluid which will activate it.

"They noticed that as a child I was more open. They came more often and they didn't stun me as often, for I didn't understand what was happening. But as I became more adult, these people would put me in a different state of mind. My conscious mind was still hanging around, but my subconscious or something of that nature was shut off.

"They would take me to their dimensions or their place, where they did the procedures on me. It was like what they were doing was just helping me out, making sure that things were going as smoothly as possible.

"I always wanted to go home. I never felt that I fit in here. I always wanted to be with my extraterrestrial friends. I wanted to stay on the platform. I did not want to come back to this little body."

Learning Tricks

The younger sibling seems to have been more kinetic, a little mischievous, more inclined to play tricks. When someone bothered or disturbed him, something the person valued would break or disappear.

Both could just think on an object and it would move. If they got really excited or scared, objects or pieces of paper would sail across the room, and they wouldn't know why.

"One curious thing: any metallic watches we wore would become magnetized, become solidly fused.

"Another one of the tricks we learned from experiencing other people in the universe was how to use our gifts to heal each other, to direct that energy for good.

"We learned certain tricks, how to move air by just thinking about it. We found that by putting two hands together, keeping them spread and at a 90° angle to each other with the two thumbs, one up right and the other at a 90° angle, then moving the hands away, we could create a breeze between our hands and keep the electrical charge in our bodies."

Consciousness Holds the Universe Together

Both had a strong affinity for wild animals, a strong grasp of, and understanding for, the environment that these animals lived in and could call them to them at will, so they never lacked for pets.

Asda always had an intuitive way of knowing what was wrong or right, an ability to pick up on certain things.

"As a child I noticed that I picked up on high emotional states. I knew I did not fit in with the normal public in general. One instance of not fitting in was that, as a child, I had an unusual artistic ability and my art differed from others.

"In school, instead of picking a normal topic, I talked about planets. I remember calling a certain planet Jet-ton, with a reptilian type of people. Most kids never understood why I picked that topic.

"When we were around other people like us, people that had psychic abilities, we could communicate with them freely. We had a sense about these individuals, that they were different in ways more similar to our understanding in our consciousness. We would talk a great deal with these people and in discussions we would become very technical, touching on the sciences.

"My sibling and I would discuss what we learned from other people in other parts of the universe, that consciousness basically holds our reality together, holds the universe together as a whole. We understood these things when very young. Like a kid understands how to put a puzzle together, but it takes time to understand the whole picture.

Learning to Control the Noise

The telepathy was always a problem. He heard the voices of people mainly when they were present. When they were communicating, he could actually understand what the individuals were saying. As his abilities grew, he began hearing more and more people. If he couldn't get away from the voices, he would sit down in a quiet place alone.

He described it as:

"If I had a thousand audible voices, in order to listen to just one, I had to tune out everybody else so my mind would not go crazily racing, trying to figure out what was going on and thinking of all topics at once.

"One of the worst side effects were headaches and stress. I had low energy because it just zapped me. I have learned now to control it to an extent. If I listen to one station, I can quietly turn it up if it is something I really want to hear. I can always put up a veil or a kind of shield or cloak to protect myself. That is part of keeping on my toes, another part of the growing experience, growing into this new life.

> "I always had a worldly status about myself, a nice manner. I had to learn as a child. I always wanted to know how things work. All children explore their environment, but I had this extra added dimension inside of me that brought out more of an adult, logical, loving, soothing manner, more adult."

Assistance With Survival

When Asda was young, he had two molars that were completely flat in the lower part of his jaw which did not have any roots. They did not have any bulk or size to them; they were very thin.

Asda attributes this to some of the genetic changes that may have happened over the years because the ETs have been adding genetics as he was growing up.

At critical moments in life, when a person is very young and when reaching puberty, the body changes, and Asda believes that would be the most opportune time to put the changes into action.

"These people found that by doing this, they could help out my ability to survive in this environment, the emotional environment, the conscious environment, and my altered state. Sometimes I reach a state of incredible loneliness."

Seeing It Another Way

Loneliness has always been his greatest problem. He sometimes goes into a state where he has no feeling whatsoever, and just observes the world in a detached way.

Puberty, high school and the teenage years were very difficult for him. He intensely disliked most of his teachers, for he had a different way of looking at things. This made it almost impossible for him to learn subjects as taught.

> "I used to sit in class and the teacher would just totally bore me to death. I did not know what to do. If I wasn't doing something exactly their way, just because I looked at it from a different angle, they would punish me.
>
> "I knew I was right when I did this. I would get a response from the teacher, not in a negative sense. It was as if I knew I was in the right position, but was looking in the wrong direction according to the teachers. They weren't going to do it that way. They went by the old rule. They took the position that they were right and I was stupid."

Loss and Grief

The accidental death of his sibling after they were adults was a terrible blow for Asda. It was a separation of the minds—what his ET friends called "drought of the mind." He went through months of grief and misery.

He said;

"I had no clear telepathy on a level that I could understand. The right vibrations or the right awareness that we had before, the ability to talk freely and emotionally, without having my mind flooded all the time, was gone. The biggest reason I hated it was because one of us would cover the other, be able to block out stuff. With two people it was easier to make a static field around us so that nothing could penetrate that field of thought. Then the mind wasn't scattered wherever it might be, all over the universe.

"This brought me closer to my ET friends. Like second parents, they have shaped my life in such a way that I have more understanding of what my purpose in life here is. There are still some answers that I don't have, may never have, but I have learned to more or less cope with my problems."

The Storms of Sexual Awareness

Perhaps the most helpful advice Asda had to give to others growing up in the divided awareness was to talk about the storms sexual awareness brought.

"I have noticed that sometimes sexual fantasies, for a teenager, are a little bit more in depth. People's needs and wants can be read. It is almost a changing of the colors of the aura as an emotional statement. If it can be imagined as emotions being the colors inside the person's mind or the aura around them. They beam out and the various colors, the colors in a rainbow, can be seen. As the different feelings get more intense, they tingle, and tend to stand out more. In a person that can see this, it can be a really intense, stressful type of situation.

"Everybody has needs and wants, and when a person has this it seems as if they can pick up on every little thing. When they are in a certain mood, in a loving mood, they pick up on those loving feelings around them from people who are giving it off.

"They are usually sexually attracted or sexually excited more. A lot of time even towards a male—anybody—it doesn't matter what their sexual orientation. Their sexual drives are up and down, and they pick up on it more than ordinary people. Everybody that has this [ET orientation] has the feeling that they have a deeper understanding of this type of feeling. They get very intense. Sometimes they don't realize they can go too far. They should have a little control.

"Children, teenagers of that age, go mad; they don't know what to think about it. They get depressed easily after they get turned down. They don't understand and at that age just go wild thinking that they are the only one that feels this way. Humans have the same feelings, but ours are more intense. For me, having these desires and urges as a teenager and not understanding why I was feeling them so much more than the children around me just drove me bananas. I didn't know what to think if it.

"I was so attracted to the idea—like a moth to a flame. Any place I saw a light I just went to it, and I didn't know what to think of it. Today I have more self control and understanding. I had to learn about etiquette, the way people think, that they want some privacy. The only way I can get around it is to just tune it out, tune out those most basic needs and desires.

"That is just one more of those things I don't understand, as these emotions become more intense when, for instance, the body is desiring something that it knows it can't have, it is pretty much just fantasy, but the body won't be placated. The mind is struggling with the body.

"There is a time sharing also with basic needs for sexual play time, when there is too much excitement about a feeling. When out in the field, it is easy to get carried away and the emotional statements are way out of proportion to the incidents that happen. A person is too excited and occasionally goes wild and goes too far for the social situation that they are in.

"They take that occasion way to far, to the point where they lose control for a little bit. Then as they grow older, they learn to stop themselves before they jump to the wrong conclusion about what is going on, that only they are excited about it. They learn there is the right place, the right emotion, at the right time or right occasion.

"I don't know what to think about it. It is just a thing I have had to live with. I have made mistakes and I have embarrassed other people by over-escalating situations, by not doing what I should have done.

"So growing up, teenagers go through changes, sexual changes. Drives are going to be greater and more rejection is going to be felt because of this. People go too far sometimes because they don't know what to expect, because the body is moving into the same space, this dimension, as this consciousness that is the self.

"This outer reach of psychic awareness is placating or helping or intensifying hopes. Just really getting too carried away about this is easy and that is one thing about growing up. I don't have these changes so much any more. I guess all people have these problems as teenagers, especially sexual identification. Where do you fit in?"

Feeling With Depth

"For me, there are two halves to my individual self. There is one half which I call the ETness, and there is the human half which has a large part to do with how I interact. One half is logical and really passionate, loving and caring.

"The other half, I just have to get around sometimes, because it can be a little greedy with its time. There is a clash of time sharing between the extraterrestrial entity which is in me and the human entity which I have to share. I have mood swings, at times I am really happy and at times I am really sad. Other times I am just nonchalant. That goes with my energy.

"Around the aura at times, there is a deepening when there is a lot of energy around. It can be overwhelming. I think in that mix is where we get our higher extrasensory perception. We sense things through our aura and with some part of the mind we don't understand quite yet. I don't anyway. But the deepness that I feel for individuals is not for the body. It is more for the soul hidden inside. It is like waiting in the morning when you get some hot water and a tea bag. You don't know what the tea is going to taste like until it steeps for awhile. That is like an individual as it grows up.

"This has nothing to do with gender. There is no such thing as gender involved with having these experiences. There should not be any reason why an individual having these experiences shouldn't share them openly in the context of being comfortable, to be able to open up without fear of rejection. I had thought myself to be completely alone in the universe."

Direction

Asda's contact with his ET friends is ongoing. He has been given directions to follow in life.

"One was to help out others in a non-interfering way. To not discuss what I had learned from these people in a manner that would bring about what I would term retaliation from individuals. A lot of the problem is fear or misunderstanding by people, mainly because they cannot cope or understand what they are dealing with.

"We tend to have a greater understanding of people than others normally would. A lot of people are self doubting, use poor judgment, do not have clarity about what they are doing. They do not have a focal point in life. People are walking around with blinders on, not seeing.

"There is no real blueprint of how to handle this. The positive aspects are the ability to learn a lot at a social and spiritual level. Another positive thing is most of the time there is a knowing about something that others don't have.

"There is a high energy input and output at times. They, meaning ordinary individuals, don't have this. Usually their bodies or their heads are asleep. I do not mean to be negative or downsizing of other individuals, but it is almost impossible for them to even come close to what I understand.

Emanating Positive Thoughts

"It is just that I have the ability to do things that others can't in certain ways. But, at the same time, there is the ability to change, to help the world. That has really affected my life. I have environmental statements that I carry around with me, slogans, and a positive way about presenting myself.

"One of the most positive things I have to talk about, one of my main goals here on earth, is to save this planet's reality. Or to develop a new reality, to help build upon that. My purpose for being here is to awaken people, whether it is through scientific means or just talking to people. At the college I stroll around and talk to those that are working on certain environmental projects to give them ideas. Maybe someday they will think of that idea and redirect their efforts to saving humanity.

"Everybody thinks the world is dying. If people don't carry a positive thought, put out good vibes as I call them, they don't necessarily help the problem. They have to put out the good vibes instead of the bad ones. If enough of those broadcasts are sent out, people start picking up on them and they change when others act in a positive manner and are sending strong psychic thoughts.

"When I see a topic on TV that might seem cruel, I would think it out logically with a loving emotional base behind it. Think how sad that is...if nobody listens to what is going on in the world. Our consciousness directly affects our environment.

Helping Other Children

"I have always wanted to help other people. My biggest goal is to help the children, others like me. I call them 'Children of the Belonging' and longing if you want to put it in that context.

"There is a consciousness, an essential grid to life, and when we are first starting we are not quite able to get there. It seems as if we have concrete boots on. We are not real sure who we are, not comfortable with this in our life.

"There are a lot of major changes to be made, like shedding the old self for a new self, now and then. We are growing and growing to fit into the new mold, and there are a lot of growing pains, bumps and scrapes along the way.

"Sometimes a little humility comes in handy because if a person goes out into the world thinking that they are hoity-toity and have all these things, they are bound to fail every now and then. They have to learn to take it slowly, come back to where they were and start over again. My advice to them, 'Don't give up.'

"People like us might think they are alone, but they need to learn more and more about the individual they are, about the people around them, how they act toward other individuals. Take that as a positive note, because we can always express ourselves in one way or another.

Dimensions That Others Have Not Seen

"There is the need, not a wanting, but a *need* of synthesis. I feel sometimes I cannot do enough to get something accomplished in my life, to get enough energy built out of positive aspects of this world as I know it, understanding how things are going, how things are shaping up, hoping for the most positive aspects of this stay here on earth.

"My understanding of the spiritual self, or myself, is growing in different directions. I've seen the worst side of society and some of the best side and some of the most devious sides in life. The sampling of all this and the comparison with everyday life more or less tells me that we are in some kind of real deep trouble.

We Volunteered

"I have a great understanding of life, a self belief. Sometimes we have a down side when we don't have enough self confidence in our own individuality. There have been certain times when I feel like I have been abandoned by these entities in my life.

"These people, I call them ETs, but I don't really like calling them that because of the fact that if I was out of town, I wouldn't like to be called an alien or extraterrestrial.

"It seems to me that the world has plenty of questions, but few answers, and the reason I'm here is to fill a little bit of that void, to answer what hasn't been answered towards the benefit of understanding the true deep self.

"That is the largest reason for my being here, to open doors for other people, pathways they couldn't see before. Being multidimensional does not mean that someone is just one kind of ET or has one kind of belief. It has nothing to do with faith or religion or gender or background.

"When we come into this body, this being, when we were born on this world or brought into this body, we volunteered this time for the people that are around us, for normal everyday human beings.

"However, a lot of times a part of the goal is to also interact with the multidimensionally aware. It cannot be done when really young, I found that out. I have always wanted to meet somebody more like me. It is a kind of picnic when somebody else is found. There is a certain amount of joy, happiness and belonging, that we would normally not ever feel otherwise.

Take It Slow

"My advice to the children is for them to take it slow at first, because they can't walk before they learn to crawl. If they jump too fast, they might be in for a surprise. Always have an open mind—a clear mind—about what is happening.

"When they do find out, discover who they are, they don't need to start shooting their mouth off and thinking they are God, or a Universal being, a creation of greatness. They need to learn from their experiences and build a picture of themselves here and the other self that remains, that they know remains, to be discovered.

"The main thing is to go at their own pace. Meditation often calms the yearning and focuses the ideas of where they want to be and why. They should not go out full blast. They will either wind up going broke or doing something they regret.

"Just do it at a natural pace, and if there is a seriousness or a need to be somewhere or do something, they need to take the time and plan ahead and do it. If they go rushing in headlong, they will find the doorway is a little shorter. I mean by that they may be too tall and proud of themselves and just walk into a wall.

"They have to bring about a change of individual reality. They will find that every time that they go to another person, they are going to more or less walk into situations that feel like entrapment and they must explain that to themselves. The human self and the extraterrestrial self sometimes are not going to agree on what is to be done.

Living With the Aloneness

"A lot of time I find that what I am doing, I am not necessarily enjoying, but I know it is for a good purpose. There is no better feeling than when I know the job is done and I have done something good. It is wholly fulfilling.

"In the powerlessness of feeling alone, of not knowing anyone like us, sometimes people turn to drugs, because they just don't fit in anywhere. For instance, I became extremely depressed.

"People like me have to deal with this aloneness. They do not have anyone to turn to. We can learn a positive way of release in the love, light, joy and spirit of life, and get away from the talking, screaming, feelings they feel they hear.

"The voices are not a physical hearing, but voices they pick up. It is not like schizophrenic voices telling them to do something evil, but murmurings of feelings that go through the mind.

"A lot of people don't understand that some people are gifted and multi-talented. The psychologist's best answer is that they are psychotic, or deranged. Actually it is because their minds are awakening, but they don't know what to do yet; they are at a loss to know what is going on.

"It is like being hit by a bright light and being blinded, temporarily. People can go around being blinded all their life, never realizing what is going on. It makes them want to put on a pair of sunshades to block it out.

"There is, however, no way of really totally shutting everything off, because it is always going to be there. We pick up on other people's ideas. We have thoughts that go through our minds, and we don't really know what to make of it. Others might believe their thoughts are subconscious, but when we start talking to them, we might find out the awake part of their mind is not always in agreement with the subconscious. That is one of the things we have to get used to.

Use the Gifts for Positive Benefits

"For the advanced kids, be really patient with them, for these kids are always looking for an output or an input about what is going on. These children need to know they are not alone and that their parents are paying attention to their needs. They need to know they are not misunderstood, are not crazy, but to be told, 'Yes, you have a special gift, or I think that you have.'

"Use that gift for positive benefits. Share that with people that understand it. Do not necessarily go out and yell 'yippee hooray' out loud, but, for inside, you can do that.

"Children tend to respond more to the emotions and actions of the parents than to what the parents say. A lot of times when parents don't know what to do, they punish their children for lying or tend to say to them that something is not right, they are not supposed to do that. The kid wakes up in the morning thinking he's nuts and the rest of the world around him thinks he's mad, or has gone off the deep end.

Find Others Like You

"It's a good idea to go out and meet multidimensionally aware people wherever possible in the world. There will be an overwhelming joy when this is done. It always helps to clear the picture and, like a crystal lens, bring it into focus. That helps us decide which direction we want to go.

"It could be totally different from other multidimensionally aware, but it might have similar traits or similar paths. It's good to meet many different people and have the ability to grow. It could be 'normal' people or a multidimensionally aware person in every day life. A lot of 'normal' people won't understand, but the multidimensionally aware will.

"Those that have met life mates are very fulfilled. Maybe they are both multidimensionally aware, maybe they are not. They may have slightly different ideas, different angles, but a lot of times they are aiming for the same goal, trying to bring about a change in individual beliefs in this world and in people and in spirituality.

Sharing the Planet

"Understanding where the ETs come from is another thing, finding out what sort of people are being dealt with. The extraterrestrials find us sometimes."

When asked if the time will come when we will share the planet with other people, he replied, "That's kind of a silly statement. We already are sharing with other people that are here, living with us, at this time. There are entities here that might be in human form or maintain the appearance of being human, but are here to do a job. Intermingling is already a fact.

"Many different people are here helping this planet, our consciousness, and our ability to go further in a dimensional way. That's only how I can put it. When another society is added on, that is another dimension.

"There are other ET people that contact each other, are in communication with each other through what I call a web, or a joining of the whole continuum. All are joined spiritually or mentally; there are different layers of this from different people.

"Most of the time I recognize these people when I meet them. Some do put up a shield or put a mask on to hide themselves. I notice some are more shy; they have a quiet manner about them, a soothing manner. Their energy sometimes is very high, very exciting. Some have a glassy look. Some have a twinkle in their eyes, as if they know something that others don't. Most of us, when we are together, find each other irresistible. We talk a lot in quiet circles so as not to alarm the people around us or to not stir up the ant colony, so to speak.

"I can recognize the ETs as much by feel, or sense, as I can by sight. With my ESP, higher sensory perception, I sense a deepness about them. I see them with my inner eye or heart, the consciousness of it. I am able to see them as more real, in the sense of me, because they are more or less on the same plateau as I am, the same level of understanding. They sense it.

"That ETness in an individual may vary just as much as the individuals themselves. If someone knows that they are an ET or have that ETness in them, a joining, then they learn to work with that one-half. Work with the human half, that they are studying and having to be, because most likely if they are here, they are going to have a human form. Or, be in some form befitting this third dimension.

"They are not quite in this universe, the ETness is not quite here, but the human is. It is more or less like a puppet or a bad marionette. A puppet with wood or clay around it, the body, the flesh, but the entity inside at times is quite beautiful and loves to share information with people. They seem to be able to coat people with a sense of well being and understanding.

"They are recognizable by their soft behavior. They will relate experiences that have something in common with extraterrestrials. They might blatantly say they believe in ET life or an afterlife, something of that nature. Maybe something is just sensed about an individual, not told 100%.

Students of the Understanding

"We believe in honor, integrity, love, friendliness, warmth, sharing and trust, which is given freely of the heart. None of this information we share costs any money. It is there because we know we are supposed to share it. We were given these gifts, and this body as a gift, to share with the rest of the world.

"Not to be negative, but a lot of people will put on a false front just to feel a part of that growing experience. They want to join in and truly help, more or less to take on the mold of that individual. They want to share that experience; they want to be part of it.

"A lot of individuals that have never seen ETs or their vessels really would love to be a part of this. They will most likely meet up with people and become proficient in it, because they want it for themselves. They are students drawn to this experience—students of the understanding, I call it.

A Different View

"Some aliens are not always super nice and some extraterrestrials are super good, and there are all stages in between. They all have interesting traits. They are all people; the individuals dealt with out there are individuals. Just as Earth people do, they might have different traits. They might have the same emotions we do, but they might have different views, different from the way we look at reality.

"They are trying to show us the ways in which we can look at their world, too, and so experience both sides. Time sharing, as I said earlier, is one of the major factors in dealing with this.

"When we can't deal with something, we tend to hide in a closet. I haven't found all the answers. I don't think anybody has all the answers. There is no way of understanding everything about life. Life is always changing; people are always changing. People can be dishonest. Life can be hard. Its not always going to be easy with this experience.

"There are no universities that give degrees in understanding."

The Plan is To Just Be

"At times there is going to be more power than you have ever dealt with and you have to deal with those highs and lows to be able to grow.

"What I am talking about is adding to the quality of the individual that a person is. There is no way anyone can escape being themselves and just understanding mainly the self and where they fit in the plan. If a person is not comfortable with it, then they can change. They can always say no.

"For every individual that has encountered ETs, there is a plan. People need to go out and fulfill this in a positive light. I don't know how many people there are, but people should go forth and use their abilities the best they can and that is the plan.

"The plan is basically just to be—be in action, in a certain manner of action. These qualities do not necessarily come overnight. I had to learn these from my extraterrestrial friends, this multidimensional idea. I had to mature on both levels at the same time before we could go any further.

"That is the main plan that my friends are teaching us. They have set out certain rules and plans that they hope to carry out for the benefit of ourselves and others. I am sure we have learned from our friends, our extraterrestrials, or certain entities that have bumped into our lives, to grow further and outward. It is just a neat growing experience.

"The plan works for us, in that we will more or less grow and learn enough in this particular life that we can function somewhere else. Maybe we are being sent here as a growth experience so that we can obtain a higher level or a parallel level of consciousness that will allow us to stay home or a place we enjoy.

"Maybe that is the reason they sent me here, to learn and to help people and find out that there are so many different kinds of people, to learn to accept and not necessarily judge them. That may be one of the tools I need to go forth and grow.

Live Without Judgment

"As far as my understanding of the extraterrestrials in my life, they have a real, deep love for the individual, sometimes a fatherly or brotherly or very wise person type of attitude. They understand me. If someone is not one of these individuals [the ETs] they can't really judge what the ETs are doing because they are not a part of the ET society.

"We learn not to be so judging of other people because we don't judge our friends, our ET friends. I don't anyway.

"We can grow with that understanding. We should not judge each other for our appearance. If we can just grow beyond the prejudices we have set in front of us—the little road blocks—if we can get beyond that, we have room for others to grow in a nature that is suitable for us as individuals.

"What people don't know is that a lot of people in the United States have had this experience and are in the process of opening up and germinating and blossoming into a new form of understanding, a new consciousness."

Chapter Eleven

Connecting To the Cosmos

In the beginning of this book, we stated that we would present frameworks of reference upon which others may build.

Thus far we have focused on the adept multidimensionally aware individual—their life stories, their characteristics, their abilities, their pitfalls and fallibilities. We have introduced Carol, Ian, Blanche, Rory, Renée, Posey, D. B., and Asda, who have so generously shared their life views.

Additionally, we have made statements concerning the nature of the multidimensionally aware as a group.

For the next few chapters, we will turn from focus on the individuals themselves to what they are saying concerning their abilities and some of the research which supports their information.

We present several frameworks of reference which specifically address some of the sweeping statements we have made. We will focus on an in-depth exploration of what lies behind the following statements:

- The multidimensionally aware represent staggering implications for the future of humankind,
- The multidimensionally aware perceive a world "beyond" the third dimension which few can understand,
- Advanced concepts often come to the multidimensionally aware in the form of a universal communication system, carried by light, seen as visions, symbols, numbers, or heard through unusual, and not yet quite understood, sound mechanisms,
- Multidimensional awareness is an innate human potential.

Staggering Implications For our Future

Volumes upon volumes have been written on the nature of evolution, citing as many theories for evolution as there are authors. As many disagreements appear as well, depending upon the discipline and perspective of the author—whether historical, anthropological, archeological, philosophical or religious—to name just a few.

To understand why the multidimensionally aware represent an evolutionary step for humankind, we turn to Ken Wilber's multidimensional series on human evolution, *Sex, Ecology, Spirituality* (with an apology for the brevity with which we must address this well-documented and monumental work).

Wilber bases his work upon patterns or laws of evolution which modern systems sciences have concluded are apparent in all three domains of evolution—matter, body and mind—the physiosphere, the biosphere, and the noosphere.[1]

Wilber views evolution (and all of existence—the Universe) as consisting of holons.

Arthur Koestler originated the term holon. A holon is that which is both a whole unit unto itself and also exists as a part of another whole unit or holon, depending upon the context.[2]

An atom is a whole in and of itself, but consists of part of a molecule. The holon of the atom is also whole but is part of the whole of the molecule holon.

Another example is the individual person. The person forms one holon with reference to individual self, but becomes a part of another holon when involved with others—the family unit, the community, the workplace.

Wilber explains that the context, or whole, determines and *influences* both the meaning and function of the part and that the whole is always more than the sum of its parts. That whole, simultaneously, is a part of another whole.[3]

The sentence structure (the whole or holon) determines what meaning and function a word (a holon itself by individual letters) takes on—"can" for example, a tin can or a person can accomplish something. The sentence structure determines meaning and function for "can."

1. Wilber, 1995, p. 32.
2. Wilber, 1995, p. 18
3. Wilber, 1995, p. 18.

It is through holons that everything is connected, with each new holon *both* encompassing and surpassing its previous holons.

The ascending nature of holons—which holon is built upon what other holons—is determined by what is more basic to the holon and what would remain if one holon disintegrated. For example, if oxygen disappeared, many life forms would also, but if certain lifeforms disappeared, oxygen would still exist. Oxygen is a more basic holon than certain life forms.

Transcendence

According to Wilber, evolution does not simply progress from one holon (level) to another, but occurs by means of transcendence.

To transcend is to expand beyond, to surpass, to go beyond in elevation, excellence, extent or degree, to surpass, to be above and independent of.[4]

New, not previously conceived, unprecedented, creative, unique, novel forms and ideas arise that were never before possible in the previous holon, but are possible in the expanded or "higher" holon.

As an example, on the matter (physiosphere) level two hydrogen atoms join with an oxygen atom and, the new holon—the water molecule—is formed, entirely different from, but containing, the previous holons of three atoms. The water molecule includes, but expands beyond, the capabilities of the previous wholes (atoms), which have now become parts.

Quite literally, the new holon reaches a level which allows new concepts, new ideas and a reality shift to occur which was not possible before. Water is very different from either hydrogen or oxygen atoms by themselves, and water is not possible in either the hydrogen or oxygen holon. Only by "going beyond" does oxygen/hydrogen/water exist.

Another example is the transcendence in reality—or world view shift—between travel in 1869 and 1969 when Neil Armstrong set foot on the moon. Within a 100 year time span, humankind transcended to concepts—new levels of reality—which had not been possible before.

Although many might deem this process "progress," the dynamics of transcendence are much more powerful than simply building upon already laid foundations—or a series of progressive steps. *Transcendence* leaps.

Each new, creative and inspired holon contains the capabilities of solving the problems of the previous holon, which it contains as a part. How-

4. The English Language Institute of America, Inc., 1971-72.

ever, each new holon also has its own potential for new problems or pathology.[5]

The Cutting Edge

Wilber describes in great detail previous cultural consciousness developmental stages, or world views, as archaic, magic, mythic, mental and centauric (body/mind):

"For the moment let us only note that these various 'epochs,' such as the magical or mythical, refer only to the average mode of consciousness achieved at that particular time in evolution—a certain 'center of gravity' around which the society as a whole orbited. In any given epoch, some individuals will fall below the norm in their own development, and others will reach quite beyond it."[6]

There are individuals in every level who clearly develop cognitive capacities which transcend the current, prevailing world views, not as fully developed capabilities, but as potentials for understanding and expanding a larger world view.[7]

This is an example of what Wilber refers to as the cutting edge (most advanced form) of consciousness evolution, as contrasted to the average consensus of thinking of the time.

Wilber's point is that "in each epoch, the most advanced mode of the time—in a very small number of individuals existing in relational exchange in microcommunities (lodges, academies, sanghas) of the similarly depthed—began to penetrate not only into higher modes of ordinary cognition (the Aristotle of the time) but also into genuinely transcendental, transpersonal, mystical stages of awareness (the Buddha of the time)."[8] Similarly depthed means others capable of being taught or conceptualizing the same idea, of entering the new holon.

In the magical epoch, a few shamans or those of yogic awareness demonstrated psychic awareness, in mythological the genuine saints demonstrated the subtle level, and in mental-egoic, the sages demonstrated the causal level of thinking and experience.

Transcendence, then, begins with and is promoted by certain individuals capable of "reaching beyond" the average mode of consciousness of any

5. Wilber, 1995, pp. 22-24.
6. Wilber, 1995, p. 172.
7. Wilber, 1995, p. 172.
8. Wilber, 1995, pp. 172-173.

given epoch and formulating new concepts theretofore unknown and also not previously possible.

The Vision of Things To Be

When Charles Darwin sailed to Patagonia, the crew went ashore in small boats. "The natives repeatedly questioned how they had come. Much to the crew's amazement they discovered the natives literally could not see the large ship anchored in the bay; the ship did not exist for them.

"The shaman could see the ship, and with his help (through drawings showing that it looked like a familiar object, and relating the ship's position in the bay to other familiar objects), the natives could finally see the ship. There had been nothing in their consciousness with which to compare the three masted sailing ship, and, therefore, it did not register in their minds."[9]

The native Patagonians, with the exception of the Shaman, had no *mental equivalent* (cognitive concept) of the larger ship (new holon). It simply did not exist for them, it had no reality, the existing world view did not incorporate it.

Humans cannot understand or incorporate a new world view until individual consciousness expands to include larger or different mental equivalents. Any other world view or perception simply does not exist without this development. They simply do not and cannot "get it."

The necessity of developing a mental equivalent applies to visually seeing material objects (the large ship or any completely unknown object) as well as to new ideologies.

A round world could not be comprehended by those whose mental equivalent was completely locked into the flat-world view. People had to formulate a mental equivalent to incorporate an expanding and new "round" world view.

The transcendence of consciousness in evolution, then, begins with a few who make a leap into an unprecedented, unknown and totally new consciousness (or holon) and then disseminate (teach) information, knowledge and the advantages of the new perception.

9. Bryant and Seebach, 1991, p. 178

The End of An Epoch

One of the many patterns or laws of holons of evolution is that they evidence four fundamental capacities: self-preservation, self-adaptation, self-transcendence, and self-dissolution.[10]

Self-preservation means that identity as self is maintained over time.

Self-adaptation means that, not only is a holon self-preserving, but it is also a part of other holons. As such it must adapt and accommodate itself to other whole-self holons. How well a holon fits into other holons of which it is a part is the measure of its self-adaptation.[11]

Self-transcendence means that a holon goes beyond its pre-existing self.

Wilber credits Ilya Prigogine with saying that "the various levels and stages of evolution are irreducible to each other because the transitions between them are characterized by *symmetry breaks*, which simply means that they are not equivalent rearrangements of the same stuff (whatever 'stuff' might be) but are in part a significant transcendence, a novel and creative twist."[12]

"The point is," Wilber states, "that there is nothing particularly metaphysical or occult about this. Self-transcendence is simply a system's capacity to reach beyond the given and introduce some measure of novelty, a capacity without which, it is quite certain, evolution would never, and could never, have even gotten started. Self-transcendence, which leaves no corner of the universe untouched (or evolution would have no point of departure), means nothing more—and nothing less—than that the universe has an intrinsic capacity to go beyond what went before."[13]

Self-dissolution is simply that, that which is built up can break down and the reverse order of construction most probably will be the path of dissolution.

By using a graph, Wilber explains that within the four capacities of any holon—self-preservation, self-adaptation, self-transcendence and self-dissolution—there exists two horizontal opposites (self-preservation and self-adaptation), and two vertical opposites (self-transcendence and self-dissolution).

When any of these opposites or capacities become out of balance, or irresolvable conflict arises between preservation of self and adaptation (whole-

---

10. Wilber names twenty tenants, with self-dissolution being Wilber's second tenant.
11. Wilber, 1995, p. 41.
12. Wilber, 1995, pp. 42-43.
13. Wilber, 1995, p. 44.

ness vs. partnership), conflict on the vertical self-transcendence and self-dissolution aspects will ensue. The holon either transcends to a higher holon, wherein the prior problems are solved by new ideas, or the holon self destructs.

Epochs end, according to Wilber, when the prevailing consciousness or world view no longer has the capability to integrate its predecessors (maintain its wholeness and resolve its own internal problems or pathologies) or collides with equal world views or other possibilities with which adaptation cannot be reached.

The Current World View

For those with the vision to see it, current world views (the current world holon) are already well into the collective emergence of an entirely new structure of reality or consciousness.

The new structure of consciousness has been necessitated by the inability of the world view, or prevailing consciousness, to successfully integrate its predecessors, the substructures upon which the current epoch has been built. Just as the foundations of a building must be firm, so must the prevailing holon successfully integrate its previous holons.

If the hydrogen atoms or the oxygen atom are not successfully integrated and stabilized into the water molecule, water can not remain water. The molecule would disintegrate back to the previous oxygen/hydrogen state.

Global Consciousness

Wilber cites three interrelated factors for the global nature of the needed transformation in consciousness:

First and foremost is the vital necessity of protecting the biosphere which "belongs" to all and over which no individual, nation or race has priority.[14]

For the first time in known human history, the overall sustaining nature of the Earth is endangered. Major life forms cannot continue to exist with complete environmental collapse. Throughout history and all over the Earth, humans have, with a few very notable exceptions such as the Maya, not concerned themselves with long-term environmental protection, focusing rather on short-term goals. If the short-term gain resulted in environ-

14. Wilber, 1995, p. 200.

mental disequilibrium and desecration of the natural resources, it was a result of ignorance and lack of any choice of alternatives.[15]

Previously, the world was large enough so that humans could "move over" into new areas after decimation of one space, but now, we have run out of room. We can no longer just move, we have to transcend to a new structure of consciousness, a new paradigm or face the obvious.

Wilber writes, "The main difference between tribal and modern eco-devastation is not presence or lack of wisdom, but presence of more dangerous means, where the same ignorance can now be played out on a devastating scale.... [O]ur massively increased means have led, for the first time in history, to an equally massive dissociation of the noosphere and the biosphere, and thus the cure is not to reactivate the tribal form of ecological ignorance (take away our means), nor to continue the modern form of that ignorance (the free market will save us), but rather to evolve and develop into an integrative mode of awareness that will—also for the first time in history—integrate the biosphere and noosphere in a higher and deeper union...."[16]

Wilber's second factor is "the necessity to regulate the world financial system, which no longer responds to national borders," and third, "the necessity to maintain a modicum of international peace and security, which is now not so much a matter of major war between any two nations, but between a 'new order' of loosely federated nations and renegade regimes threatening world peace....

"The situation is clear enough: these are transnational crises that have rendered national responses obsolete....

"Although each of those three factors have important material-economic components (the relational exchange of monetary-financial systems, the protection of the bio-material global commons, the physical security of nonaggression between nations)—none of those physical and material and economic components can be secured in the long run without a corresponding change in consciousness among the citizens of the nations surrendering some of their sovereignty for the transnational good.

"Thus, solutions to the various global crises certainly demand efforts on the biomaterial-economic-financial front, which is where most efforts are now being concentrated. But it's a losing proposition without a corresponding shift in world views that will allow citizens and their governments to

15. Wilber, 1995, p. 167.
16. Wilber, 1995, p. 168.

perceive the greater advantage in the lesser death (the surrendering of some sovereignty for the greater good)."[17]

In Essence

Thus far we have seen that evolution transcends to greater heights, allowing new concepts to emerge which were impossible before the evolutionary leap and which are capable of solving the prior problems of the lower or previous holon.

It is individuals who have the cognitive capacity to formulate new visions that open the doors for the mass consciousness to follow.

Not all consciousnesses, however, make the leap to the new, prevailing world view, so that there are always some behind as well as some advancing.

And finally, we are, at this time, in imbalance within the current world view holon, which either must be transcended (by the self-transcendence capacity) to a higher holon with problem solving capabilities or will self destruct.

Perceiving "Beyond" the Third Dimension

Since transcendence is preferable to destruction, and it is due to transcendental vision that new holons are formed (and existing problems are solved), how do the multidimensionally aware see the nature of their own abilities to go beyond or obtain the visionary mental equivalent for a new world view?

Hyperspace has already been defined as existing beyond, and different from, the everyday third-dimensional world which most people routinely experience.

This definition, however, seems to imply that everything "not here" is "out there." But is it?

One uniting idea that ran as a common thread among all the multidimensionally aware we interviewed is their understanding of the connection of universal forces with human physiology and intellect. The multidimensionally aware repeatedly say that humans are not separate from, but are a part of and integral to, each other, the functions of the Earth, the universe and the higher dimensions.

17. Wilber, 1995, p. 200.

Humankind has always had an inner awareness of, or an innate need for there to be "something more, something beyond" physical existence. Throughout time many humans, the shamans, the saints, the sages, have consciously ventured into those beyond, transcendental realms.

It is the cultural context of the interaction, and the individual meaning assigned to that interaction, which has differed so vastly because each transcendence had to incorporate and supersede its preceding ideologies or world view. Thus archaic preceded magic, magic preceded mythic, mythic preceded mental, and now mental precedes universal.

All transcendence, according to Wilber, is accomplished by going within.[18]

The Worlds Within

Einstein spent the last thirty years of his life trying to formulate a unified field theory—a theory that would unite all the known laws of nature, energy and matter, and the cosmos. He had a mental equivalent of a unified field, but could never discover the third-dimensional equations to define it.

Until the advent of string theory, all physical theory from the time of Faraday had been based on field theory. Even now, theorists are searching for a field theory of strings.[19]

Hyperspace Journeys into the Unified Field

After 37 years of personal out-of-body journeys and research on the extension of consciousness beyond the physical, Robert Monroe wrote in his book, *Ultimate Journey*:

"There is a broad field of energy which for convenience is called (M). It is virtually unrecognized in our contemporary civilization. It is the only energy field common to and operational both within and outside time-space and is present in varying degrees in all physical matter. Because of the tendency of (M) to accumulate in living organisms, LIFE—or Layered Intelligence-Forming Energy—is a useful acronym for one band of the (M) Field spectrum.

"In the Earth Life System, (M) is present in greater concentration, ranging from 'inert' matter through microorganisms to Human Minds. The vari-

18. Wilber, 1995, p. 272.
19. Kaku, 1994, p. 166.

ance and spectrum of (M) radiation is extremely wide by local standards, yet is only a small notch in the total breadth of the (M) Field.

"All living organisms use (M) to communicate. Animals are more aware of (M) radiation than humans, who, with few exceptions, have no awareness at all."[20]

Nothing New Except the Current Context

According to Daniel Blair Stewart,[21] for the ancient Egyptians, the word *Ankh* conveyed a deep understanding of life force, an acknowledgment of the relationship between life and mind with special understanding of and accent upon the interrelationship of all living things. Ankh referred to a unified force emanating from every living thing and both invisibly and manifestly interconnected all life.

In later civilizations, such as exemplified by the intellectual golden age of Greece, which influences philosophical thought even today, and to the Florentine scholars near Rome who reshaped philosophical thoughts and belief systems in Europe's great Renaissance, the concept of consciousness as a unified, psychic field was questioned and rejected by many.

Ancient Egyptians, however, never questioned the existence of a universal life force, fully conscious, fully accessible, internally and externally to all life; a knowledge symbolized by the word Ankh.

India's ancient Vedic literature is a rich treasure of knowledge of human-cosmic interconnection such as out-of-body experiences, past-life memories, clairvoyance, psychic, spiritual and transcendental experiences.

In *Ageless Body, Timeless Mind: The Quantum Alternative To Growing Old,*[22] Deepak Chopra, M.D., writes at length about the traditional medicine in India and its combination of science and the deeper spiritual values in Indian philosophy. They held the belief that there can be longevity without limit, because life is, in essence, immortal.

The life force, or *prana*, is channeled throughout the body of all living creatures. *The Living Webster Encyclopedic Dictionary of the English Language*[23] defines *prana* as: a noun originating in Hindu philosophy meaning the vital breath; the life principle of the living body; force; energy.

---

20. Monroe, 1994, p. 185.
21. Stewart, 1993, p. 105.
22. Chopra, 1993, p. 269.
23. The English Language Institute of America, Inc., 1972.

By its very definition, prana is the subtle life force that energizes both the physical and nonphysical aspects of the human being. This belief, held in ancient times in India and China, has filtered down into Western thinking through Christian mysticism. It is the Chinese Chi, being utilized in acupuncture, meditation techniques and various Yoga practices.

Einstein introduced relativity of all things. Modern physics has demonstrated relativity in matter and basic particles which are themselves interactions and events rather than things.

Holograms are an excellent example of the interference pattern of all things, actions and thoughts in the manifest universe.[24]

Chopra writes in *Quantum Healing*, "Einstein did not step outside the river of time, except mentally.... His search for a unified field that would embrace all of time and space was a strictly mathematical enterprise.

"To the rishis [seers of ancient India], this is the very attitude that makes physics incomplete. We are not onlookers peering into the unified field, they said—we are the unified field. Every person is an infinite being, unlimited by time and space. To reach beyond the physical body, we extend the influence of intelligence. As you sit in your chair, every thought you are thinking creates a wave in the unified field. It ripples through all the layers of ego, intellect, mind, senses, and matter, spreading out to wider and wider circles. You are like a light radiating not photos but consciousness."[25]

The Misconception of the Material World

Since insight into the mechanics and workings of creation is the special domain of the multidimensionally aware, they explain that not only does the unified field exist, but that humans and all of existence are contained completely within and are a functioning part of that field.

Perhaps the biggest misconception of the prevailing Western world view is that of viewing all of reality as some form of matter. The nonphysical is viewed in exactly the same manner as the physical world, expected to obey the same "laws" and evolve in the same way.

This perspective applies to consciousness, the paranormal and supraconscious abilities—including psychic phenomena, mental energy manipulation and being multidimensionally aware—confining and defining it all in terms of third-dimensional matter (physiosphere).

---

24. Bryant and Seebach, 1991, p. 176.
25. Chopra, 1989, p. 217.

Ingo Swann clearly points out this fallacy in thinking in *Natural ESP*:

"The greatest drawback to any progress in comprehending extrasensory perception, at the individual level and in parapsychology, is trying to make ESP fit into the reality we think is the only reality. We are used to viewing the physical reality with our consciousness. What we can perceive with our physical senses and what we can think about with only our conscious minds has come to constitute the one and only reality.

"The other parts of our minds—the unconscious or the supraconscious, for example—predominantly have been thought not to have any reality of their own, but to exist in some sort of a subjective arrangement that depends upon our consciously perceived reality."

Three statements dispel this concept.

- First, the concept emerged in Western science as a result of ideas of enlightenment and has been tenaciously clung to.
- Second, this polarized concept has not been adhered to by the majority of other cultures.
- Third, the evidence of Western science, such as quantum physics and psychology, clearly indicate the existence of another reality.[26]

This other reality, second universe or hyperspace is the substance, glue, thought form or hologram which is the nonmaterial matrix from which all matter of the physical universe is formed and organized into a harmonious whole.[27]

In Essence

The error of Western thought then, we and the multidimensionally aware agree, is in attempting to incorporate the nonphysical into the physical, attempting to find the material laws to define the nonphysical source only in terms of the view that some form of matter is all that exists. Nonphysical does not equate to nonexistence.

This other reality, or the second universe, is the ultimate unified field, or the basic holon upon which the material, third-dimensional holon is built and is nonphysical.

It is into the unified field, or hyperspace, that the multidimensionally aware journey into the reality of the nonphysical beyond.

---

26. Swann, 1987, p. 46-47.
27. Swann, 1987, p. 48.

Chapter Twelve

Communicating With the Universe

It is through the unified field that human consciousness can interact with all that is, all that ever was or that which will possibly be. Advanced concepts often come to the multidimensionally aware in the form of a universal communication system, carried by light, but that transmission is often distorted.

In the Western world view, the concepts most generally associated with supraconsciousness (psychic awareness or multidimensionality) equates this phenomena with that of electromagnetic radiation and utilizes the same nomenclature—vibrations, frequencies, and energies. Telepathy is thought of as having a "sender" and a "receiver," healing energies are "sent," etc..

Some of the earliest work disproving this association was done by L. L. Vasiliev, a Russian professor of physiology at the University of Leningrad in the 1920s. Vasiliev's experiments showed that no amount of electromagnetic shielding could prevent telepathy and there were instances where "reception" sometimes took place before "transmission."[1]

Since that time, Russian research has followed Vasiliev's path of discovery formulating the new field of "psychoenergetics," while the West continued with the electromagnetic frequency ideology of sender/receiver.[2]

Within the reality of the second universe, knowledge is instantaneously available through the holographic nature of the unified field in which the most minuscule part contains the entire whole.

1. Swann, 1987, pp. 49-50.
2. Swann, 1987, p. 50.

Human Interactive Communication Systems

Because the unified field is infinite, we are forced to limit our discussion to only a few pertinent "information systems" through which humans access knowledge from the unified field.

These three information systems are: cosmic-light information systems, life-unit psychoenergetic systems and electromagnetic radiation (EMR). These system types vary greatly in information, emotional content and the effect on life forms.

Due to the prevailing Western world view equation of supraconsciousness to EMR, the English language becomes limiting. We have attempted to clarify meaning in the best available terms.

Technically, cosmic light and electromagnetic radiation refer to third-dimensional energy movement and have very well-defined meanings within science. Our use of these terms here is simply to differentiate source, as well as impact.

The Transducer Function

The multidimensionally aware understand and interact with the non-physical properties of these transmission systems.

Planets, stars, humans, plants, rocks—all things which exist—have movement or energy.

All movement is equipped with, or works in concert with, a natural *transducer function*. In other words, there exists within all things a natural ability to convert the energy of one transmission system into the energy of another.

Because of the transducer function, it is possible for human awareness to enter the cellular awareness of a plant. An information exchange can take place at the cellular level, which can be a beautiful experience. See the inter-dimensional communication "The Standing People" on page 170.[3]

Since all matter exists within the unified field, the energy movement of one individual or planet or rock can be acquired through the transducer function (internal receptors) of another intelligence across space/time.

The Cosmic Light Connection

One of the best explanations of the understanding of interaction with cosmic light transmission systems is given by Dr. José Arguëlles in *The*

3. See also Cowan, 1995.

Mayan Factor: Path Beyond Technology, which was published after years of study of the Mayan civilization, with special focus on the Mayan Great Calendar. Clearly, the ancient Maya understood the nonphysical properties and utilization of cosmic light.

Arguëlles writes, "Two Mayan terms, *Hunab Ku* and *Kuxan Suum*, are essential in providing us a galactic view which synthesizes science and myth.

"Hunab Ku is usually translated as 'One Giver of Movement and Measure'; it is the principle of life beyond the Sun. In this regard, Hunab Ku is the name of the galactic core, not just as a name but as a description of purpose and activity as well. Movement corresponds to energy, the principle of life and all-pervading consciousness immanent in all phenomena. Measure refers to the principle of rhythm, periodicity, and form accounting for the different limiting qualities which energy assumes through its different transformations.

"Kuxan Suum, literally 'the Road to the Sky Leading to the Umbilical Cord of the Universe,' defines the invisible galactic life threads or fibers which connect both the individual and the planet, through the Sun, to the galactic core, Hunab Ku. These threads or fibers are the same as the luminous threads extending from the solar plexus described by the seer, Don Juan, in Carlos Castaneda's series of Yaqui wisdom books. According to the extant Mayan texts, *Popul Vuh* and *The Annals of the Cakchiquels*, the Yaquis were the first of the Mayan tribes to separate from the rest of the clans following entry into this world. The purpose of the Yaquis in so doing was to keep at least some of the original teachings of the Maya relatively pure and in a remote place.

"In any case, the fibers, or Kuxan Suum, define a resonant pathway, like a walkie-talkie, providing a continuing channel of communication, a cosmic lifeline. Through Kuxan Suum, each of us has a connection that extends from the solar plexus through the reflective membrane of the planetary field on to the Sun and, ultimately, to the galactic core."[4]

According to Dr. Arguëlles, "So-called sun worship such as is imputed to the ancient Maya [and Egyptians] is in actuality the recognition and acknowledgment that higher knowledge and wisdom is literally being

4. Arguëlles, 1987, p. 52.

The Standing People

...a communication received while meditating in a forest
at the base of an ancient Ponderosa pine.

Little One, why are you the first to pause at my feet and seek my wisdom?

A thousand two-leggeds have passed here intent on getting somewhere,
Possessed with the idea of arrival,
While ignoring the wisdom of silence that can be found in a pause.

Thank you for seeking the Wisdom of the Standing People.

It is our sacred honor to stand where we sprout
And to play our part in the great balance.

It is our sacred honor to welcome the energies of
Father Sun and Grandfather Sky,

And to use these energies to clean the wind as it passes through our bodies.

It is our sacred honor to anchor the soil on the slopes,
So that the watersheds can bear fruit,
And so that the swimming ones can breathe.

Ours is a consciousness that is shared by all of our kind.
When one of us falls, all of us know.

We feel the receding edges of our forests, and we mourn.

Ours is a consciousness that extends unbroken in our memory
To the very dawn of time.

We remember the millions of years that we stood,
Balancing the components of the air and water until
This sacred planet could sustain

Beings that needed not to root in soil,
Beings that could run and shout,
Beings that could move away when fires came.

We gave your kind life, and our continued balancing keeps your kind alive.

Without us, Mother Earth will lie still,
A lifeless orb drifting in the blackness of space.

We remember when the first moving creature stirred.

We remember when the first awkward land crawlers emerged from the sea.

We remember how we rejoiced
When four-leggeds began to roam our forests,
And when flying ones first gathered in our crowns.

We remember how our branches sang in the wind
When two-leggeds first stood in awe below us and gave us honor.

And we remember when the first two-leggeds lived in balance with us,
Using our bodies for shelter, and encouraging our seeds into the earth.

We are an ancient people,
And your kind has been able to live here only a short while.

We do not understand the moving sharp teeth
That your kind uses to break our spines.

We do not understand what you do to the air
That makes our needles burn when it rains.

We are your Mother.

We do not deserve your anger.

We are the Standing People.

We cannot flee when you attack us.

We are at your mercy,
And we ask that you return to balance with us.

The Earth is becoming unbalanced,
And we need to make it balanced once again.

Our forests need to be larger.
They need to be diverse, with living things of all kinds.

Please take this wisdom to your kind, Little One,
And ask your brothers to stop and seek Wisdom, too.

by Dr. Brian Crissey

transmitted through the Sun, or more precisely, through the cycles of the binary sunspot movements."[5]

Communication Through Harmonic Resonance

"Looking through this galactic telescope of vibratory lenses," Arguëlles continues, "rather than an atomistic world of space and time, distance and separateness, the Mayan Factor brings into focus a world of coherence and unity, a resonant matrix within which information transmission is virtually 'instantaneous.' If we were to give a modern name to this process of galactic focussing and transmission of information it would be the principle of *harmonic resonance.*"[6]

"...*Resonance* means the quality of sounding again. To resonate is to reverberate. Reverberation implies give and take, the definitions of communication which is always simultaneous and between at least two agents. Any communication implies an exchange of information. People talk about the 'information age,' but what is it? From the perspective of resonant harmonics, information is the form-vehicle of qualities of energy passing between two agents or parties. As a sounding again, resonance *is* information.

"The essence of information, then, is not its content, but its resonance. This is why feeling or sensing things is so important. To sense the resonance of incoming information creates a coresonant field. If we try to conceptualize experience before we have actually resonated with the experience, the field is off or even broken. If the field is broken, it means the Kuxan Suum is obscured at the solar plexus—in a word, we've stopped feeling things and our resonance has been damped!

"When people speak of resonance, they also speak of frequencies and tones. Frequency refers to rate of vibration. As everybody knows, there are higher and lower rates of vibration, while all vibration is pulsation of waves. A frequency held for but a single wave-cycle, otherwise known as a beat, becomes a tone. A tone, then, is any sustained frequency, whose level determines which of our sense organs may be affected. In other words, touch has its tones; perfume is a tone of the sense field 'smell'; even 'mind' experiences its high-frequency sensory tones.

5. The Tzolkin, or Sacred Calendar, is a means of tracking the information through knowledge of the sunspot cycles. The Tzolkin is also the information matrix that is communicated by at least two star systems, creating a binary communication field through the sunspots.
6. Arguëlles, 1987, p. 54.

"Inclusive of all the sense-fields, harmony is the synchronization of two or more tones. The skill in synchronizing tones and synthesizing sense-fields is an art much as it is a science. The practice of this science yields opportunities unthought of from a materialistic perspective, which, for instance, leads one to think that flying is the airborne passage of a physical body between two points. But what is flying to the sense-fields of the passenger in the airplane? The coarse, vibratory shudder of jet engines, the odor of jet fuel, and a microwave meal. What if flying is, instead, a capacity to identify consciousness with resonance and ride the frequencies of different levels of reality?

"Indeed, harmony *is* a science. Those who practice this science are the real artists, the diviners of harmony, for it is they who transmit—not as any doctrine but as reality itself—the principle of harmonic resonance.

"If this world view sounds Pythagorean—music of the spheres—it is! Yet the difference between the Pythagoreans and the Maya is this: the Maya demonstrated to no uncertain degree that this is not merely a philosophy, but the basis for an entire civilization. Such a civilization based on the principle of harmonic resonance is obviously different in nature and purpose than a civilization such as ours, which is based on the acquisition of material goods and the defense of territory."[7]

The multidimensionally aware have, like the Maya, once again tapped into the principle of harmonic resonance through their transducer function or internal receptors. Each expresses their method of internal knowledge in different terminology, but the underlying concept is their ability to resonate with and transduce nonphysical information transmission systems.

Life-unit psychoenergetics

The second information system we will discuss within the unified field is generated by life-unitthought forms or psychoenergetics.

Life units may be human, plant, animal or other intelligences on other dimensions and are differentiated, for our purposes, from cosmic light sources such as planets, stars and unmanifest creation.

---

7. Arguëlles, 1987, pp. 54-55.

Thoughts Forever Spreading

Monroe suggests that thoughts and emotions constitute bands or energies within the unified (M) field. Within the unified field is contained all thought, emotion or energy generated by conscious life forms from all time and throughout all dimensions.

He states, "[H]umans are subject to constant (M) input from other sources, *without the conscious knowledge of either sender or receiver*"[8] [italics ours] and "*Group thought, especially when it is primarily emotion-inducing, can be highly contagious, owing to the extreme amplitude of the radiation.*" [Again, italics ours].[9]

Given humankind's recorded history, it is not surprising that many of the transmission bands closest to Earth have a violent, emotional content.

All the emotional content of all the wars ever fought, all conquests—the Crusades, tribal wars, revolutions and revolts, World Wars One and Two, Korea, Vietnam and the Gulf War—have set up very destructive bands of energy which still exist, encircling the Earth, and which still influence human consciousness.

Conversely, contained within the bands are the energies developed by the experiences of peaceful cultures and "higher order" civilizations and humans.

An example of this is the harmonic resonance left by the Mayan civilization.

"To understand the Maya and their scientific base as an alternative to our present disorder," Arguëlles writes, "we must pursue the description of such a civilization even further. For instance, what would a civilization founded on the principle of harmonic resonance have as its goals or purpose? Could it be anything else but to place the system Earth in resonance with the Sun as an evolving member of a larger galactic family...?

"Precisely, because it is based on the principle of harmonic resonance, a civilization such as the Mayan can be described as *galactically informed*. That is, by the principle of harmonic resonance, there is a two-way information wave that ripples to and from the individual being to the collective or planetary mind, and from the planetary mind through the Sun to the galactic core."[10]

---

8. Monroe, 1994, p. 186.
9. Monroe, 1994, p. 187.
10. Arguëlles, 1987, pp. 54-55.

Transmissions From Time and Space

Time can be transcended, as well as space, through venturing into the unified field. The limitations experienced in third-dimensional Earth do not apply.

Thus, past and future knowledge is as readily available as going to a library. This library is just immensely larger.

It is not uncommon for people to have vivid experiences of a remembered or reenacted nature when visiting old ruins or places where historical events transpired.

The psychoenergetics of events do not dissipate with the passage of time, but enter the unified (M) field. Those sensitive to psychoenergetics can reexperience the emotional content, especially if there is a connecting memory involved.

The Psychoenergetics of Teotihuacan

Alice traveled extensively in Mexico when researching her book, *The Message of the Crystal Skull*. Having enjoyed the various ruins, she was surprised to find that at Teotihuacan she was depressed.

One night she found herself mentally back at Teotihuacan many centuries ago, in the male body of a soldier.

"I was on the Avenue of the Dead, about a third of the way from the Temple of the Moon, going toward the Temple of the Sun. It was filled with fighting men using short swords. There was blood everywhere. I was filled with such pain of loss that I was relieved to die with the others. The next day I 'saw' the avenue, and it was filled with dead bodies from side to side."

Semi-waking from the experience, she returned to this dimension sobbing and crying, suffering a mental anguish such as she has seldom known. Subsequent regression sessions revealed that she had lost her belief system at Teotihuacan.

Beings from another space/time had come and taught, and she as a soldier had been a willing and cherished pupil. When they departed, the group of priests could not hold the Light. The dark forces overwhelmed them and overran the temple.

Because of this defeat, the soldier came to believe that the belief system did not work, that the dark forces were stronger.

This scenario is borne out in the history of the site. Many historians believe that the priests themselves destroyed the art works and sacred artifacts in the temples, rather than let them be taken and used by the enemy.

Alice learned from this that her strong faith of this lifetime comes from the experience of learning that to lose one's belief system is far, far more painful than the death experience.

Nonlearning Transmissions

As well as life-unit "memory" psychoenergetics, prevailing world view thoughts of any epoch enter into the unified field and remain as well.

The 100th monkey syndrome was documented and established as scientific fact when simultaneous, spontaneous behavioral changes in monkeys occurred across distinct island chains after the 100th monkey "learned" the initial behavior.

In *Your Nostradamus Factor,* Ingo Swann states, "In short, so the theory goes, if a hundred monkeys learn something, all monkeys will soon acquire this knowing even in the absence of any sensory contacts with the learned monkeys. An unknown form of 'learning transmission' is thought to exist, which would explain all this. Such learning transmission is presumably *psychic,* since it is of some nonsensory quality. Critics say this is all bunk, but the facts remain. With a wide expanse of ocean separating them, monkeys learned something in a way that no standard or prevailing explanation can account for.

"It is rather well known that humans possess psychic states that influence those around them. And there is also a phenomenon of people separated by vast distances 'having the same idea at the same time.'"[11]

He further observed that "...the hundredth monkey syndrome appears operative in negative as well as positive respects. *If a lot of us forget or ignore one of our powers, eventually the rest of us, by 'dis-learning transmissions,' may do so also.*" [Emphasis ours].[12]

It may be there is another dynamic associated with the 100th monkey syndrome, one which concerns qualitative phenomena as contrasted only to quantitative phenomena.

Perhaps it was not that 100 monkeys projected a particular learning transmission psychoenergetic.

One clear, life-unit psychoenergetic could first reach a few others, who would then accompany *in concert,* but not originating, the same information loads. The initial life-unit energetic would be capable of being received

---

11. Swann, 1993, p. 27.
12. Swann, 1993, p. 28.

across great distances and synchronizing the thought patterns of others, bringing the learning transmission to conscious action.

Two-Way Transmissions

Because information transmission is a two-way highway, thoughts, ideas and emotions are constantly being added to the unified field as well as received.

These additions, though, are not all of equal magnitude or intensity.

According to Monroe, "[T]he organized (M) Field radiation of a *single individual* [emphasis ours] and, if broad-banded enough, may be many thousand times greater than that of the group. Whatever the source, reception can influence any mind and/or body that contains resonant receptors [open transducer function]."[13]

Negative Energy

Both individuals and groups can generate positive or negative thought forms and can have a very profound influence on those who are "open" because of internal receptive mechanisms or transducer functions in their own bio-minds.

All people, especially the multidimensionally aware, are capable of holding a strong, personal psychoenergetic transmission system, but not all individuals have the well being of others as their priority. Some can emanate very destructive thought forms, which can strongly impact other individuals.

These negative thought forms, projected into the unified field, can impact the physical DNA, cause severe illness and even physical death. A person who is open to them internalizes the energy of destructive influences and embodies them as their own thoughts.

To embody is to integrate an externally generated idea, thought or energetic into cellular memory to the degree that it becomes a core belief (belief system) upon which other concepts are built. The message can either be given verbally, nonverbally through actions, or transmitted through thought-form emission.

Many people embody beliefs which are never reexamined and they may be unaware that many of their reactions are based upon the embodiment of an ideology which may or may not be true.

---

13. Monroe, 1994, p. 187.

Other people's opinions and judgments can be embodied to the point that a person may build their entire life upon someone else's ideology or opinion.

Embodiment is the result of repeated exposure, i.e. a parent constantly telling their child that they are bad, stupid, ugly, etc., or through the absorption of thought forms existing in the unified field.

Internal Receptors

All individuals have internal factors which determine how information is received in conscious awareness. These factors, which we discuss in depth in Chapter Thirteen, are the automatic thought processes, or types of barriers, which define how information is internalized in the subliminal or unconscious.

Medical journals contain many instances where patients were misdiagnosed with a fatal disease and died simply because they were told they would. These people had a belief in the infallibility of the medical profession, internalized the misdiagnosis and acted upon the erroneous information.

Many people, and certain societies, hold beliefs in spells and curses, and they form resonant receptors in their minds. Thus, they are susceptible to existing thought forms from someone who they believe might "cast a spell or curse" on them.

Monroe states, "Through experience, methods that prevent reception of undesirable thought radiation may be learned, often painfully. It is a matter of phasing. Shut off the aligning receptor thought-form and there is no influence. This holds true both in physical and nonphysical environments."[14]

From Chaos To Cure

On the other side of the coin, the same dynamics can be utilized in positive ways. Prayer, healing thoughts and positive emotional emanations can be influential toward miracle cures, spontaneous remissions, receiving good fortune and instilling happiness.

Because of their strong personal life-unit psychoenergetic capability, the multidimensionally aware can transmit information to others in nonverbal ways on the mental information system.

---

14. Monroe, 1994, p. 187.

One important information emission is the knowledge of how individuals can align their own internal structures to resonate with the cosmic light in the same manner as the multidimensionally aware. Or in other words, people can learn to transcend from those who have done so.

The loving, multidimensionally aware firmly anchor their resonate thought forms in the Earth plane, keeping open the pathways to the infinite. Others can realign their own receptors and also journey in the unified field.

These cosmic light harmonic resonances, which are being anchored into the Earth, are now forming the new holon, the invitation to step up the ladder of evolution. Because of this input, people are beginning to reflect on the environment, world harmony, peace, and to care more for humanity. The current world predicament can be changed by the presence of these strong emanators.

When the light or cosmic information can be accessed, more information, or higher mental equivalents, can be obtained and people can change, expand and become capable of things previously thought impossible. They, too, can participate in the formation of the new holon.

Electromagnetic Radiation

The third type of system in the unified field is electromagnetic radiation.

One of the American pioneers in the study of effects of electromagnetic radiation on life forms was Robert O. Becker, an orthopedic surgeon who investigated the electrical system of living organisms.

Although the Russians had been studying the effects of electromagnetism on the biosphere since 1933, American scientists largely ignored the research until the 1970s when Russia opened its doors through *détente* for some exchange of scientific information.

In speaking of electromagnetic radiation, Becker and Seldon write:

"Each energy wave consists of an electric field and a magnetic field at right angles to each other, and both at right angles to the direction the wave is traveling. The number of waves formed in one second is the frequency; the distance the energy travels (at the speed of light) during one oscillation is its wavelength. The higher the frequency, the shorter the wavelength, and vice versa."[15]

15. Becker and Seldon, 1985, p. 272.

Electromagnetic radiation (EMR) spans an enormous range of frequencies: gamma rays, X-rays, ultraviolet waves, visible light, infrared heat, microwaves and radio frequencies. The microwave and radio frequencies are broken down into a range from extremely high to extremely low frequencies.

With the exception of visible light and infrared heat, the other frequencies are only perceived *subliminally* by humans.[16]

Where Did That Idea Come From?

Human consciousness subliminal receptivity of frequencies has been of great interest to many governments, research groups—including both scientific and advertising—and individuals.

One deliberate utilization of human receptivity to "unseen broadcast transmissions" is illustrated by subliminal messages transmitted through various wave functions, sound and visuals given so briefly that the conscious mind does not perceive them, but the subconscious mind does. Everyone is susceptible to subliminals.

Negative subliminals contain encoded sequences and are indicated by inexplicable feelings of unease, or negative thoughts, about a particular subject. Some subliminals instill a gradual change or development of an attitude concerning certain issues, groups of people, modes of behavior. These subliminals are strong, and not likely to be detected. Ideas are embodied without there ever having been a conscious consideration of the issues.

It is up to the individual to train themselves to discern that they are receiving a subliminal, and there are far more subliminals being used than people are aware of.

Nonlethal Weapons

For decades various governments, including the United States, have developed electromagnetic weapons of a wide variety, including electromagnetic mind control.

According to Becker and Seldon, "The Central Intelligence Agency funded research on electromagnetic mind control at least as early as 1960, when the notorious MKULTRA program, mostly concerned with hypnosis and psychedelic drugs, included money for adapting bioelectric sensing methods (at that time primarily the EEG) to surveillance and interrogation,

16. Becker and Seldon, 1985, p. 278.

as well as for finding 'techniques of activation of the human organism by remote electronic means.'"[17]

In a 1994 report from the Strategic Studies Institute at the U.S. Army War College in Carlisle Barracks, Pennsylvania, authors Steven Metz and James Kievit point out that emerging technology and innovative ideas which were *utilized in the Gulf War* appear to herald a genuine revolution in military affairs.

The new technology includes: sensor technology, electronic identification implants [electronic individual position locator device—IPLD], robotics, biotechnical antimaterial agents [affecting "things"], nonlethal weapons (mind control techniques and biotechnical agents [affecting humans]), high energy radio frequency guns and electromagnetic pulse transformer bombs.[18]

The Electropollution Threat

Becker and Seldon very ably summarize the electropollution threat, not only to humans, but to the biosphere as well:

"Three dangers overshadow all others. The first has been conclusively proven: *ELF electromagnetic fields vibrating at about 30 to 100 hertz, even if they're weaker than the Earth's field, interfere with the cues that keep our biological cycles properly timed; chronic stress and impaired disease resistance result.* Second, the available evidence strongly suggests that regulation of cellular growth processes is impaired by electropollution, increasing cancer rates and producing serious reproductive problems. Electromagnetic weapons constitute a third class of hazards culminating in climatic manipulation from a sorcerer's-apprentice level of ignorance.

"There may be other dangers, less sharply defined but no less real. All cities, by their very nature as electrical centers, are jungles of inter-penetrating fields and radiation that completely drown out the Earth's background throb. Is this an underlying reason why so many of them have become jungles in another sense as well? Is this a partial explanation for the fact that the rate of suicide between the ages of fifteen and twenty-four rose from 5.1 per 100,000 in 1961 to 12.8 in 1981? Might this be an invisible and thus overlooked reason why so many governmental leaders, working at the centers of the most powerful electromagnetic networks, consistently make decisions

17. Becker and Seldon, 1985, p. 320.
18. Metz and Kievit, 1994.

that are against the best interests of every being on Earth? Is the subliminal stress of electronic smog misinterpreted as continual threats from outside—from other people and other governments? In addition, if Teilhard de Chardin's noosphere exists, our artificial fields must mask it many times over, literally disconnecting us from life's collective wisdom. This is not to ignore the plain fact of evil, but it often seems there must be some other reason why today's power elite are so willing to bring the whole world to the brink of so many different kinds of destruction. Maybe they literally can't hear the Earth anymore.

"Everyone worries about nuclear weapons as the most serious threat to our survival. Their danger is indeed immediate and overwhelming. In the long run, however, I believe the ultimate weapon is manipulation of our electromagnetic environment, because it's imperceptibly subtle and strikes at the core of life itself. We're dealing here with the most important scientific discovery *ever*—the nature of life. Even if we survive the chemical and atomic threats to our existence, there's a strong possibility that increasing electropollution could set in motion irreversible changes leading to our extinction before we're even aware of them."[19]

In Essence

The three types of universal transmission systems we have discussed include cosmic light, which ties all of existence together and through which "higher order" information is available.

Psychoenergetic transmission systems are both projected and internalized whether or not people are aware of it.

Psychoenergetic transmissions do not disappear with time, but remain forever in the unified field and, thus, can be accessed at any time.

Psychoenergetic thought forms are both positive and negative and can either have beneficial or detrimental affects.

Electromagnetic radiation is received subliminally and has a profound effect upon all living forms. Overproduction of EMR constitutes a major threat to planet Earth.

---

19. Becker and Seldon, 1985, pp. 327-328.

Chapter Thirteen

Putting It All Together

In *Quantum Healing*, Deepak Chopra points out the most obvious, but also the most hidden connection to the unified field:

> "Our senses are not prepared to see emptiness as the womb of reality, being tuned in to a grosser level of nature populated with flowers, rocks, trees and our families. It is said that the human eye can distinguish 2 million shades of color, each of which occupies a narrow band of light energy, but our optical mechanism nevertheless doesn't register these energy vibrations. Much less do we register a chunk of solid marble as vibrations, although at bottom that is what it is, just the same as color…."
>
> "Every quantum gradation is slight, but it implies a completely new reality at the grossest level of molecules and living things. The spectrum of light is like a long, continuous string, vibrating slower at one spot and faster at another. We make our home on a tiny part of the spectrum, but it takes the entire length for us to exist. Beginning at zero vibration, shakes of the string are responsible for the light, heat, magnetism and countless other discrete energy forms that fill the universe. It is just a few steps on the ladder of creation from empty space to inter-galactic dust to a sun and finally the living Earth. What this shows is that emptiness, the point of zero vibration, is not a void but a starting point for everything that exists. And this starting point is always in contact with every other point—there are no breaks in continuity…. We experience the void every time we think."[1]

1. Chopra, 1989, pp. 126-127.

The great Greek philosopher Plotinus saw in humanity a vast potential for development above their current level. Yet, most were unconscious to the incredible potentials and the higher levels of being which all could actualize and bring into being.[2]

Speaking for his own views, Wilber says:

> "I think the sages are the growing tip of the secret impulse of evolution. I think they are the leading edge of the self-transcending drive that always goes beyond what went before. I think they embody the very drive of the Kosmos toward greater depth and expanding consciousness. I think they are riding the edge of a light beam racing toward a rendezvous with God.
>
> "And I think they point to the same depth in you, and in me, and in all of us. I think they are plugged into the All, the Kosmos sings through their voices and Spirit shines through their eyes. And I think they disclose the face of tomorrow; they open us to the heart of our own destiny, which is also already right now in the timelessness of this very moment and in that startling recognition the voice of the sage becomes your voice, the eyes of the sage become your eyes, you speak with the tongues of angels and are alight with the fire of a realization that never dawns nor ceases, you recognize your own true Face in the mirror of the Kosmos itself: your identity is indeed the All and you are no longer part of that stream you are that stream."[3]

Living In the Quantum World

Every human then, as we have seen, is part of the unified field, or second universe, as the unified field is the nonphysical void or space interconnecting every bit of matter.

Chopra refers to the unified field or second universe as the quantum world and explains very elegantly how humans are both quantum and physical, thus multidimensional at the same time.

The physical portion lives in the physical world where the body is subjected to all the forces of weather—heat, cold, wind, rain, hail, snow, balmy and perfect. The body is subjected to all physical pleasures and assaults—the feel of silk on the skin, cozy fireplaces in winter, cool sea shores in summer, good and bad food, and disease from bacteria and viruses. All of which is "out there."

2. Wilber, 1995, pp. 337-338.
3. Wilber, 1996, p. 43.

Simultaneously, a person occupies the quantum w
there" things change and count for naught.

Consciousness and memories do not get wet in the rain,
ter or roast in summer.

The quantum events of the physical form the quantum mechanical body, a body which functions by direction of the unseen universal laws. The quantum mechanical body is part of all that exists; it is the motion of awareness, guided by the infinite intelligence.

Humans are quite "at home" in both the quantum and physical body, completely interacting in both "universes" constantly without any or very little thought about it at all. Humans are constantly multidimensional.[4]

Tapping the Unified Field

Humans interact with the void, or the second universe, at all times, but the interaction is mostly through the unconscious. However, interaction sometimes occurs in a direct, uninhibited manner as happens with the multidimensionally aware.

Based on years of research and exploration of the potential of the human mind, Ingo Swann in his book *Natural ESP*, provides a clear understanding of the processes involved in tapping into the unified field through the deeper self.

> "The capabilities of this deeper self are quite astonishing." Swann writes, "We can by now, I think, appreciate how the deeper self participates with the interconnected information universe, the second reality [hyperspace]. The deeper self runs on its own realities—which we might assume are in keeping with the workings of the second reality. Waking consciousness has to become 'awake' to it through focusing and training."[5]

Such training has not been readily available in Western civilization. The prevailing world view has downplayed the nonphysical, esoteric world to an almost nonexistent state. It has been an orientation away from nonmatter.

Special education and a different orientation will be necessary for the integration of both the physical, third dimension and the internal, nonphysical world.

4. Chopra, 1993, pp. 286-287.
5. Swann, 1987, p. 54.

_e Deeper Self

The deeper self, according to Swann, is in contact with the unified field, or "all else that exists," although this contact is normally barred from everyday consciousness. The deeper self emerges into conscious awareness in pure form spontaneously from time to time.

Barriers exist between the deeper self and the conscious mind, otherwise the input from the second reality would flood the mind with overwhelming information. Swann equates this to attempting to listen to 1,000 TV and radio stations simultaneously.

Indeed, this is exactly the case with people who spontaneously, for unknown reasons, open the pathway to hyperspace. They become mentally drowned in the vastness and quantity of information accessed. The natural inhibiting barriers are, for some reason, eradicated.

Swann also points out that "these extrasensory intrusions affect the individual's biosystem, although the exact information does not reach consciousness. People 'feel' apprehension, which is unexplained, and only afterward find out a loved one was in danger or dying."[6]

Free-floating anxiety is often the case of psychoenergetics at work in the individual. As was pointed out in Chapter Twelve, all life forms both are and can be affected by all kinds of energetic input.

The ESP Core

Based on years of in-depth research and examination of his own internal psychoenergetic processes, Swann developed a model for what he terms the ESP core.

The ESP core constitutes the pathway or route, consisting of several layers, that information (cosmic, psychoenergetic and EMR) must negotiate to come from the second reality into conscious awareness.

"I think," Swann states, "we will have to understand that the core itself is something quite intangible. But if it is a universal human endowment, then one should be able to elicit common, respectable efforts that can be identified in anybody. Once these common core fundamentals are observed and studied, then understanding the core seems quite simple. Talent cores seem to possess a common integrity to produce similar or identical phenomena in different individuals—even in the raw state."[7]

---

6. Swann, 1987, p. 57.
7. Swann, 1987, p. 62.

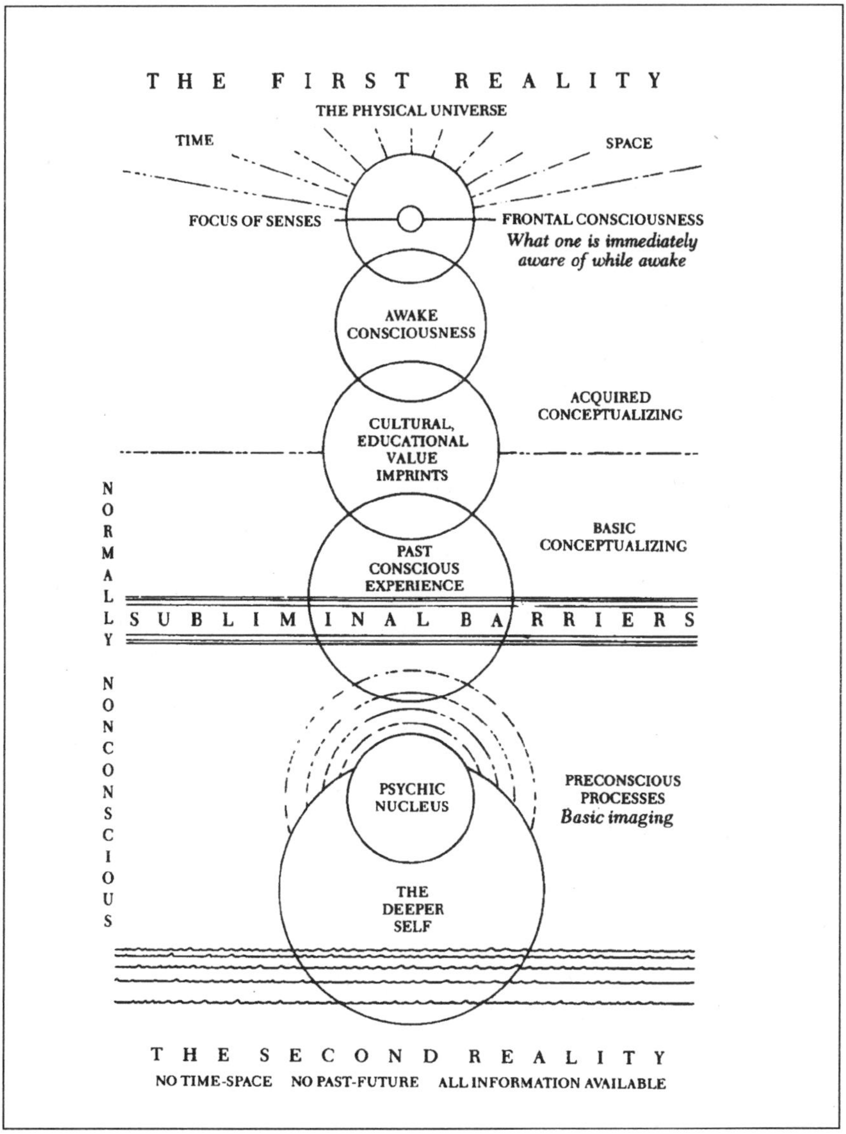

FIGURE 1. *First and Second Realities. Reprinted with permission of Ingo Swann.*

Swann's elements of the ESP core include: the psychic nucleus, the preconscious process, the subliminal barrier, and an area identified as "past conscious experience."

> "Incoming psychic information often makes its way through all the mental processes that can interfere with it without being impeded. In such cases, the impeding mental processes either are not influencing the psychic information at all, or are working in harmony with it. In cases of spontaneous high-stage ESP, the impedance process probably has been overthrown by unconscious factors not yet well understood."[8]

The accomplished multidimensionally aware are capable of working in harmony with both conscious and unconscious processes so that neither impedes the information they obtain from hyperspace.

> "When high-stage psychic information [as in multidimensional awareness] arrives in one of the consciousness areas, it does so *already* formed. This indicates that either the psychic nucleus is capable of exact perception of information and presentation of it, or that associated to the psychic nucleus are a series of preconscious processes that accomplish the work for it."[9]

The information received into conscious awareness did so by means of unconscious and unknown spectra. The correct and already formed information first passed through the preconscious processing area, where it was given form and was projected directly into consciousness.[10]

The Preconscious Process

When incoming information is not projected directly and clearly into conscious awareness, the information goes through the preconscious process. This process takes the direct input through idea-creativity formation in order to take on basic forms that can be recognizable to logic and analysis. In this manner the general idea of the incoming data is generated, but is less exact than high-stage or direct awareness.

---

8. Swann, 1987, p. 66
9. Swann, 1987, p. 60.
10. Swann, 1987, p. 68.

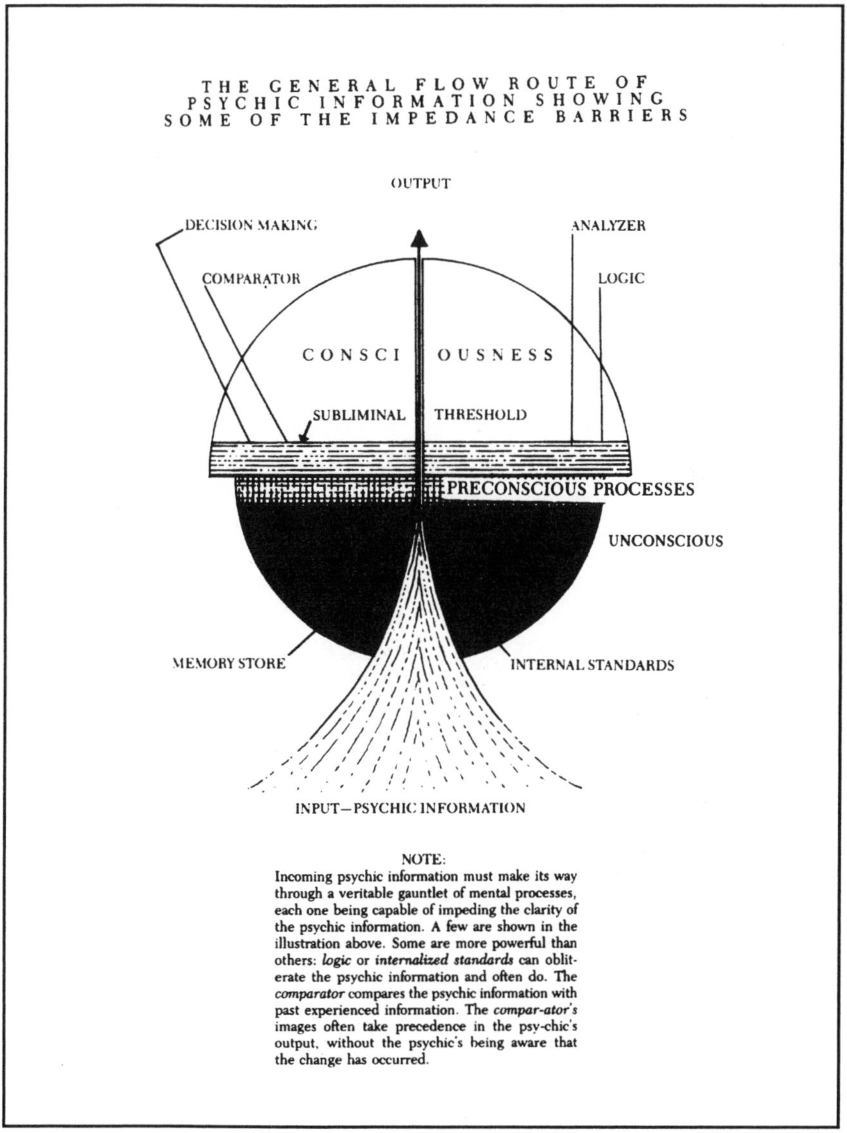

FIGURE 2. *The Unimpeded Route. Reprinted with permission of Ingo Swann.*

Many of the results of ESP experiments show preconscious processing, which constitutes the next best thing to high-stage perception.[11]

11. Swann, 1987, p. 61

Scientists are bringing new information to light regarding how much of human awareness is a product of preconscious processes, which are both unknown and uncontrolled by waking, conscious thought. It is in these hidden realms that core ESP clearly operates.[12]

Subliminal Barriers

In between the conscious awareness of third-dimensional reality and the nonconscious awareness of the unified field, lies a layered band of mental processes, any one of which can stop or heavily distort the incoming information. Swann refers to these automatic thought processes as subliminal barriers.

When information is not directly perceived in consciousness (direct route) the information then "filters" upward toward consciousness as raw data. If a person is adept at perception, this raw data can be rescued before it runs the gamut of subliminal barriers, or goes through "the idea forming area."

"The idea-forming route shows that the information was rerouted through a conscious idea generation component of the mind. When it goes through this route, the mind *adds* interpretations which are frequently incorrect."

Therefore, there must be present in both the direct and idea forming route a process of creativity. The creative process allows participation by the individual in a creative sense.

"It is probably at this level of interaction that the psychic information acquired a good deal of its 'noise.' The creativity channels are closely connected to a multitude of analytical thought process, the emotions of the individual and the visionary elements of his or her dreams, preoccupations and education. If the psychic information pops up through these multifarious channels, it is easy to see how it can become impeded with other random mind elements."[13]

The Automatic Processes

Swann lists eight types of automatic thought processes, or types of barriers, which interfere with information input by means of misinterpretation or

12. Swann, 1987, p. 64
13. Swann, 1987, p. 68.

misinforming. Information filtered through these thought processes comes out in erroneous results influenced by mind manifestations.

- Belief Barriers
- Label Barriers
- Memory Comparison
- Creative Additions
- Imagination
- Random Uncontrolled Thoughts
- Idea Making
- Intellectual [analysis] and
- Decisioning (guessing)[14]

For people developing and utilizing the pathway to the second reality or hyperspace, the first issues to be examined are the barriers which each individual has erected that prevent, inhibit or distort the arrival of second reality or hyperspace information directly into consciousness.

Universal Imaging

Because all people are capable of tapping into the same manner or form of universal information from hyperspace or the second reality, there must exist a basic "psychic or universal language."

This psychic language takes the form of psychic picto-language, or simply picture drawing.

According to Swann, before language there is a world of mental images possessed by all humans which is cross-cultural and universal.

"Basic imaging occurs long before words are learned to describe those images. Imaging, then, is closer and more intimately connected to the psychic nucleus and the ESP core.

"Any information derived psychically from the second reality by the deeper self is first processed as imaging. Later, in the chain of interpretation, the images are translated into the language the individual normally uses.

14. Swann, 1987, p. 69.

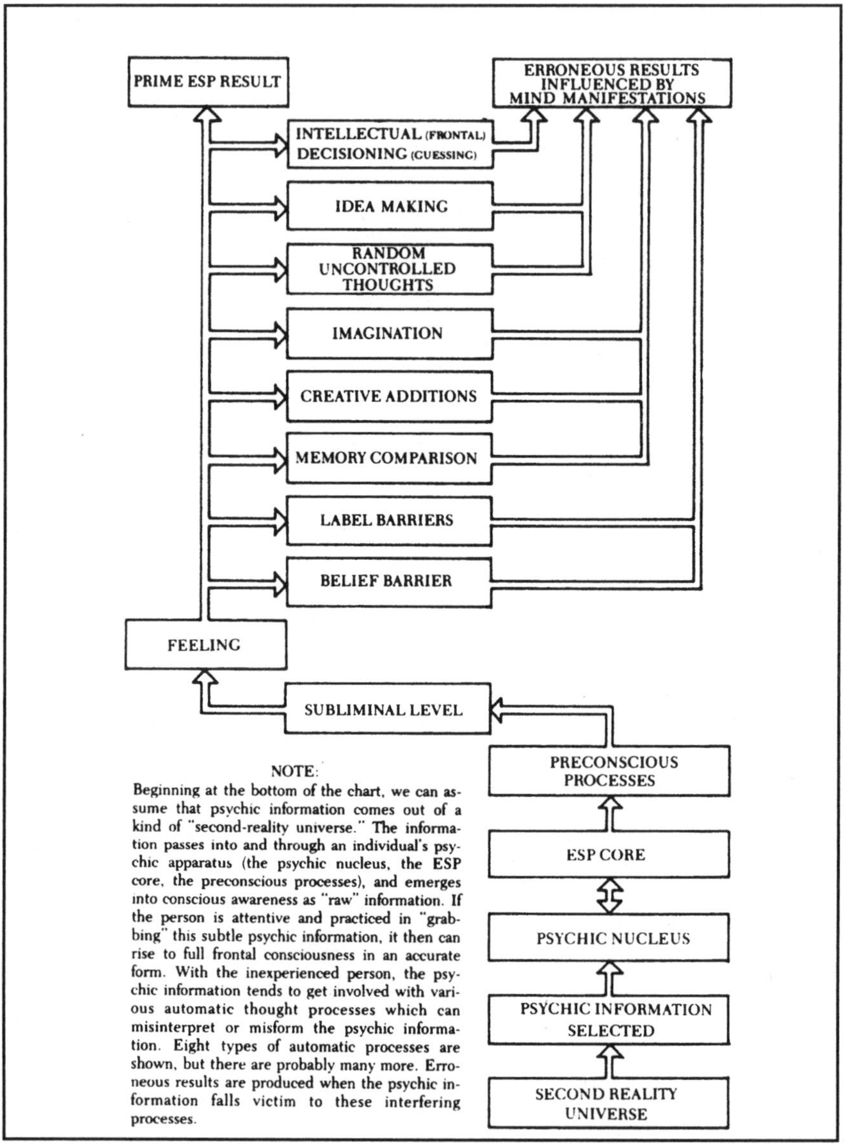

FIGURE 3. *Psychic Information Flow. Reprinted with permission of Ingo Swann.*

"This is not to say that all languages do not exist in the general information pool the second reality represents, for there is evidence that very high-stage ESP can also process languages totally unknown to the individual. But all the evidence points to the fact that when you are first trying to contact your own basic ESP core, it is more progressive to undercut the difficulties imposed by languaging, and allow the basic imaging processes to provide the first and most natural work."[15]

Picture Drawing

The basic imaging process can be easily accessed by the conscious mind by psychic picture drawing.

Picture drawing translates the incoming information into basic forms and shapes which the individual psychic system and conscious recognizes and relates to.

Psychic picture drawing is closely aligned with the artistic attempt of small children, idle doodling and rough diagrammatic sketches preformed during the idea formation stages of projects, buildings, layouts, etc.

Psychic picture drawings have a commonality which does not change over time or from individual to individual. Picture drawings made over a hundred years ago are virtually identical to picture drawings of today.

"Pristine examples of picture drawing," states Swann, "are all a kind of psychic imaging shorthand, truncated, brief, and to the point. With experience, picture drawings do become more precise as to details and relationships, but the shorthand quality remains the same. It is this basic shape-form characteristic that causes all picture drawings to resemble each other. It is the commonality that tells us that we are dealing with a psychic language of some kind and not an individual's artistic bent."[16]

The Ignored Proof

In the winter of 1882-1883, a young psychic named George Albert Smith working at the Society for Psychical Research in London produced the first picture drawings while involved in psychical research.

Smith was attempting to perceive a selected "target" from a friend located in another room. During these experiments, Smith began drawing what he perceived. These drawings were startlingly accurate, so much so that a great scandal ensued upon their emergence. There were charges of collusion.

15. Swann, 1987, p. 74.
16. Swann, 1987, p. 187.

Later, the Society for Psychical Research studied several people using picture drawing with a great degree of success. Other studies were conducted in Paris, Berlin and the United States, all with very promising results. Upton Sinclair's book, *Mental Radio*, published accounts of the psychic picture drawing experiments of his wife, Mary Craig Sinclair. *Mental Radio* caused quite a stir when published in 1930, but the prevailing scientific attitude in America was not bent toward psychic phenomena in any form.

In 1971, Ingo Swann spontaneously began drawing his impressions while working with OBE research at the American Society for Psychical Research in New York.[17]

Picture drawing was later developed as an underlying basis of Controlled Remote Viewing (CRV) at Stanford Research Institute. The methods were developed into protocols for CRV.

Appendix A gives details of picture drawing techniques.

Controlled Remote Viewing

While working at Stanford Research Institute, Dr. H. E. Puthoff, Ingo Swann and others researched and developed Controlled Remote Viewing as a model, which produced high increases in accuracy and could be taught, involving a training period of one year.

Not All Training Is Equal

The method was utilized by government agencies to some extent during the Cold War. The U.S. Army funded a program for CRV for several years and when this elite corps left the Armed Services, some set up in private practice. Speeded up training for non-CRV Remote Viewing sometimes varies very much from the original CRV method.

According to Swann, "Seven or so days of so-called 'intensive training' cannot and does not make a CRViewer. All the so-called 'intensive training' achieves is to induce both mental and physical fatigue into the trainee, and which might render the trainee into a suggestive, hypnoid-like state which is well known in brainwashing techniques."[18]

The suggestive, hypnoid-like state is conducive to the trainee having an induced telepathic overlay. An induced telepathic overlay is the actual basis

17. Swann, 1987, p. 34.
18. Swann, Ingo. correspondence with the authors. April 14, 1996.

for "consensus RV." A consensus is naturally obtained when several ostensible viewers work under the guided imagery control of one person.

"Regarding this," states Swann, "futurology researchers established (at the Rand Corporation in the early 1970s) that consensus even among experts was often completely in error and that consensus of and in itself is worth nothing."[19]

Strict Protocols

Proficient remote viewers actually "travel" in the same manner as the multidimensionally aware.

In CRV strict protocols are set up and viewers usually work with a monitor. There are two types of monitors: the training monitor and the session monitor. These may be the same person, but their roles are entirely different regarding the two situations.

During training, the training monitor certainly does control the training sessions at the start-up of the training. But the ultimate goal is to shift absolute control to the viewer. When this is achieved, the training monitor is practically silent throughout, which is also the case regarding a monitor in an operational session.

Controlled Remote Viewing methods are very clearly defined and strictly adhered to, requiring CRViewers to have a high degree of discipline.

There is No Interpretation in CRV

Spontaneous, or random, forms of RV will probably occur in certain multidimensionally aware individuals, but CRV *must* be learned. People with natural remote viewing abilities can go to specific locations, but the information they receive is at times random. This is not true for CRViewers.

People who access hyperspace often need to interpret what they are seeing and the meaning of the information they obtain.

There is no interpretation in CRV. Information obtained by CRV can be corroborated by duplication of results by different viewers and information gained by "on-site" inspection feedback.

CRV always focuses on obtaining information concerning a specific place, event or person. Regardless of what the subject is, it is designated by a set of coordinates. These numbers are usually the only information given to a coordinate Remote Viewer.

---

19. Swann, Ingo. correspondence with the authors. April 14, 1996.

According to Swann, "There is only one type of data to be obtained by any format or mix of remote viewing personnel, and that is *correct data measured against feedback.* A datum has to be correct in order to be called a datum, since data are expected to correspond to facts. Erroneous 'data' are, of course, not data, even though people persist in using the term to refer to everything including their visions and illusions. In such case, the term 'data' should be preceded by the term 'dirty'—hence 'dirty data.' Just because an ostensible viewer produces something is no sign that it is data."[20]

CRV was not designed to be deployed regarding situations for which feedback was not going to be possible—which is to say it was designed to penetrate hard targets which sooner or later could be checked out.

Regarding this, it was the continuing correctness of the data which accounted for the long duration of the active project, some fifteen years. Had RV or CRV produced dirty data, then Swann says, "We would have been out of business within a week."[21]

Hard, Semi-Soft and Soft Subjects

The multidimensionally aware need to distinguish between hard, semi-soft and soft subjects, or sites, to be viewed.

Semi-soft and soft subjects are ones for which feedback is not possible, and may never be possible, and so there is no real way to determine if data acquired about this is dirty or otherwise. Semi-soft RV stands a chance of eventually achieving feedback.

CRV is only related to hard, immediately available feedback. There has been no CRV developed for soft and semi-soft subjects.

Monitors

Swann continues, "If the CRViewer is a highly perfected one, it does not matter whomever (monitor and/or viewer) knows before hand what the site is. Indeed, the perfected CRViewer will have no interest in what is known or not known, since all that is completely irrelevant—excepting sites utilized for training purposes, in which case the training monitor knows but the trainee never does.

"Solo viewing (a session without a monitor) is tolerable only after the viewer has established a quite long and openly verifiable track record of cor-

20. Swann, Ingo. correspondence with the authors. April 14, 1996.
21. Swann, Ingo. correspondence with the authors. April 14, 1996.

rect CRV against adequate hard feedback, and which record must include precision reference to many details as contrasted only to vast perhaps even imprecise generalities. Solo viewing was never permitted regarding functional operational sessions, even concerning my humble self."[22]

Validation

Replication of results is one of the criteria in science, and Remote Viewing provides this avenue. Controlled Remote Viewing is structured in such a way that verification is built into the procedures themselves. Verification is judged against feedback. Where no feedback is available or possible, there can be no verification.

Because of their natural abilities, the multidimensionally aware probably would make excellent Remote Viewers. They must, however, have the capability to conform to the discipline necessary to follow the protocols and to stay within the CRV structure. Those multidimensionally aware people who can incorporate the discipline benefit greatly in many aspects from CRV training.

Validation of multidimensional experiences is one of the greatest rewards, for validation is one of the multidimensionally aware's most intense needs. To be multidimensionally aware is to have very powerful inner resources, but to be in the awkward position of not being able to present scientific proof or even to have validation except in results.

They tend to spend hours in telephone conversations with people who are experts in a given field in order to obtain validation of the material they are obtaining in hyperspace.

In Essence

All humans are a part of and integral to the unified field. Much of this interaction is subconscious or subliminal.

Emotions and thoughts are entered into and become a permanent part of the unified field. Both time and space can be transcended within the unified field, thus knowledge is not limited in third-dimensional manner.

People are able to have spontaneous, clear instances of information contained within the unified field, which comes directly into conscious awareness.

---

22. Swann, Ingo. correspondence with the authors. April 14, 1996.

Other information is filtered or blocked by an individual's own automatic thought processes or types of barriers, which interfere with information input by means of misinterpretation or misinforming.

Transducer functions are those functions which allow communication between two divergent energy systems. People with adequate transducer functions (and few, if any, automatic thought processes that block information) are able to communicate with all other forms of creation.

Development of these skills can be learned by anyone who desires to do so as evidenced by the success of Controlled Remote Viewing. However, training programs currently available do not have the standards of CRV as built into CRV protocols.

Chapter Fourteen

Wisdom From Within

Within the unified field are many bands of knowledge transmission systems. These bands contain information which is not affected by space or time. We have discussed cosmic light, designating higher order, universal knowledge; psychoenergetics, designating energy emanating from a life unit; and EMR, designating various forms of electromagnetic energy emission, whether occurring naturally or generated by machines.

There exists one other type of knowledge transmission system very pertinent to humans—the knowledge and information contained within the DNA.

Intricate Correlations and Interdependence Exist Between the DNA of Humans, the Earth, Time and the Universe

Recall that one uniting idea among all the multidimensionally aware is their understanding of the connection of universal forces with human physiology and intellect.

Research in several different disciplines adds further information concerning how human physiology is designed in a universal pattern and is interconnected on all levels.

Sacred geometry shows a definitive progression of geometrical shapes upon which *all* forms of creation are built, and which are interrelated, including both physical and nonphysical.

A few examples of the interrelatedness are:

A form taken from a Toras Tube placed inside a glass tetrahedron casts a shadow which corresponds to the 19 letters of the ancient Hebrew alphabet which corresponds to the shape of the 19 amino acids of DNA.[1]

In much the same way that the ancient Hebrew alphabet corresponds to the 19 amino acids, Martin Schonberger discovered that the 64-unit DNA code corresponds to the 64 hexagrams of the ancient divination tool, the *I Ching*.[2] Terence L. and Dennis J. McKenna, in *The Invisible Landscape*, regard the universe as a hologram, created by the interaction of two hyper-universes, just as an ordinary hologram is created by the interaction of two lasers. (They see the third-dimensional physical universe as being created out of the unified field, or a second nonphysical universe.)

According to Terence McKenna, there are 64 time scales in the hologram of the universe, each related to the *I Ching*. Consciousness, or mind, is a standing wave form in these 64 time systems.

As the two hyper-universes making up the hologram of the known universe interact in time, "mind/man" manifests further in the time continuum. Sixty-four evolutionary waves are all mounting toward a cosmic awakening, like the omega point suggested by Teilhard de Chardin.[3]

Scientifically Speaking

The scientific definition of DNA, or deoxyribonucleic acid, is that it is a complex chemical/molecular structure contained within all living cells. Inherited traits are transmitted through DNA genetic coding.

Structurally, a double spiral, or helix, is formed of two strands of a phosphoryl-deocyribose polymer, bonded by attachment between nitrogenous bases and the polymer.

The specific genetic information, encoded by the molecule, depends upon the sequence of nitrogenous bases. A gene is a segment of DNA which encodes the cell's synthesis of a specific protein. These are composed of hundreds of codons, or sets, of three base sequences. The codons formulate a specific amino acid in the protein.[4]

Matter vs. Life

This is a third-dimensional description of DNA, but the physical DNA of the body alone does not make "life." Life only occurs when a mysterious and intelligent force found within the void of the second universe brings its activating energy to direct or energize the physical DNA.

---

1. Melchizadek, 1991.
2. Schonberger, 1979.
3. McKenna and McKenna, 1994.
4. *The New Encyclopedia Britannica*, 1990.

How this occurs, how basic atoms and molecules form into physicality, especially advanced, autonomous beings with consciousness, has been the unexplained mystery since the concept of life itself was perceived.

Chopra writes:

> "[A] baby begins as a speck of DNA sitting in the middle of one fertilized egg cell; over time that cell multiplies until a ball of cells is formed, large enough to begin to sort itself out into the beginnings of tissues and eventually organs, such as the heart, stomach, spinal cord, and so on; then the entire nervous system, digestive system, respiratory system, and so on, emerge, and finally at the moment of birth the millions of cells in the newborn are precisely coordinated to sustain the life of the whole organism without the mother's help.
>
> "But if DNA is the bottom rung of this next step ladder, what makes DNA unfold in the first place? Why does it initially divide on the second day after conception and begin to make a nervous system on day eighteen? As with all quantum events *something inexplicable happens beneath the surface to form the all-knowing intelligence of DNA.* [Italics ours] The point is not that DNA is too complex to understand, being a super-genius molecule; what makes DNA mysterious is that it lives right at the point of transformation, just like the quantum. Its whole life is spent creating more life, which we have defined as 'intelligence tied up in chemicals.' DNA is constantly transferring messages from the quantum world to ours, tying new bits of intelligence to new bits of matter."

DNA is the stage manager in charge of the entire production. It sends its messages in the form of neuro-peptides, hormones, enzymes and all the other body regulating and defense mechanisms. In addition, it receives all incoming information at the same time.

"How does DNA manage to be the question, the answer, the silent observer of the whole process at the same time?" Chopra asks. [Italics ours][5]

From the free-floating organic molecules with which it is surrounded, DNA extracts the appropriate building blocks of physical matter and choreographs the entire organism. The free-floating molecules are formulated into adenine, thymine, cytosine and quanine—the four codes of DNA—A, T, C and G. With this simple, four-letter combination, DNA forms infinite combinations, some short like the three letters coded into amino acids or extremely long ones such as the poly-peptide chains.

---

5. Chopra, 1989. pp. 104-105.

DNA's silent intelligence manufactures the exact chemical message, then manufactures an almost exact duplicate of itself, ribonucleic acid (RNA), which in turn travels away from the DNA to produce the more than two million proteins to build and repair the body.

Chopra states:

> "DNA does not work just from rote memory. It can invent new chemicals at will.... Exactly how this is accomplished is not known, although molecular biologists have found the spacers that separate different words, or genomes. It is also well established that only 1% of the genetic material in DNA is used for its complicated coding, self repair and manufacture of RNA, leaving *99% doing nothing that science can account for.* [Emphasis ours]
>
> "This puzzling silence has stimulated a great deal of curiosity, especially among people who believe that humans do not use their full intelligence. William James ventured to guess that we use only 5% of our intelligence—he meant mental capacity—with an Einstein utilizing up to 15% or 20%. How this percentage translates into usable DNA is unknown, but we can venture to say that DNA is keeping a large vocabulary in silent storage—one geneticist has calculated that the number of molecular "words" produced in a single cell, if translated into English, would fill a thousand-volume library. And that is the product of just the active 1% we have managed to understand. Thanks to the discovery of recombinant DNA (pieces of genetic material that can be shuffled in and out of sequence on the DNA strands), the potential vocabulary may be infinitely larger than we suspect; already combinations of 'letters' encoded on DNA are sufficient to create every life form on Earth from bacteria and molds to all plants, insects, mammals and people."[6]

According to the multidimensionally aware, life only occurs when the soul brings its activating force to imprint and activate the physical DNA. The lifeprint, soul or spiritual DNA, gives life force the physical DNA by an interactional exchange between physical and soul DNA in the body. Together, these two DNAs form the complete entity. The term DNA is then defined in terms of the physical genetic carriers and the incorporated, activating lifeprint of the soul.

6. Chopra, 1989, pp. 150-151.

The spiritual DNA is the mechanism through which a person can access higher order information and knowledge concerning the cosmos and Creation and constitutes the Oneness or "linkage" of self and Creator.

Accessing the DNA

Because the multidimensionally aware can interact directly with the unified field, or hyperspace, they also have the capability to interact with and transduce the information contained within their own DNA.

Contained within each cell of every biological organism is an entire data bank of information. This data bank not only produces, regulates and heals the physical aspect, it contains "memory" going back to the beginning of creation.

An example of this is the formation stages a human embryo undergoes during development. First amorphous blobs form, then stubby knobs extend. Aquatic, reptilian, amphibian, animal and then human forms emerge in distinctly defined sequences, all of which is retained in the DNA.

Opening the Time Capsules

In the 1970s, Dr. Marc Lappé of the Institute of Society, Ethics and the Life Sciences in Hastings, New York, made reference to "walled-off genes." These genes contain genetic information which goes back for millennia and are quiescent until activated.[7]

This has led to the speculation of "time capsules," or internal clocks, contained within the genes, time capsules which remain unchanged for eons until activated to release the abilities and knowledge therein.

What can be found when these time capsules within the DNA are opened by the multidimensionally aware who can journey inside their own DNA?

All the knowledge for all time which is contained within DNA can be allowed to come forward into consciousness.

Through accessing of DNA knowledge, increased information concerning ancient wisdom, the meanings within artifacts, and the knowledge possessed by early earth inhabitants from other space or time frames can be brought forward. Not only the multidimensionally aware, but many people are coming into an awakening, a vast expansion into their own past knowledge to be utilized in the present time.

---

7. Lansburg and Lansburg, 1975, p. 38.

Stored Knowledge

By allowing the DNA information to come into consciousness, people can follow the pathway to their own DNA source information.

In many instances, the "knowing" people have comes from the information within the DNA. Because the DNA is an intrinsic part of a person, accessing the information therein can be an automatic, unconscious act, and will not feel in any way strange to them. They simply "know" by calling forth the stored knowledge.

Conscious, deliberate exploration within the DNA can lead to some very interesting and unusual information, since history, as it is currently written, may not conform to the reality of accessed information.

A person may find a reality basis for events or abilities, which have been deemed myth rather than history.

DNA Knowledge

There are ways to help people discern the difference between reaching their own DNA and other associated phenomena. If the knowledge is brand new with no previous association, the knowledge comes from hyperspace. If the knowledge has a familiarity to it, a feeling of remembering something forgotten, it is DNA recall. If strong visual images come with intense emotion, it is a reincarnational or soul-memory experience.

The accessed information may have a profound affect on the person. Memory of a home planet other than Earth is a frequent revelation for people who have explored their DNA roots. For those with ET DNA, the memory will incorporate the home planet of the ETs, knowledge of how earth was colonized, and the cultural development of the original species.

By being able to internally travel backwards in time through their DNA, the multidimensionally aware are able to trace human evolution in ways that differ from those of archeology.

The Stored Experience of Cellular Memory

According to the multidimensionally aware, cellular (DNA) memory is very real. Emotions, especially traumatic experiences, embody at the cellular level and remain there to be passed on through genetic coding from generation to generation.

As Renée expresses it, the songs of the ancestors sing in the living cells. These songs are not always quiet; they speak loudly to the deeper self.

Within every being, the memories of all ancestors reside, waiting for their chance to speak—and speak they will.

Cellular memories enter into the ESP core and surface in the same manner as knowledge from the unified field. They are subject to the same routing as direct knowledge. They can enter consciousness as a complete, fully developed "knowing," or they can appear as visions, symbols or (inexplicable) feelings.

Genetic Predispositions

Cellular memories are also subject to the same gamut of interpretive functions as unified field knowledge. DNA information, however, may also be an integral part of the formation of the eight types of automatic thought processes or types of barriers which interfere with information input.

Cellular memory may, in fact, be a major contributing factor to what kinds of barriers are formed by contributing a genetic predisposition of how information is processed.

Often gifted individuals will have an ancestor who had the same gift. Part of their inheritance was the ability to access the ESP core and process the information clearly. The cellular memory not only contains the predisposition toward a talent, but also codes the *access processing methodologies as well.*

To Swann's list of barriers, we then suggest the addition of the DNA predisposition factor. This factor may greatly enhance the abilities for clear reception of information into the conscious awareness, or it may hinder it.

Like all the other barriers, a genetic predisposition can be overcome if it presents another barrier to clear access.

Changing the Code

By working at the cellular or DNA level, many healers, as well as the multidimensionally aware, are able to initiate changes which can completely alter the physical form.

In releasing the stored memory of injury, trauma or embodied emotions which outpictured as disease (dis-ease), the cell DNA can return to pretrauma conditions of wholeness.

Changing the actual structure of DNA is not such an unthinkable concept when understood in terms of matter being formed from nonphysical universal energy. By approaching the DNA through the unified field energetics, the physical will outpicture the pattern given it.

Because the DNA has memory, the original "healthy" pattern still exists. It becomes a matter of reinserting the original instructions, or coding, back into the cells from the energetics of the unified field.

It is an energy to matter to energy concept. The energy applied through the unified field alters or reinstates the physical matter of healthy cells, which then produces the energy (instructions) to continue healthy cell replication.

The same approach can be utilized to reconnect any genetic material which may have been disconnected, which is dormant or which has mutated due to electromagnetic pollution.

Conscious Activation

The process of reaching matter through the unified field is the exact, reverse process of bringing information into the conscious from the unified field.

The "directive" from the conscious must negotiate through the levels of mind barriers, past conscious experiences, the subliminal barriers, the preconscious process to the psychic nucleus.

Only then can the input enter directly through the unified field back into the cellular level. Simply "thinking" of something will not achieve the end results. Utilizing repetition, meditation and picture drawing techniques will enable the process to work.

The Multidimensionally Aware Perspective

The electromagnetic nature of today's world and consequences to the DNA have been given serious consideration by the multidimensionally aware. Blanche[8], particularly, has addressed this:

> "In my study of physics, and in understanding cosmic forces which dictate its law of energy and matter, I find that our extremes in creation of electromagnetism and its artificial light have saturated our physiology, the environment, the atmosphere and the cosmos.
>
> "This saturation has brought all the stresses of disequilibrium to full potential. Because of artificial induction of light, the body can no longer internalize and properly utilize sunlight. We can no longer utilize light and the kinetic energy it contains for two reasons: mis-

8. See "A Multidimensionally Aware View of Life" on page 21.

alignment of our skeletal structure and the distortion of the angle of light's reflection through the atmosphere.

"From an internal perspective, the properly aligned bones of the skeletal system form perfect angles, either concave or convex, that reflect light through the system to the cranium or skull, feeding the convolutions of brain tissue.

"The angles of skeletal alignment, in addition to the conductive nature of the calcium phosphate and copper in the bones, transfers kinetic energy. The variations of bone induce the reflections or diffractions necessary to penetrate the mass of the internal organs, particularly those which store, contain and manufacture blood. The skeletal structure conducts and reflects potential energy to areas with the highest concentration of blood.

"I theorize that blood flows by magnetic momentum of polarity dictated by the light, not by the contraction of the heart. Magnetic momentum is stimulated by the bipolarity, which is the human skeletal framework.

"The costal and intercostal spaces within the body reflect light in a circular motion, maintained as the reflection whirls (vorticulates) and reflects from the position of the sternum into the thoracic cage, then directs light (energy) into the heart to cleanse the blood.

"The concentration of light and multiple angles of the skeleton direct energy through the heart chamber, thus purifying the blood for exchange in the excretory systems and re-oxygenation to flow once again to body cells.

"The heart is not the pumping mechanism, but a holding chamber wherein the kinetic energy of light induces cleansing and purification by evaporation. As hydrogen breaks free of oxygen, CO_2 is released in respiration, and venous circulation through viscous nature and gravity removes impurities through the excretory systems.

"As hydrogen attaches to oxygen, its now-rich nature feeds every cell, restimulating balance for cellular vibration, or life, at the atomic level—photosynthetic potential to equate cellular physics."

Electromagnetic Mutation

"It is obvious our blood is toxic with heavy metals, and the wave of electromagnetism has offset bonding and cellular vibratory rates. These ferric metals are mutating our genetic code.

"If anatomically, the skeletal framework reflected the potential of light, this ferric condition in the blood would fracture spontaneously. Light, with its ability to induce oxidation, would become a catalyst for energy exchange at the atomic level, fracturing the ferric domain, releasing trace metals, freeing the DNA of mutation.

"Our internal nature is magnetic. Electrical potential exists on the periphery of the skin or cutaneous membrane. If we shut down the external electrical nature of our energy source—electricity—then our being will emit the glow of potential energies equal to the kinetic input.

"The PH balance will react only with magnetic affinity of the elements, as natural light reacts to the cutaneous protective layer of our bodies. Because we are magnetic, the concentric rings of gravity emit magnetic potential in rings of color to form pure light.

"Our bodies are a prism to reflect the energy within the light, and our elemental composition of energy is pertinent to manifesting balance and maintaining life.

"Cellular vibratory rate originates within the subatomic level in its atomic bonding. The nature of penetration of electromagnetism's wave of light is the opposite of magnetism's light penetration, which is more linear.

"Therefore, if every atom were based on a monopole, the light would penetrate its nucleus and every atom, by weight of its magnetic affinity, would react accordingly. Thus, magnetism would guide each atom in molecular formation, cellular structure and vibration, disallowing mutations.

"Hypotheses are simplistic, but the need is to reach theoretical conclusions and to apply the thoughts based on these premises in principle. Then, and only then, can we begin to unravel the complexities of our creation.

"Time helps, or forces, the confusion, but our minds will transcend space and time, bringing out its reality."

In Essence

The coded language of the universe found in sacred geometry forms the basic structure of all material forms. DNA acts as the "conductor" for the formation and function of all living things. DNA also contains pathways to the past, all the way to Creation.

Information accessed through the DNA often leads to knowledge differing from the current scientific beliefs, including ET origin. Recoding at the cellular level is possible in order to correct illness and mutation. Electromagnetic pollution has mutated the DNA, and the living organisms on Earth are toxic.

Understanding the natural workings of the body from a unified field viewpoint will lead to better methods for correcting these ills.

Chapter Fifteen

We Are Not Alone

In our many, many hours of conversation with the multidimensionally aware, there were certain aspects of those levels of reality beyond our known time/space which were repeatedly discussed.

The exploration of the dimensions, and those who access the vast information available there, would not be complete if we did not undertake a further journey into those fathomless realms.

Some might deem these next chapters "politically incorrect," but as every serious investigator knows, all things (especially something as vast as the infinite) have many aspects and points of view.

So, we will now step out into a more in-depth look at some of the revolutionary ideas which have already been touched upon by the multidimensionally aware in presenting their stories.

The Prevailing World View on Extraterrestrials

The official stance held by the United States government (*Project Blue Book,*[1] *the Condon Report,*[2] etc.) is that UFOs, and, therefore, extraterrestrials, do not constitute a threat to the United States.

This stance has dominated the prevailing world view held in the United States to the extent that many people believe UFOs and extraterrestrials do not exist and are certainly not visiting Earth.

Other countries, however, are far more open to the reality of UFOs. Investigative reporter Jamie Maussan of Mexico states that over 2,000 inde-

1. Steiger, 1976.
2. Condon, 1969.

pendent video recordings have been made of discs appearing in the skies over the Mexico City area since 1991.[3]

Sightings by citizens, police, airline pilots and military personnel continue world wide, almost on a daily basis.

The ET Connection

In addition to current sightings and reports of ET/human experiences, several modern day writer/researchers such as Zecharia Sitchin,[4] José Arguëlles,[5] and José Cabrera Darouea[6] have brought new information regarding records and monuments from ancient times which document that beings from other space/time civilizations came to Earth. In ancient times, the ET purposes were multiple and they often interacted with humans.

Due to their ability to read and translate ancient records, these researchers have been able to retrieve the precise information left by ancient civilizations who either came to Earth and then left, or colonized and intermingled.

From Monuments to Activators

Some authors—specifically Zecharia Sitchin, Brinsley Le Poer Trench, Barbara Marciniak and Alexander Collier[7]—have written extensively about the idea of human/ET lineage, as well as human genetic engineering and manipulation by ETs.

In support of these findings, several of the multidimensionally aware have been able to access their own DNA and have found DNA material of

---

3. Elders and Maussan, 1996.
4. Sitchin, 1993.
5. Arguëlles, 1987.
6. Cabrera Darouea, 1989.

   The Engraved Stones of Ica tell the story of an ancient civilization with medical technology only just now being developed in the modern world. That they also tell of human and dinosaur interaction has left a great question mark as to who the engravers were, when they existed on Earth, and where.

   Supposedly man did not ride and hunt dinosaurs and for that reason, mainstream scientists have dismissed the stones as fakes, for they most definitely do not fit into the present conception of pre-history. Yet, only recently, history was rewritten when John Anthony West geologically concluded that the Sphinx in Egypt is far older than was first believed.

   If the stones were faked, it would be the most elaborate forgery for the least monetary gain ever perpetrated on the civilized world. Peasants, barely literate, would have carved accurate depictions of plants and animals extinct for hundreds of thousands of years. Correct surgical procedures, many of which, such as organ transplants, have only been developed in very recent decades, are shown on the stones. The one person who confessed to carving one, did so when faced with a large fine and years of imprisonment due to Peru's laws regarding the artifacts of antiquity.

   While they are not fakes, what they are is open to interpretation. Some of the oldest strata of rock on Earth are close to the surface in Peru. Laboratory analysis has shown the Engraved Stones of Ica to be from the Mesozoic Era, volcanic in origin, with a high specific gravity.
7. See: Sitchin, 1976; Le Poer Trench, 1960; Marciniak, 1992 and 1995; and Collier, 1995.

ET origin. By tracing this back to their home world, they were able to retrieve information concerning those civilizations.

Among the many, many possibilities this knowledge represents, one possibility is that the activation of ET genetic material also affects—perhaps in a major way—the way in which information is processed.

It is most probable that beings advanced enough to have traveled to Earth, process information in a way quite different from present-day humans. Most essentially, the ETs are knowledgeable of multidimensionality.

Genetic Engineering

Several current, popular books advocate the abduction theme, the taking of egg and sperm—the basic genetic material—presumably in order to reproduce hybrid offspring.

The multidimensionally aware, and some current authors, present a different perspective on the utilization of this genetic material and genetic engineering, that of *genetic reinstatement*.

We, as well as some of the multidimensionally aware, believe genetic reinstatement is not necessarily detrimental.

The thought of genetic engineering is very frightening to most people. However, to begin with, many people cannot formulate a concept of genetic engineering having been performed throughout the course of human evolution.

The altruistic genetic engineering taking place today, we suggest, is an upgrade, a reactivation of the already existing genetic material humans possess. These genes, and the qualities they bring to a person, have been in recess or not activated. Perhaps the benevolent ETs are rewiring our structure so that we can more fully utilize what is ours innately.

The benevolent ETs could be doing this because, with more capabilities—and by this we mean more psychic abilities and more ability to enter into awareness of the dimensions—we will be able to effectively address a future of galactic interaction.

Genetic Upgrade

The ETs are aware that we are in trouble on this planet, and it is possible that in an effort to assist us, the ETs, probably other than the greys, are taking egg and sperm because therein is contained the basic DNA which can be activated.

One possible explanation is that the upgraded, activated genetic material is inserted back into our own bodies so that it can begin replication. This is why, we believe, the majority of people who have had encounter experiences have an inexplicable increase in ESP and in psychic awareness of all kinds. Their own innate abilities were activated within their own DNA.

Experiencers begin to process information in a different manner than before their experiences and usually develop a new world view, a higher holon.

A Future Race?

Other forms of genetic engineering are more questionable, however.

The disappearance of fetuses has been one of the most highly debated subjects in all the field of Ufology. There are as many theories as there are people presenting them.

Another possible scenario is that the most commonly spoken of type, the greys, are preserving human DNA. Through cross breeding, they could continue the evolution of the human race in the event that humans are destroyed through an atomic cataclysm, an atmospheric disaster or violent Earth changes.

One long-time experiencer, a multidimensionally aware individual, offers her perspective after having gone through several "interrupted" pregnancies.

> "Even if none of the experiences were really traumatic, it was the weirdness of them that shattered reality. I was scared because all of this was so unfamiliar. I would find myself in a situation with beings—nothing frightening me, nothing harming me—but I was scared because it was so strange.
>
> "I began having mystical experiences that I felt moved me into the Christ Consciousness. I knew I was pregnant again and this time it was more like, what are you going to do? I knew they were going to take it.
>
> "I felt I had to change the outcome, change how I responded. So, the first thing I did was just give it to them, lovingly, for them not to have to take it. [I would] give it instead of having it taken. I began preparing myself for that. I knew they were coming, but they wouldn't have to forcibly take me or it. It was decided.
>
> "I was wide awake when they came that time. I didn't have a multitude of entities around my bed. There were only two. They said it is time, let's go, and we went. I remembered and it was a wholly

different experience. It was loving because I allowed it to be. Before, I was not open to being loving.

"While it was a very loving experience, I don't believe I am going to be doing that anymore. They have their agenda; I have mine. My agenda was to think and behave in the Christ Consciousness about it.

"I believe they are trying to help themselves. I feel they are doing genetic experiments, genetic manipulation, in order to get back physical sexuality and emotions which have been bred out of this particular race of beings. I think that is one aspect of it.

"They are not going about it in an effective way, for the way they are doing it doesn't make sense. The present way is not successful and not effective. There was an agenda of hybridization they thought was necessary for some reason.

"I think there is discord among them about how to do this, that they are not all in agreement. Perhaps they realized it wasn't necessary and it wasn't working as they wanted it to, anyway. I think the hybrid children, the surviving ones, are on ships.

"I believe it is the greys that have done this. They are the ones that are not coming here anymore. It's not that we won't be working with them again, it's just that this way didn't work out.

"I feel there are many aliens here, many different kinds passing for human. No one is native to Earth; this is an island of free port. Everybody's origins are elsewhere. It is a matter of remembering, to get back to that. It's not that they are so different; they just came in for different experiences. Which is better, second grader or fifth grader? We don't want to look at our sameness. Everyone wants to be different.

"We are two very different civilizations. They are very technical, unemotional, and of a oneness consciousness. We are very emotional, individualistic and not of a oneness consciousness. A parallel evolution is going on. Actually, it would work better if we would cooperate on some level."

More Disinformation

There is reason to believe that the popular version of abduction is not a true representation of ET/human interaction. Of the 139,914 letters received by Whitley Strieber after the publication of *Communion*, only 20% described negative encounters and only 3% mentioned hypnotic regression sessions with UFO researchers. Nine out of ten of that 3% viewed their encounters as negative. That is a very small percentage of the entire population.[8]

One of the strongest arguments against the popular abduction scenario is that the population sample, with which the current abductionists do their research, is both a small and biased sample.

It is our own experience that the vast majority of people interacting with the ETs find their lives changed in positive ways. Much more research of the encounter phenomenon needs to be done before accurate conclusions can be made.

Retroactive Rereading

There is growing evidence that children who have interacted with aliens or ETs from their earliest childhood, may have experienced probings and examinations. Later in life they came to believe they were victims of incest, when, in fact, the event did not include a parent or relative at all, but was the confusion in the child's mind with what constituted an authority figure.

There is a great need for open-mindedness among counselors, for if they do not accept the ET theory as a possibility, they may inadvertently lead the experiencer toward the more commonly accepted incest as a cause of childhood trauma, a direction which induces more trauma.

In *A Brief History of Everything*[9], Ken Wilber makes a very valid point in stating that as individuals evolve and formulate new mental concepts (new personal holons), past events are analyzed through the perspective of advanced knowledge. Past events can rarely be viewed from exactly the same perspective as that in which they initially occurred.

Wilber writes that all of us

> "will retroactively reread the earlier events in our life from this new perspective [attained after developing higher mental concepts], and we tend to imagine that is the perspective we had from the start. When we think of ourselves at age 4 or 5, we think of the people around us at that time—our parents, our siblings, our friends—and we picture what they were thinking about us, or how they felt about certain things, or what was going through their minds, when in fact we could actually do none of that at the time! We could not take the role of other at that age. So we are automatically (and subconsciously) 'retro-reading' our entire life from the perspective of a

8. Strieber, 1995, p. 96.
9. Wilber, 1996.

recently emerged world view, and imagining all of this stuff was present from the start!

"Needless to say, this totally distorts what was actually occurring in the earlier periods. Memory is the last thing you can depend on to 'report' childhood. And this leads to all sorts of problems. Romantics imagine childhood is a wonderful time where you see the world just like you do now, only in a marvelously 'spontaneous' and 'free' fashion. Archaic is non-dual paradise in the non-egoic core, magic is holistically empowered wonderfulness, mythic is alive with spiritual powers, and, gosh, it's all so marvelous and free. Whereas they, the Romantics, with access to the higher world view of reflexive awareness, are simply reading all sorts of wonderful nonsense back into a period which, if they could *actually* see it (on videotape, for example), they would deny any reality to it at all!

"The impressions of various childhood events are certainly present, sort of like bruises in the psyche. And these impressions retain the world view of the level that was present when they were laid down—usually archaic or magical.

"But when these impressions are recalled by adults, the impressions themselves are thoroughly interpreted in terms of the higher world view now present. And then all sorts of present-day concerns can be injected back into these original impressions, and it vividly appears that these concerns were there from the start. It doesn't seem like you are reinterpreting these early impressions, because that is done subconsciously or preconsciously, and so you only see the conscious result of this extensive reworking.

"In certain intense states of regression—with certain therapies, certain meditative practices, certain drugs, certain intense stresses—these original impressions can be accessed (precisely because the higher paradigm is temporarily decommissioned), but even then, a few seconds or a few minutes later, the higher world view returns, and people begin extensive retro-reading of these impressions. And we have to be very careful about that."[10]

Thus, in any regression to recover childhood memories, the current perspective (personal world view) will subconsciously "correct" a former perspective (world view held at a particular age) to accommodate the new world view.

---

10. Wilber, 1996, pp. 176-77.

Using Hyperspace

There are certain phenomena associated with hyperspace that are relevant to ET encounters. Many authors have documented that UFOs have an affect on automobiles, radar tracking devices and computers, most notable *Visitors From Time* by Marc Davenport. Monroe and Becker, and many others, have documented that humans are affected by various wave functions and that certain tones and frequencies entrain the brain, causing altered states of consciousness.

Taken together, this research indicates that energy emanated by UFOs might also affect the human mind, causing an altered state of consciousness. The person is, effectively, opened up to hyperspace.

The mind is accustomed to functioning in the third dimension, but if opened to hyperspace, events are experienced on another dimension. Due to unfamiliarity with multiple dimensions, the event is interpreted in third-dimensional reality and can be extremely confusing.

Is Seeing Believing?

Screen memories are often associated with ET encounters. Screen memories are usually discovered in conjunction with an encounter event, but this is not the only time a person will develop a screen memory.

A screen memory is a consciously recalled sequence of events which overlay another, more accurate memory of any paranormal, traumatic or very bizarre occurrence. The human mind will immediately and automatically attempt to relate anything experienced to known reality. It will draw upon mental equivalents already present in the memory.

A screen memory is formulated by the same barriers which function to distort incoming information from the ESP core.

This is a completely subconscious action. The eye sees, sends sensory signals to the brain; the subconscious identifies what is being seen and informs the conscious mind. The conscious mind then makes a decision as to what action must be taken, prompted by the intensity, or lack thereof, of the subconscious message.

In encountering something which has no mental equivalent, the subconscious mind will first attempt to relate the unknown to a known memory. As an example, many screen memories of animals—deer, owls, rabbits—are found in a forest setting. The mental expectation is that it is highly possible to see an animal while walking in the woods.

The first instinct, upon seeing a form, would be to identify that form in the context of a known, expected form. Thus, a deer, owl, rabbit etc., would be the first impression sent to, and registered in, the conscious mind.

Subconscious Processing

Initial identification with the known is a normal, human response. Faced with the truly unknown, the subconscious will do one of two things:

If it can vaguely associate, but not well, it will send a signal of a "composite closeness," a sort of manufactured similarity signal. However, if the object seen or encountered has no mental equivalent what-so-ever, then the subconscious will register the image, but no signal will be sent to the conscious mind. Nothing will be registered as having been seen.

This is called the exclusion factor and takes place because there is no mental equivalent. The Patagonians could not see the ship because there was no mental equivalent, and the mind excluded the visual image from consciousness.

It may be possible that some ETs do not instill a screen memory themselves, but instead utilize this normal human reaction and enhance it.

In an altered state of consciousness, however, the conscious and subconscious are far more synchronized and the conscious mind does register the imprint without it being suppressed by the subconscious.

The energy created by a UFO, or some other mechanical means, could cause the mind to open into hyperspace and encounter strange images in these spaces.

Many times experiencers will not relate some of their experiences except to a very few, trusted people, because they are just too bizarre. Placed in the framework of multidimensional experience, these encounters begin to make more sense.

In encounters, exploration of the idea of a multidimensional event should also be considered. There is a difference between an actual encounter with a physical UFO and a hyperspace experience, but both are real.

The Multidimensional Perspective

D. B. Valdez offers a different and unique perspective on the entire UFO/ET phenomenon:

> "People of deep spiritual awareness never have problems with the brothers of either side. The greys cannot approach us in the

purity of essence, because they are dealing with things of denser vibrations.

"Many people have said that the others can walk right through doors, glass, everything. They only do that to scare the living hell out of people, to show that if the intellect doesn't understand this ability, then automatically the intellect says the others are more powerful, which is wrong!

"They are afraid of our thoughts more than they are of our weapons, because we can manipulate them more with thought than they can us. That is the reason they show such frightening scenarios, to scare people.

"From a strictly intellectual viewpoint, they don't succeed in scaring anyone. What scares people the most when they are scanned? The needles, the cold operating table or creatures that come out of our own subconscious to scare the living daylights out of us? If people could truly see, they would see there are no differences.

"People try to differentiate between the kinds of visitors. People talk about channeling this one, or that one. It takes a golden spade to shovel through all this to find the little nuggets of wisdom. Even though many people allow their inner self to perceive these things, they are still perceiving out of their subconsciousness, so the little bug-eyed greys are the ones everybody sees.

"The reason is because the more prolific we are in talking about them, the more people are able to see them, or to visualize them in their mind. Then when something out of dimensionality that they don't understand comes to them and touches them, the image that is called forth from the brain is the image they have already perceived. On the other hand, if they are a very religious person and the same thing happens, what they see is Mother Mary or angels.

"Concerning the perceptions of who our brothers are, out there, it has helped me so much, being multicultural, being able to understand more than one language. Take five points of perception, put them together, and a person can come up with a new perception. The American populace gets only one point of view. That is why the government is so adamant about making only one common language."

Knowing Only What We Are Told To Know

"The extraterrestrials have as much to learn from this as we do. They can't buy the knowledge like they bought our government with technology. The government traded themselves over, because they realized there were people in the universe that had more technological power than they did.

"As long as the government does not tell people about this, so they can awaken to do something, people will not do anything. The reason we can't get information from the government is because the government has already been told that if they say certain things are true, then the aliens, instead of being surreptitious, will come out in the open.

"It has been predicted that the information will be filtered out into the third world countries. In the United States, we may think we have a great, all ranging society where we can see what is going on all over the world, but, in actuality, we only see what is given to us.

"If you cannot go to another plane and observe for yourself, you can be told anything and believe it. Don't believe the media."

Little Bits of Truth At a Time

"Some of the channeling coming out now is accurate, but what I call contrails have been laid out by disinformation sources to keep people from understanding it. There are those who do not want the general populace to know about this.

"People get stuck in the micro perception. In order to really expand, you have to let your consciousness flow over the entire universe and see the big picture.

"The movie *Stargate* has a dimensional plot. When they wrote it, it was plucked from the consciousness. Humans still try to use technology to get through to the dimensions.

"Technology has to adhere to the laws of the universe. You can't stretch from one point of the universe to another because of the kinetic energy concept. Like a rubber band stretched as far and long as it will stretch eventually has to go back.

"One of the arguments we are having now concerns things people are being told about the Pleiadians. They are told that Pleiadian ships can go up to a certain apex point above us, then are able to travel to the Pleiades in a few minutes. You cannot break the laws of the universe in order to travel in these perceptions. You have to travel through the dimensional gates. When you travel through the dimensional gates, you are not using any kind of perceived energy, because you are not going anywhere."

Predicted Earth Changes

One of the things which most concerns the multidimensionally aware is the present state of the environment and the eventuality of some form of Earth movement, whether it be a pole shift, massive earthquakes or depletion of the atmosphere.

Earth changes and damage to the environment are frequent topics of ET encounters and much has been written concerning the information given to individuals on these topics.

The multidimensionally aware are, however, working at a furious pace to help correct the imbalances humankind has brought to this planet.

Additionally, they do not see major disaster as inevitable, only *probable* under present conditions.

D. B. Valdez has some refreshing views on predicted Earth changes:

> "It irritates me to see people accept prophecy. I tell them prophesy is only fulfilled when they let it become fulfilled. If people do not understand that they have the ability to change prophesy, then they are not working in the right direction. They are waiting to be sacrificed, instead of finding a way to stop the sacrifice. *Prophecy is a warning to change what is possibly going to happen.*
>
> "The people that understand have been working to see why certain prophesies have been perceived as prophesies. In order to explain this to people, I have to sit down and tell them slowly.
>
> "Look at this. You understand how molecules and the distribution in the atmosphere is used to carry a TV signal from a tower to your antennae, to your TV set? This is a basic, very simple, premise of altering the three primary colors for a color set. There is the TV screen where it fires from the three cathode tubes at the back. It fires to the screen, then each one of those little dots is assigned a number, a plus or minus. That is what gives the perception, and everything that happens on the TV screen can be seen.
>
> "It is the same thing when dealing with dimensionalities, except it is to a higher degree. These things can be perceived without the help of the sending unit.
>
> "For instance, suppose we make a film about multidimensionality and put it on the airways. Nostradamus, 550 years ago, was able to see the things he put in his prophecies. We are challenging that now, on the basis that the things he saw were perhaps not the things that were real, but the things that were made up by us, living in this time, such as films.

"Nostradamus would see certain things, but he could have been making his prophecies based on things that here, in his future, are not real. He could have been seeing a movie. Looking at the movies we have made, wouldn't Nostradamus say he saw certain things, like Doomsday, the Earth ending, because we made movies based on the prophecies? He would not understand it as a movie, because they did not have that capability.

"Therefore, he thought he saw the future and put that in his prophecies. Perhaps what he saw was skipping—in CB talk. CBs only have a certain range, but when there is a skip, the radio signal hits the ionosphere and skips up and up, before it skips back down. The signal reaches thousands of miles away when it was supposed to only reach a few miles.

"When dealing with light, we are dealing with the same kind of thing. Perhaps what is happening right now is being put into the universe in picture form and is what is being bounced back to the past. Prophets that could see it would not be seeing a true idea of what was happening on Earth, but seeing a false idea, a fiction.

"See what happens about self-fulfilling prophecies? We read the prophecies at a later time and say, 'Oh! This is going to happen,' and we are filling our consciousness with false ideology. Your belief system absolutely formulates your perception."

Working Together

Other multidimensionally aware individuals have developed a working relationship with ETs, gaining insight and knowledge which they have applied to helping others here.

Once, in deep meditation, one such person was working on a healing and realized that the person in question, in a psychological sense, really "had no backbone." She knew, in that altered state of consciousness, that if she could visualize a physical backbone for the person, their psychological state would be healed also.

She mentally lined up backbone vertebrae, but had difficulty keeping them aligned. Suddenly, over her right shoulder, someone handed her a perfect backbone. Assuming it was a medical person, she thanked them, then turned to look. To her consternation, the entity was reptilian. She is sure that, in her shock, her jaw dropped.

The entity said in a very gruff voice, "We serve the same God," which reassured her. Then he added, "I don't think you are very beautiful, either."

Negotiating With Other Worlds

Hurtak adds further information on his beliefs about other life forms, which may be dimensionally different from us and how they may assist us:

> "We must understand that within our space and time, and as we go into other realms of space-time, there may be certain life forms we will not immediately understand because of different dimensional frequencies. They may be watching us, but we may not be conscious of them because they operate from bodies of quantum mechanical corpuscles of Light or from a different vibratory frequency. In other words, we may encounter our brothers and sisters in space, not simply in terms of a physical constitution, but through a different type of nucleogenesis. We may be bio-transducers of a slower vibration of chemical 'letters' when compared with their consciousness interdependence from our biological strata.
>
> "Within the space happenings at some future time, humanity as a race will perhaps experience the higher evolutionary Light forms of superluminal Intelligence, but we may not immediately relate to them because of different dimensional frequencies. More advanced forms of life may exist, in addition to corporal forms of intelligence in our immediate universe, who, like us, are restricted to one evolutionary form.... They [these higher life forms] may be able to create a planetary and transplanetary Renaissance by virtue of giving us the gifts of a new biotechnology and the ability to program our own DNA-RNA, or to open new planets to us as educational centers—not through culture shock or negative experimentation, and not through a lift-off of Pioneer 10 or 11 from Cape Canaveral. Rather, it would come instead from a 'lift-off' within our own inner consciousness, and through our inner consciousness, we would see that the body and the mind is a collage of super holographic possibilities."[11]

11. Hurtak, 1990 pp. 27-28.

Chapter Sixteen

In the Vastness of the Universe

The multidimensionally aware generally acknowledge that they have roots not from planet Earth, but that they came here to be of assistance to humanity, particularly at this time.

Dr. Scott Mandelker, in *From Elsewhere: Being ET in America*[1], undertook an in-depth study of people who were aware that they had come from other systems, that their origin was extraterrestrial. They either were born into a human body (Wanderers) or came to Earth by a walk-in process (Walk-ins).

Wanderers constitute the main group of ET souls on Earth, are far more common and grounded than Walk-ins, and many are multidimensionally aware.

According to Mandelker, a walk-in process takes place when there is a second soul entering the body/mind system, and the soul may be of either extraterrestrial or more evolved human origin. The walk-in personality is usually more spiritually aware and very definitely more oriented toward service to humanity than the previous personality.

Not the Only Truth

In his study Mandelker found that in this group there was no overt pathology present, despite the fact that many therapists may have a problem with people who say they are not from Earth.

Holding a doctorate in East-West psychology, a Master's in counseling psychology and trained in comparative religion, Mandelker astutely writes, "Therapy, for humans or ETs, can be a potent force for change and healthy

1. Mandelker, 1995.

growth—for individuals, couples and families. But modern psychology does not explain everything.

"The problems come about when psychologists or psychiatrists begin to believe that their model of the mind—a very Western one—is the only true model. They believe that the human self stretches from head to toes, that life and death are opposites, that genetics and social conditioning are the greatest forces shaping personality. Unfortunately, this model of how the mind works labors under the same limitations that cripple their model of the universe. It's why so many clinical therapists spend so much time trying to understand how UFO crop circles, ET sightings, alien abductions, ESP, telepathy and out-of-body experiences are all 'psychological events.'

"The lengths to which therapists go in explaining such paranormal experiences as psychological are often absurd. ...Keep in mind that psychological definitions, no matter how exact, are only one way of seeing it. They are not the only perspective.

"Human denial and fear of the unknown are immense and often hide behind the mask of authority. It might be interesting one day to read a psychological study of those 'psychologizers,' those researchers who've arrived at such presentable, westernized conclusions....

"Because there is much that does not compute in the rational, materialist world view, which is the basis of our western civilization, and, now, our global culture, how can we be surprised when the experts scramble for psychological explanations of everything mystical and nonordinary?"[2]

"The presence of ETs has rarely been given any real analysis or serious research. The experience of ET identity has rarely been addressed and often gets lost in a medley of strange and fascinating tales. The personal conflicts, the struggles and accomplishments of those with non-Earth origins, their transition from confusion to confidence—all of that has been given far too little attention by academics or the mainstream public."[3]

It Is a Process of Becoming Aware

In a questionnaire, Mandelker lists twelve traits most clearly associated with those who are aware of extraterrestrial origins. Many multidimensionally aware share the same characteristics, but not all the people Mandelker

2. Mandelker, 1995, p. 4-5.
3. Mandelker, 1995, p. 6.

interviewed showed multidimensionally aware characteristics as we have described.

Comparison With Mandelker's Questionnaire Characteristics

Numbers 1 through 12 are Mandelker's characteristics, followed by our discussion.

1. *You were often lost in daydreams of ETs, UFOs, other worlds, space travel and utopian societies as a child. Your family thought you were "a bit odd," without knowing quite why.*

The multidimensionally aware young are very knowledgeable about the realities of the higher dimensions, but do not necessarily *focus* on ETs, UFOs or space travel. Conversations with hyperspace intelligences are very common, but these beings may not always be ETs. Most commonly the little ones will delve deeply into more futuristic, often scientific knowledge.

2. *You always felt like your parents were not your true parents, that your real family was far away and hidden. Perhaps you thought things around you were somehow "not the way they should be," and reminded you of life somewhere "far away." These beliefs may have caused you a great deal of pain and sorrow. You felt "out of place."*

The multidimensionally aware's most common complaint was that no one understood them, that their awareness set them far apart from most of humanity, and that they were aware of other realities very different from this one which other people did not believe exist. Many felt as if they did not belong to their parents.

3. *You have had one or more vivid UFO experiences (in a dream or during waking hours) which dramatically changed your life: they helped resolve doubts, inspired confidence and hope, and gave you meaning and greater purpose. From then on, you knew you were a different person. Like a spiritual wake-up call, it changed your life.*

There was conscious UFO involvement with some of the aware, however, this involvement appeared to be ongoing and only part of their many hyperspace experiences.

4. *You are genuinely kind, gentle, harmless, peaceful and nonaggressive (not just sometimes, but almost always). You are not much interested in money and possessions, so if "someone must do without," it is usually you—such is your habit-*

ual self-sacrifice. Acts of human cruelty, violence and perpetual global warfare seem really strange (shall we say, alien?). You just can't figure out all this anger, rage and competition.

In the majority of the multidimensionally aware that we interviewed, these qualities were very prominent. Conflict of any kind was generally not understood and generally abhorred.

Ian stated, "It was hard learning about conflict and to understand why people had to do those things to each other, why that was necessary."

5. *You have a hard time recognizing evil and trickery; some people call you naive (and they are right!) When you do perceive genuine negativity in your midst, you recoil in horror and may feel shocked that "some people really do things like that." In a subtle way, you actually feel confused. Perhaps you vaguely sense having known a world free of such disharmony.*

Because they are so psychically attuned, the multidimensionally aware generally know when a person is saying one thing and actually doing or meaning something else. The difficulty they encounter in these situations is a lack of understanding why people act in the manner they do.

6. *The essence of your life is serving others (be they family, friends or in a profession) and you cherish great ideals, which may also be somewhat innocent and naive (in worldly terms), but you sincerely, deeply hope to improve the world. A lot of disappointment and frustration comes when such hopes and dreams don't materialize.*

Service to others and to the planet was almost always the highest priority of the multidimensionally aware. They, however, brought the added gifts of futuristic technological knowledge to implement their ideas. Those who have come to terms with their abilities excel in highly competitive fields, such as developing free energy sources, alternative medicine advancements and inventions, as well as being able to have deeper insights into such workings as human mind functioning, social evolution and energy transformation.

7. *You completely embrace the scientific temperament, with a cool, reasonable and measured approach to life. Human passion and red hot desire seem strange; you are baffled. Romance and the entire world of feelings are truly foreign to your natural way. You always analyze experiences, and so people say you're always in your head—which is true! [Note: This type of Wanderer is less common. Such an "odd bird" is probably a brilliant scientist.]*

Embracing the scientific temperament comes naturally to the multidimensionally aware because they have such incredible vision into the inner workings and universal flow of things.

Very deep feelings of love were also found. Interpersonal relationship problems arise from the multidimensionally aware, being extremely busy doing their work and focusing in hyperspace, thus leaving the partner somewhat alone, both physically and mentally. It takes a very emotionally well-balanced individual to have a successful relationship with a multidimensionally aware person.

Mandelker's "odd birds" of scientific bent are probably some of the multidimensionally aware!

8. *You easily get lost in science fiction, medieval epic fantasy (like The Hobbit) and visionary art. Given a choice, you'd much prefer to live in your dreams of the past or future than in the present. Sometimes you consider your Earth life boring and meaningless, and wish you could go to a perfect, exciting world. Such dreams have been with you a long time.*

Because the multidimensionally aware actually access different time/space continua, the temptation to spend their entire life there is almost overwhelming. They do find Earth life rather boring and one of their greatest challenges comes in focusing here. When they read, they tend to read highly technical journals seeking to add to their wealth of knowledge, rather than to escape into fantasy.

The multidimensionally aware are the Jules Vernes and H. G. Wells.

9. *You have an insatiable interest in UFOs, life on other worlds or previous Earth civilizations such as Atlantis or Lemuria. Sometimes you feel like you've been there, and may even go back someday. (Actually, this question is a give-away, since only Wanderers and Walk-ins have profound, undying curiosity about worlds beyond—and for good reason!)*

Profound interest in ancient civilizations and accessing ancient knowledge is a hallmark of a multidimensionally aware individual. Worlds beyond *are the very life* of the multidimensionally adept.

10. *You have a strong interest in mystic spirituality (East or West), both theory and practice, with a deep sense that you used to have greater powers and somehow lost them.*

The majority of the multidimensionally aware we interviewed are very spiritual beings, for they are aware of the many facets of the human being and the connection to higher selves. Conversely, the successful multidimensionally aware have not lost their greater powers of the mind, but utilize these abilities to a high degree.

11. *You have become a conscious channel for ETs or some other non-Earth source—and you realize that the purpose of your life is to help others grow and evolve.*

Most multidimensionally aware do not channel in the commonly utilized sense of receiving information from another person. They have gone to the next step—direct access to information. They may converse with other intelligences, but it is a conversation in the way of a consultation.

In addition to helping people grow and evolve, many are concerned with and work in the areas of new and different technology, innovative ideas and inventions to advance civilization in an environmentally compatible way.

12. You feel, and *perhaps all your life have felt*, tremendous alienation and a sense of never quite fitting in. Maybe you hope to be like others, try your best to be "normal," or imagine yourself like everyone else—but the bottom line is that you *simply feel different* and always have. There is a very real fear of never finding a place in this world. (Which you might not! Note: This is *the* classic profile of Wanderers.)[4]

This is very true of the multidimensionally aware who have not yet understood their capabilities. Those who have accepted them no longer worry about being different. They know who they are; they know what they are to do here, and, therefore, put all their energy into accomplishing their tasks.

Being From Or Just Being Is Truly Not Important—Doing Is

One thing the adjusted multidimensionally aware and Wanderers or Walk-ins have in common is that neither see their abilities or origins as something special. Almost all focus on their life's work, rather than who they are, per se.

Renée captures the overall feeling quite well: "If you are here for a reason that is different from everybody else's, and are here with the knowledge of that difference, having a human experience, you must be busy doing what you are here to do, nothing else is even to be entertained. Though for some, the investment is to be the freak, be the weird one, experience trauma drama. If you truly know what you are here to do, you cannot do."

It Is Not as Uncommon as People Think

Basing his computed figures on information received in 1981 that the current incarnated ET population of Walk-ins and Wanderers was 65 mil-

4. Mandelker, 1995, pp. 207-209.

lion, Mandelker estimates that by a little calculation, we "can assume the number is much higher today, almost fifteen years later, amidst an ongoing influx of souls coming to help the transition into the New Age. If we estimate, the figure can be revised to a current population of about 100 million—probably one of the strangest secrets of the universe."[5]

It is not known, and can not be estimated, how many multidimensionally aware are here.

Barbara Marciniak believes that many more multidimensionally aware children will be born after 1994.

Futurist Gordon-Michael Scallion stated in an article in September 1995, that the forthcoming Blue Star will cause a vibrational change on Earth, and the physical body will change to reflect the higher vibration. According to Scallion, "Blue, violet and indigo shall rule the next cycle and the next root race. All children born after '98 shall be telepathic at birth and many born prior shall exhibit such abilities."[6]

Herman writes, "[M]any of the children are wise, advanced souls from far distant civilizations. Just as a great number of you came as representatives of distant races and civilizations to influence and participate in the grand experiment on planet Earth, so are many of these beautiful souls. There is a new seeding; a fresh infusion of Spirit taking place on Earth. Not only are you, as the old vanguard, bringing in and anchoring on Earth the energies and wisdom, but these wonderful young ones are bringing a new wisdom and knowledge so advanced, so outlandish to you at this time, that you cannot even comprehend it."[7]

"A Stranger in a Strange Land"

Being different, being alienated, being too radical or nonconformist has usually been the pathway for the multidimensionally aware and those "from elsewhere" alike. Because of their differentness, each felt a deep sense of isolation, a not belonging which went to their very core being.

This difference stems from the absolute internal knowing each one has about the realities beyond the third dimension.

Mandelker writes of one person he interviewed, "Because of his experiences as a child, Soren knew from an early age—although he didn't fully understand—that there was another state of being and that this planet was

5. Mandelker, 1995, p. 2.
6. Scallion, September, 1995.
7. Herman, 1997.

not the only place to be. He already knew that what most of us take to be the only possible reality is just a relative state, a single frequency on an endless band of signals."[8]

8. Mandelker, 1995, p. 177.

Chapter Seventeen

And So It Begins

For many, the concepts we have presented will be startling, even shocking perhaps. That is the nature of a new holon. Ideas never before possible become reality.

Over the three-and-a-half years of researching the multidimensionally aware and the material we have presented, we found ourselves struggling with some of the concepts. We, too, had to formulate new mental equivalents to accommodate the world view of the multidimensionally aware in order to fairly present that world view.

The New World Holon of Multidimensionality

In every epoch there are those whose vision transcends the prevailing world view and opens the doors to allow new concepts, new ideas and a reality shift to occur which was not possible before.

The new holon which the multidimensionally aware represent includes:

- A revolutionary paradigm shift in what constitutes "reality"—movement beyond the confines of the third dimension.
- An evolutionary leap for humanity.
- An opening of doors to advanced human mind potential.
- An unlimited potential for new, pure energy technology.
- The enhancement of a psychoenergetic approach to disease and health.
- An avenue by which "history" can be rewritten in light of knowledge of prior extraterrestrial presence and interaction on Earth.
- A new way to access and process information which is more closely aligned with a galactic perspective.
- The ultimate transcendent shift from materialism to mentalism.

Prototypes of Human Potential

The multidimensionally aware are living examples of human potential. They have consciously surpassed material, third-dimensional, controlled and limited information transmission systems to reach unlimited, unified field information transmission systems.

What the multidimensionally aware are not is nonhuman beings. They have only accessed levels of awareness in themselves others are discouraged from discovering and experiencing.

In other words, they are prototypes of larger human potential. They are examples of the old adage, "Anything is possible, if you know how." The adept multidimensionally aware know and share the "how" of tapping into the unified field.

Eradicating the Barriers

Earth has always been contained within the unified field; therefore, humans have always received knowledge transmissions, but have repressed this knowledge from conscious awareness, relegating cosmic information input to the deeply buried mind dynamics of the subconscious.

Successful multidimensionally aware individuals have simply eradicated the barriers between the conscious and subconscious input. They have opened pathways between the two mind centers and expanded their 5-15% conscious awareness factor by an untold amount.

Stuck In a Mind-Set

The current holon of human conscious awareness—prevailing world view—has been stuck or blocked into a "dis-learning" mind-set, which has short-circuited human mind functioning potential.

The prevailing band of thought form energy in the (M) unified field is one of closing, rather than opening, individuals to new information and awarenesses available in the second universe.

The multidimensionally aware have made the adjustment necessary to unlock the mind-set (overcome the prevailing world view) and, once free from that state of nonawareness, can access higher dimensions.

Teaching Others

Accomplished multidimensionally aware individuals can effectively teach individuals they come into contact with by emanating learning transmissions. In concert, they can reach millions who, acting on the learning transmission themselves, could also access the dimensional pathways.

Individual, conscious awareness of and overcoming of mental barriers, and a conscious, internal search for the learning, rather than dislearning, transmissions, are keys that allow the mind to expand.

Seeing Past the Mind Blocks

The importance of breaking free of third-dimensional world view mind blocks and individual barriers is, very simply, that humans have radically altered the planet's environment without radically altering themselves on a conscious mental level.

The result is a quest for material comfort and the irrational utilization of Earth's resources in this pursuit, and it has already caused irreparable damage.

If humanity continues in the current destructive mind-set, Earth *cannot* continue to support human life. The blocked mind-set does not allow this knowledge of Earth's inability to support burgeoning human life to become readily apparent, due to an inherent belief system, a dislearning transmission, that "Life will always continue this way."

Those who have escaped the mind blocks and accessed the unified field can see the rapidly approaching end of material resources. Humans are decimating those resources at an astronomical rate. When Earth's resources are exhausted, all that will be left is the damage.

Overpopulation

> "At the core of the global warming and pollution issues lies the real culprit—human overpopulation that has stretched the world's resources to their limits. To be sure, the world's human population has grown exponentially in the modern era, doubling from about 2.5 billion in 1950 to 5 billion in 1991, and estimated to hit 10 billion by 2010. During the first half of the 20th century, we consumed more non-renewable resources than in all of our previous time on Earth, stretching the planet's carrying capacity to its limits. In 1994, Worldwatch, a private, non-profit research group that monitors population growth and natural resource supplies, issued a report that warned of potential food shortages in the years ahead. "As a result of our population size, consumption patterns, and technological choices, we have surpassed the planet's carrying capacity." Their study indicated that the slow growth in the world food supplies is evidence that the

planet's biological limits have been reached. This is in sharp contrast to what mainstream science has been telling us. In spite of such warnings, many scientists continue to say that the world can continue to produce enough food to feed all its inhabitants, due to improved agricultural technology.

"But the Worldwatch report says that such technology cannot keep up with the population explosion in third-world nations. They point out that fish harvests from the world's oceans have leveled off at about 100 million tons a year and may possibly not be exceeded. As more bodies of water become highly polluted, freshwater shortages are beginning to occur around the world. Grain production has slowed dramatically in the last few years, and in some cases, as with rice, corn and wheat, the per capita output has fallen since 1984. Even with massive programs of deforestation in many areas of the world, crop land has only increased 2% in the last decade as topsoil has disappeared and farmland has given way to factories."[1]

New Holons Always Bring Solutions

The obvious question then becomes, "How does a multidimensional vantage point contribute solutions to the many environmental and human ills (disease, starvation, war)?

It must be comprehended that the environmental and human predicaments are a product of materialistic world view mind-sets, which are caused by lack of knowledge of:

1. *matter first being pure energy,*
2. *the human mind effects on pure energy,*
3. *a misutilization of pure energy and*
4. *ignorance of the effects of the energy created when the energy of matter is changed.*

1. *Matter first being pure energy:* Everything which exists is first an idea (pure energy), then material matter (formed energy) is acquired by means of the (energy formed idea of) money, work, time and effort.

The creation is then "made" by assembling the matter in a certain structure, with the structure being "the end product," without regard to the potential of the transformed energy except as more matter (i.e. profit or consumer goods).

1. Lewels, 1997, pp. 285-286.

The third-dimensional vision dynamic is matter to matter, not energy to matter to energy.

2. *Human mind effects on pure energy:* Humans constantly create energy forms in their minds by means of their thoughts. Mind blocks (belief systems) misinform that these thoughts are self-contained within the mind and "go nowhere."

This constitutes the greatest fallacy of the current world view. It has been proven over and over again in all the scientific disciplines from nuclear physics to astronauts resonating mental messages from the moon to Earth, that thoughts have a definite physical impact on and over matter, including other individuals.

3. *Misutilization of pure energy:* Because of the belief system that thoughts "go nowhere," the prevailing thought forms of a negative nature are negatively impacting all of Earth.

Negative thought output adversely effects all life forms because of information exchange psychoenergetics of which most humans remain unaware, but are constantly producing.

4. *Lack of knowledge of the effects of the energy created when the energy of matter is changed:* Historically, massive experiments and testing of weapons has occurred worldwide.

Scientists *do not know* the long term effects these experiments and tests will have on the planet and all life-forms. These tests continue, despite vast amounts of scientific documentation and research on the detrimental effects of nuclear radiation, electromagnetic radiation and the depletion of the ozone layer.

These experiments include, among others:

- Nuclear testing both above and below ground and in the atmosphere.
- The launching of space exploration vehicles, missiles, satellites and high flying jets which affect the ozone layer.
- Weather control experiments.
- The High-frequency Active Auroral Research Project (HAARP) on the northern slope of Alaska includes experiments in ionospheric heating of heretofore unknown magnitude and the bouncing of electromagnetic waves off the ionosphere to Earth, plus many other related "studies."[2]

2. Begich and Manning, 1995.

The Mind-Set of Materialism Can Be Reversed

Technology, not of third-dimensional materialism which depletes Earth's resources, but a technology of mental energy and unlimited information transmission and access, can restructure human focus and activity and restore Earth's environment.

Consider the following two tables:

TABLE 1. Multidimensionally Aware Perspective

Access to pure information transmissions	Unlimited access to higher order information	Clear vision of energy to matter to energy	Clear action on energy to matter to energy	Future positive results: Positive utilization of energy to matter to energy
→	→	→	→	

TABLE 2. Third-Dimensional Awareness Perspective

Generated 3-D material information system	Limited access controlled by the mind block. "Secrets" kept.	Vision of what the control deems fit to fulfill self interest. Denial of existence or importance of pure energy and thought forms.	Action of matter to matter	Focus depletion of existing matter. Negative environment, life form impact.
→	→	→	→	

Unlimited Information Access

By having unlimited information access, the multidimensionally aware can view energy working and can also trace the energy paths from source to end results. Thus, they can determine positive or negative outcomes of material creation and the progression of the energy to matter to energy change dynamic.

This is not futuristic science fiction; it is the reality available by breaking free from world view mind blocks and individual barriers, by being able to access mental energy technology and then apply that technology in third-dimensional, physical space.

We Are All Multidimensional Beings

Mental energy concepts and abilities are humans' innate birthright, which humankind, for themselves, must dig from the graveyard of their own deeply buried psychic minds and activate.

Because all matter, including humans, exist as part of the unified field, learning to access the unlimited information available is a potential possessed by every human.

Forerunners of human mind potential have mapped the territory by developing proven methods for accessing these vast regions.

People can learn by meditation, practicing picture drawing techniques and by attuning to the learning transmission systems available in the unified field.

Becoming a multidimensional being simply means that consciousness is aware of other levels of self existence beyond time and space.

Bringing the Dimensions To Us

By learning of the realities of the existence of the second universe, the unified field, we can begin to integrate those higher dimensions into the third dimension.

Integration of the dimensions is movement of consciousness, for the physical body is consciousness and more—the unified field. Integration is the infusion into consciousness of a wider spectrum of energy and dimensional experience.

Each influx, each expansion, brings a fuller spectrum, a wider range of consciousness, an enlivened physicalness to the individual.[3]

The Dimensional Shift

With an integration into consciousness of other realities, the third dimension would not cease to exist. Experience would simply incorporate other dimensions and realities blended together. It would be a multidimensional experience, an integrated Earth experience.

It would be a new dimension of experience which is multidimensional, fully conscious, fully expressed and fully understood.[4]

As consciousness integrates multidimensionality, the physical body would begin to manifest changes dictated by increased awareness. Human

3. For an interesting and enlightening perspective on multidimensionality see: Moore, 1996.
4. Moore, 1996, p. 31.

form, beginning at the genetic level, would change in accordance with input from the unified field.

A dimensional shift brought about in this manner would be gradual and is already in the process, beginning with the multidimensionally aware.

Galactic Citizenship

A shift in consciousness would allow Earth's inhabitants to move *peacefully* into an already populated universe.

If the world view toward both humans and extraterrestrials is not changed, the "them vs. us" prevailing, warring mentality will spread from Earth out into the galaxy.

By a change in the way information is accessed and processed, humans can move into a mental equivalent equal to those of non-Earth, nonaggressive civilizations.

If the ETs mindset had been that of Earth's prevailing, warring world view, Earth would have been conquered long ago.

In lieu of war technology, humans can acquire higher order information and knowledge. This, in turn, could lead to wisdom.

The multidimensionally aware have opened the way for transcendence into the new holon. They have set up the information transmission resonance on the highways of the unified field, the highways which can lead to freedom from a destructive world view and a much higher quality of life for all.

A Final Thought

The creation of this book has been a fascinating experience. During the course of the three-and-a-half years of research, we, ourselves, began to experience some of the phenomena described. We experienced the process of being able to access altered realities by being in the presence of the emanating energies of the multidimensionally aware (described in Chapter Twelve).

We both experienced visions of things "beyond" and instant insights after assimilating the "how" of it.

Because of our own experiences, we can attest to the realities we have presented.

In all probability, you will now begin to meet multidimensionally aware individuals in your daily life. We hope that you will find the experience of knowing these individuals challenging and exhilarating, as we have.

Our highest hope, however, is that when you meet a special, bright child with a shine in their eyes, that you will stop, look them in the eye and validate them mentally by saying, "I know who you are and I appreciate you."

Appendix

Learning the Techniques

The success of those following the instructions published in *Natural ESP* and *Your Nostradamus Factor* and the success of Controlled Remote Viewing has proven that anyone can learn to access the ESP core. The following is taken from *Natural ESP* and is a very abbreviated version of Ingo Swann's excellent instructions.

Picture Drawing Techniques

Very basically, another person places a very simple object or drawing in an unseen location. The object or drawing is designated as a "target" or focus of the experiment.

Distance between subject and target does not matter, except for the availability of immediate feedback on results.

The subject sits comfortably at a table with plain white, unlined paper in front of them. Distractions should be kept to a minimum, such as radios, TVs, other people, etc..

The subject then draws, very rapidly, any impressions he or she may have of the target. The rough, first sketches are usually the best in the beginning as the conscious mind is learning how to access the ESP core.

Commonalities

There are four commonalities to all picture drawings. These commonalities include: error contributions, associations, lack of fusion and accuracy.[1]

Analysis of the drawings compared to the target is where most of the learning takes place. Unlike most techniques which focus on accuracy, errors

1. Swann, 1987, p. 139.

are most important to the learning process. Error contributions are barriers which must be addressed and identified in order to develop.

Common Errors

Swann lists four of the most common error contributions:

1. Some other thoughts that have nothing to do with the target or experiment.
2. No contact or correspondence at all (barriers).
3. Illusion or imagination.
4. False guesses, or just guessing.[2]

Associations

In addition to error contributions, associations are formed when information gets far enough to elicit an internal response - emotion, feeling, taste, smell, etc.

Four major types of associations are identified:

1. Not the object itself, but things associated with it, o, in some cases, things that might be expected in association with it.
2. Associations of feelings, etc.
3. Something the object (or location) reminds you of
4. An image of something similar to the object.[3]

Lack of Fusion

Swann believes that "lack of fusion is one of the more important concepts that needs to be understood. In terms of the ESP core and the pathway, it means that the components of the target are being perceived, but that they 'won't go together' to form an understandable image or concept.

"The picture drawing emerges as bits and pieces, but will not evolve into a distinct image. The subject usually experiences some kind of stress or confusion when this happens, and can become so irritated that the whole ESP core collapses as a result. Normally we would think of this as definitely destructive. But not if you really look at what is happening.

"Lack of fusion frequently occurs without imagination or associations poking into the response. The incoming psychic information is not being

---

2. Swann, 1987, p. 140.
3. Swann, 1987, p. 149.

diverted into these 'helpful' channels. In fact, lack of fusion shows that the ESP core is trying to cope with the information on its own - without assistance.

"Thus, when lack of fusion emerges in the picture drawings, it is a hopeful and positive signal that the ESP core has been activated, and that the whole system pathway is retreating from trying automatic resolutions to the information. When lack of fusion does occur then, it is an indication that soon the activated ESP core will 'learn' to cope on its own with shape-form, etc. Conscious extrapolation has retreated or ceased, and so false imaginings soon go away."[4]

Careful Analysis

Finally, carefully analyze the picture drawing, identifying which error, association or lack of fusion occurred. Circle the correct portions with a red pen and write in a blue pen beside the incorrect portions which type of commonality it is (error, association or lack of fusion).

Individuality

Swann's advice to those learning the art of tapping into their ESP core:

"At first, any or all of these characteristics can be found in picture drawing. There is no particular order in which they are to be encountered. But as the psychic pathway becomes stronger and more integrated into the system (of the unconscious and consciousness), a lot of these random manifestations simply disappear. The individual's intuitive system appears to take over, and the picture drawings become more and more organized.

"One of the things that does appear to happen, though, is that the system grows by leaps and bounds. These may be a first spontaneous high-stage result, followed by a series that is plainly a mess. Suddenly, the system makes another jump in quality, followed by yet another difficult period. This can happen several times before the system levels out and begins working in a predictable harmony with the psychic nucleus.

"We can assume that during these jumps and starts, the ESP mind mound is reorganizing itself based upon actual self-experience of the activated ESP core. So do not be dismayed if after doing well, your experiments suddenly appear to collapse in confusion."[5]

4. Swann, 1987, p. 157.
5. Swann, 1987, p. 184.

About the Authors

Alice Bryant

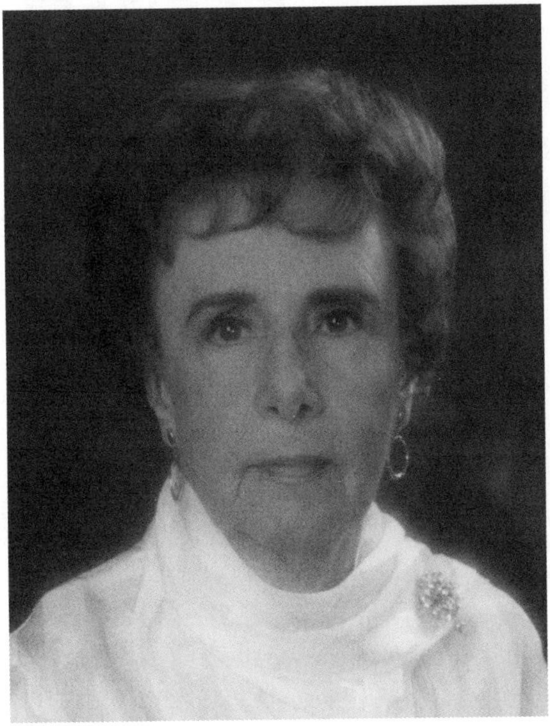

Early in life Alice began a journey on the metaphysical path which led her to the write *The Message of the Crystal Skull*. Subsequent to this, she and her daughter were guided to write *Healing Shattered Reality* that has brought much needed understanding of the contactee phenomenon in Ufology. She has traveled extensively in the United States and in Mexico visiting the ancient monuments. As a student of new age philosophy, she believes that UFO experiences can be exhilarating and not traumatic, that healing can be accomplished in all things, and that we are on the threshold of a new planetary age. Researching and presenting material about other dimensions, unusual phenomena and what it means to the world has become her life's work.

LINDA SEEBACH

Linda earned her Bachelor of Arts degree from the New Mexico Institute of Mining and Technology and her Master of Social Work degree from the University of Denver. In 1984 she began working with Vietnam veterans with post-traumatic stress disorder. A long time student of metaphysics and new age thinking, she incorporated empowerment methodologies into her counseling and utilized innovative means to bring people back into the knowledge of who they truly are, to help them get in touch with their deepest selves, and to assist them in formulating a future worth living. Along with her mother, Alice Bryant, she co-authored *Healing Shattered Reality* which utilized her therapist skills and her new age philosophy and brought enormous healing to experiences who up until this time had no information on which to rely. Linda has recently become an ordained minister and once again in a collaborative effort seeks to bring further enlightenment to the world about multi-dimensionals.

Acknowledgments

Alice Bryant

I wish, with heartfelt gratitude, to acknowledge the contributions to this work by the following people:

Richard Linder for sparking the original idea for the book and nourishing the first tender shoots of creativity. Special gratitude goes to my daughter and co-author, the Rev. Linda Seebach, for her unflagging energy, dedication and exceptional inspiration. I deeply appreciate the editorial advice, as well as the contributions of my dear friend, Ingo Swann, artist, author, philosopher. Thanks too, to the patience of the publishers Pam Meyer and Brian Crissey, who saw the potential of the manuscript and suffered through the many re-writes. My appreciation to Blanche McLanahan for giving me a first hand look at a multidimensionally aware family, the great love and the great difficulties in adjustment. My grateful thanks goes to all the multidimensionally aware who gave so generously of their time and knowledge. By sharing their intimate life stories they will help others have a greater understanding of how to cope with being a traveler in these vast realms.

Rev. Linda L. Seebach, M.S.W.

I wish to express my deepest gratitude to my mother, Alice Bryant with whom I had established a working and living relationship during the creation of our first book, *Healing Shattered Reality: Understanding Contactee Trauma,* which served us well as we co-created *Opening To The Infinite.* I am deeply grateful for her commitment to this work—it would never have been achieved if it were not for her years of seeking and finding the multidimensionally aware, of patiently acquiring material and laying the foundations.

As the multidimensionally aware entered my own life, I found true soul mates, fellow travelers on the same path. Through them, I learned who and what I, myself, am; what all of humanity is and can learn to be. My own dimensionality became very clear to me. For this, I bless each and every one of them. I deeply appreciate my very blessed friend Hank Sanders. M.S., who journeyed so many times to those other dimensions to assist in this work by easing my tension and realigning my being. As I went to bed with an aching back and awoke renewed because of Hank's thoughts and projection abilities, great validity was given to our work in the other dimensions.

I wish to thank my spiritual sisters, Blanche and Renée for holding the frequency of Light and Love, for being a part of my life and journey. My love and appreciation go to my Earthly sister, Rebecca Ryan, because she understands what words can never express. And most of all, my deepest appreciation and heartfelt gratitude for the loving generosity of Ingo Swann without whom this work would never have been what it is.

Glossary

- **ACCESSING THE DNA:** Ability to access the DNA evolutionary pathway, thereby experiencing circumstances and/or other space/time continua that are unique to a person, an ancestor or another civilization.
- **ACTIVATE:** Energies and abilities which have been dormant are awakened or suddenly brought into consciousness and begin to be experienced and utilized.
- **ARCHETYPE:** An archetype, according to Jung, can not really be described, for it is something perfectly empty, but capable of assimilating a tremendous variations of a certain kind of material, always associated with a certain archetypical quality. Archetypes were originally derived from mythology, fairy tales, legends and religious forms of thought. The original pattern after which a thing is made.
- **ASTRAL BODY:** Soul aspect; ethereal, identical to physical but of a non-physical form.
- **COLLECTIVE UNCONSCIOUS:** Jungian term designating a mass psyche, the collective experience of humans. A "band" within the "M" field, second universe or hyperspace.
- **CONSCIOUS:** Day to day, third-dimensional perceptions, thoughts, ideas and experiences, as well as the analytical and emotional thought process. All or portions of subconscious information can be brought to conscious mind for interpretation and analysis or as direct information from the unified field.
- **COSMIC LIGHT:** For our purposes is defined as an information transmission system for higher order knowledge.

- **DEEPER SELF:** The subconscious mind, a nonphysical mind which is in contact with the unified field or "all else that exists," although this contact is normally barred from everyday consciousness. The deeper self emerges into conscious awareness in pure form spontaneously from time to time.
- **DIMENSIONS:** Levels of existence having boundaries outside the known time/space continuum. The third is but one of many dimensions.
- **DNA:** Singular unique make-up of each individual; also a total evolutionary link extending to the beginning of creation.
- **ELECTROMAGNETIC RADIATION (EMR):** Used for our purposes to designate one of three types of information transmission systems. Physical energy waves consist of an electric field and a magnetic field at right angles to each other, and both at right angles to the direction the wave is traveling. The number of waves formed in one second is the frequency; the distance the energy travels (at the speed of light) during one oscillation is its wavelength. The higher the frequency, the shorter the wavelength, and vice versa. Electromagnetic radiation (EMR) spans an enormous range of frequencies: gamma rays, X-rays, ultraviolet waves, visible light, infrared heat, microwaves and radio frequencies. The microwave and radio frequencies are broken down into a range from extremely high to extremely low frequencies.
- **EMBODY:** To integrate a belief system into cellular memory to the degree that it becomes a core belief upon which other concepts are built. Many people embody beliefs which are never re-examined, and they may be unaware that their reactions are based upon the embodiment of an ideology which may or may not be true.
- **ENGRAM:** A genetic memory trace associated with the Genome Racial Memory, as discussed by Immanuel Veilikovsky in *Mankind In Amnesia.*
- **ESP CORE:** The pathway or route, consisting of several layers, that information must negotiate to come from the second reality into conscious awareness.
- **EXTRATERRESTRIAL (ET):** Nonterrestrial; not of Earth origin.
- **GROUNDING:** The ability to completely incorporate the mind focus into the physical body, thus focusing attention directly into third-dimensional reality and day-to-day life. The ability to be fully and completely aware of all conscious processes and the third dimension at the same time.
- **GROUP MIND:** Interdependent mentality of shared thoughts, goals and activities.

- **HARMONIC RESONANCE:** Resonance means the quality of sounding again. To resonate is to reverberate. Reverberation implies give and take, the definitions of communication which is always simultaneous and between at least two agents. Communication implies an exchange of information. Information is the form-vehicle of qualities of energy passing between two agents or parties. As a sounding again, resonance is information.
- **HEMISPHERIC SYNCHRONIZATION:** Synchronizing the two halves of the brain, enabling a person to enter an altered state of consciousness.
- **HOLON:** That which is a whole, but also contained as a part of another, larger whole. In evolution, the next higher stage of evolution which encompasses and supersedes the previous stages of evolution.
- **HYPERSPACE:** The spatial dimensions beyond time and the reality known as the three dimensional world, defined by height, width, depth of space and time; multiple dimensions; unified field; second universe.
- **KEY PHRASE:** A harmonic resonance which acts as a guide to delineate specific areas of knowledge to be accessed in hyperspace.
- **KINETIC ENERGY:** Electromagnetic energy emanating from an individual which can affect other electromagnetic and electric systems.
- **"M" FIELD:** A term coined by Robert Monroe to designate a broad field of energy, which for convenience was called (M). Virtually unrecognized in contemporary civilization, it is the only energy field common to and operational both within and outside time-space and is present in varying degrees in all physical matter. Used interchangeably with hyperspace, the unified field or multiple dimensions.
- **MERGING**: Becoming multidimensional by understanding that other parts of self exist on other dimensions.
- **MULTIDIMENSIONAL:** Multiple, diverse levels of reality existing in more than the third, physical dimension.
- **MULTIDIMENSIONALLY AWARE:** A person who can consciously access hyperspace (the second universe, the unified field) including their own DNA. These people can and do access technical, advanced information not commonly known, (i.e. Albert Einstein).
- **OUT-OF-BODY EXPERIENCE (OBE):** Separation of the physical and astral body with conscious awareness being in the astral body; astral travel.
- **PAST LIFE MEMORY:** Memory of self being in another space/time in a different physical body.

- **PSYCHIC:** The natural human ability to collect information from physical and nonphysical realms through the ESP core.
- **PSYCHOENERGETIC:** Used for our purposes to define the energy emanated into the unified field from a life unit available for transduction into human consciousness. A specific energy signature unique to all life units which exist.
- **RENEGADE ALIEN:** Those extraterrestrials who do not have humanities' best interest in their agenda.
- **SECOND UNIVERSE:** An identical universe which exists in the nonphysical, the unified field, hyperspace, multiple dimensions.
- **"SEEING":** Conscious internal visualization and perceptions of other time/space dimensions. A seer.
- **SUB-CONSCIOUS MIND:** Repository of all knowledge including every detail and nuance of individual experience; also the link with the unified field where all information can be obtained.
- **SYMBOL:** A designation for something which can only vaguely be characterized or designated otherwise. A symbol only approaches the meaning by utilization of certain designs. In its original utilization, the Greek word symbol meant creed, which is the closest humans can approach to certain intuitions and beliefs; symbols were the only expression of the greatest mysteries of life and eternity, and were always sacred.
- **TIME TRAVEL:** Travel out of linear time to other past/future circumstances.
- **TONE:** Harmonic resonance which resonates within the human mind, opening communication throughout the Cosmos.
- **TRANSDUCER FUNCTION:** A natural ability to convert the energy of one transmission system into the energy of another. Energies can be passed from one form to another by various transmission systems.
- **UNIFIED FIELD:** The nonphysical "glue," origin from which all matter springs, the All That Is. Used interchangeably with hyperspace, second universe, multiple dimensions, the "M" field.

Bibliography

- American Psychiatric Association, *Diagnostic and Statistical Manual of Mental Disorders*. 3rd Ed. Washington D.C.: American Psychiatric Press, 1980.
- Arguëlles, Jose Ph.D., *The Mayan Factor: Path Beyond Technology.* Santa Fe, New Mexico: Bear and Company. 1987.
- Becker, Robert O. and Selden, Gary. *The Body Electric: Electromagnetism and the Foundation of Life.* New York: William Morrow and Company, Inc. 1985.
- Begich, Nick Ph.D. and Manning, Jeane. *Angels Don't Play This HAARP: Advances in Tesla Technology.* Homer, Alaska: Earthpulse Press. 1995.
- Braden, Gregg. *Awakening to the Zero Point: The Collective Initiation.* Questa, NM: Sacred Spaces / Ancient Wisdom. 1994.
- Bryant, Alice, and Seebach, Linda MSW. *Healing Shattered Reality: Understanding Contactee Trauma.* Mill Spring, NC: Wildflower Press. 1991.
- Cabrera Darouea, Jose Ph.D., *The Message of the Engraved Stones of Ica,* First English Edition by Dr. Cabrera. Lima, Peru. 1989.
- Chopra, Deepak M.D., *Ageless Body, Timeless Mind: The Quantum Alternative To Growing Old.* New York: Harmony Books. 1993.
- Chopra, Deepak M.D. *Quantum Healing: Exploring the Frontiers of Mind/ Body Healing.* New York: Bantam Books. 1989.
- Cohen,Barry M. ,ed. and Esther Giller, Lynn W.. *Multiple Personality Disorder from the Inside Out.* Baltimore, Maryland: The Sidran Press.1991.
- Collier, Alexander. *Global Government: The E.T. Connection, Extraterrestrial Overview from Andromeda,* video tape series. 1995.

- Condon, E.U. *Scientific Study of Unidentified Flying Objects*. ed. Daniel S. Gilmore. New York: E.P. Dutton and Co., Inc., 1969.
- Cowan, Eliot. *Plant Spirit Medicine*. Mill Spring, NC: Swan-Raven & Co., 1995.
- Dennis, Caryl, and Parker Whitman. *The Millenium Children: Tales of the Shift*. Clearwater, FL: Rainbows Unlimited, 1997.
- Elders. Lee and Maussan, Jamie. "Voyagers of the Sixth Sun" video. Genesis III. Tucson, Arizona. 1996.
- Feldman, D. H. and Goldsmith, L., *Nature's Gambit*, New York: Basic Book Publishers. 1986.
- Fuller, John G. *Arigo, Surgeon of the Rusty Knife*. New York: T.Y. Crowell. 1974.
- Grenwell, Bonnie L. Ph.D., *Energies of Transformation*, Saratoga, CA: Shakti River Press. 1995.
- Herman, Ronna. *On Wings of Light: Messages of Hope and Inspiration from Archangel Michael*. Alpine, California: Star Quest. 1997.
- Hunt, Roland. *The Seven Keys To Color Healing*. San Francisco: Harper and Row Publishers. 1971.
- Hurtak, J. J. Ph.D., *Negotiating With Other Worlds*, Los Gatos, CA: The Academy for Future Science. 1990. Original copyright (c) J.J. Hurtak, 1978 (cassette recording).
- Kaku, Michio Ph.D., *Hyperspace*. New York: Oxford University Press. 1994.
- Landsburg, Alan, and Landsburg, Sally. *The Outer Space Connection*, New York: Bantam, 1975.
- Le Poer Trench, Brinsley. *The Sky People*. London: Neville Spearman Limited. 1960.
- Lewels, Joe Ph.D. *The God Hypothesis: Extraterrestrial Life and Its Implications for Science and Religion*. Mill Spring, NC: Wildflower Press. 1997
- McKenna, Terrence L. and McKenna, Dennis J., *Invisible Landscape: Mind, Hallucinogens and the I Ching*. San Francisco: Harper.1994.
- Malchizadek, Drumvalo. *The Flower Of Life Workshop*. Volume 6. Dallas, Texas. 1991.
- Mandelker, Scott Ph.D. *From Elsewhere: Being E.T. In America*. New York: A Birch Lane Press Book. 1995.
- Marciniak, Barbara. *Bringers of the Dawn: Teachings from the Pleiadians*. Santa Fe, New Mexico: Bear and Company. 1992.

- Marciniak, Barbara. *Earth: Pleiadian Keys to the Living Library.* Santa Fe, New Mexico: Bear and Company. 1995.
- Metz, Steven and Kievit, James. *The Revolution In Military Affairs and Conflict Short of War.* Carlisle Barracks, PA.: Strategic Studies Insitute, U.S. Army War College 1994.
- Monroe, Robert A. *Ultimate Journey.* New York: Doubleday. 1994.
- Monroe, Robert A. *Far Journeys.* New York: Doubleday. 1985.
- Moore, L. David, Ph.D., *The Joy of Knowing We Are One: Transformational Conversation Among the Masters and Erik Myrmo.* Atlanta, GA: Pendulum Press, 1996.
- Pfeiffer, Eric. *Disordered Behavior, Basic Concepts in Clinical Psychiatry.* New York: Oxford University Press. 1968.
- Puharich, Andrija. M.D. *Beyond Telepathy.* Garden City, New York: Doubleday. 1962.
- Puharich, Andrija M.D.*Uri: A Journal of the Mystery of Uri Geller;* Garden City, New York: Anchor Press Doubleday and Company. 1974.
- Ring, Kenneth. *The Omega Project: Near Death Experiences, UFO Encounters and Mind at Large.* New York: Morrow. 1993.
- Scallion, Gordon-Michael. 'The Blue Star. It's Origin'. *The Earth Changes Report.* Chesterfield, New Hampshire. September, 1995.
- Schonberger, Martin. *The I Ching and the Genetic Code: The Hidden Key to Life.* Translated by D.Q. Stephenson. New York: ASI Publishers, 1979.
- Sightings. Paramount Pictures Corporation "Sightings" Broadcast, November, 1994.
- Sitchin, Zacharia. *The Twelfth Planet.* New York: Avon Books. 1976.
- Steiger, Brad. *Project Blue Book.* New York: Ballantine Books. 1976.
- Stewart, Daniel Blair. *Akhunaton: The Extraterrestrial King.* Ukiah, CA.: Mind's Eye Productions. 1993.
- Strieber, Whitley. *Breakthrough.* New York: Harper Collins Publishers. 1995.
- Swann, Ingo. *Natural ESP: A Layman's Guide To Unlocking The Extrasensory Power of Your Mind.* New York: Bantam Books. 1987.
- Swann, Ingo. "The Panoramic Consciousness Tutorial To Extend Awareness Conduits Toward Natural And Indwelling Peak Human Performance. General Introduction" 1993.
- Swann, Ingo. *Your Nostradamus Factor.* New York: Fireside. 1993.

- The English Language Institute of America, Inc. *The Living Webster Encyclopedic Dictionary of the English Language. Chicago. 1971-72.*
- *The New Encyclopedia Britannica.* Vol. 4. Chicago: Encyclopedia Britannica. 1990.
- Veilikovsky, Immanuel. *Mankind In Amnesia.* Garden City, NY: Doubleday. 1982.
- Weaver, Andrew Thomas. *Freefall's Fantastic Journey.* 1994.
- Wilber, Ken. *A Brief History of Everything*. Boston: Shambhala Publications Inc. 1996.
- Wilber, Ken. *Sex, Ecology, Spirituality: The Spirit of Evolution.* Boston: Shambhala Publications, Inc., 1995.

Permissions

We gratefully acknowledge permission to reprint from the following works:

- Barbara Marciniak, *Connecting Link,* 1992. Reprinted with permission of Barbara Marciniak.
- *Beyond Telepathy* by Andrija Puharich, M.D.. Copyright ©1962 by Andrija Puharich. Reprinted with permission of Doubleday and Company.
- Chopra, Deepak M.D. *Quantum Healing: Exploring the Frontiers of Mind/ Body Healing.* New York: Bantam Books, 1989, p. 217.
- *Freefall's Fantastic Journey* by Andrew Thomas Weaver.1994. Reprinted with permission of Kurt L. Weaver.
- *From Elsewhere: Being E.T. In America* by Scott Mandelker, Ph.D. Copyright ©1995 by Scott Mandelker. Reprinted with permission of Scott Mandelker.
- *Hyperspace* by Michio Kaku Ph.D.Copyright ©by Michio Kaku, 1995. Reprinted by permission of Oxford University Press, Inc., 200 Madison Avenue, New York, NY 10016.
- Ingo Swann, correspondance with the authors 1993 and 1996. Reprinted with permission of Ingo Swann.
- *Natural ESP: A Layman's Guide To Unlocking The Extrasensory Power of Your Mind* by Ingo Swann. Copyright ©1987 by Ingo Swann. Reprinted with permission of Ingo Swann.
- *Negotiating with Other Worlds* by J.J. Hurtak, Ph.D. The Academy For Future Science, P.O. Box FE, Los Gatos, CA 95031, 1990. Original copyright ©J.J. Hurtak, 1978 (cassette recording). Reprinted by permission of The Academy For Future Science.
- *On Wings of Light: Messages of Hope and Inspiration from Archangel Michael through Ronna Herman.* Star Quest 1485 Midway Court, Alpine, CA. 91901. Copyright ©by Ronna Herman 1996. Reprinted with permission of Ronna Herman.

- *Sex, Ecology, Spirituality* by Ken Wilber, ©1995. Reprinted by arrangement with Shambhala Publications, Inc., 300 Massachusetts Avenue, Boston, MA. 02115
- "Sightings", Paramount Pictures Corporation. Broadcast November 1994. Copyright ©by Paramount Pictures Corporation. Reprinted by permission of Paramount Pictures Corporation.
- 'The Blue Star. Its Origin' by Gordon-Michael Scallion. The Earth Changes Report. Chesterfield, New Hampshire. September, 1995. Reprinted with permission of Gordon-Michael Scallion.
- *The Joy Of Knowing We Are One. Transformational Conversation Among The Masters and Erik Myrmo*. Compiled and edited by Dr. L. David Moore. Copyright ©1996 by L. David Moore and Erik Myrmo. Reprinted with permission of L. David Moore.
- *The Mayan Factor: Path Beyond Technology* by Jose Arguélles, Ph.D.. Reprinted with permission from *The Mayan Factor: Path Beyond Technology* by Jose Arguelles, Copyright ©1987, Bear and Company, Santa Fe, New Mexico.
- "The Panoramic Consciousness Tutorial To Extend Awareness Conduits Toward Natural And Indwelling Peak Human Performance. General Introduction" by Ingo Swann. Reprinted with permission of Ingo Swann.1993.
- *The Seven Keys To Color Healing* by Roland Hunt.Copyright ©by Roland Hunt. 1971. Reprinted with permission of Harpercollins Publishers.
- *Ultimate Journey* by Robert A. Monroe. Copyright ©1994 by Robert A. Monroe. Reprinted with permission of Doubleday and Company.
- *Uri: A Journal of the Mystery of Uri Geller* by Andrija Puharich, M.D.. Copyright ©1974 by Andrija Puharich. Reprinted with permission of Doubleday and Company.
- *Your Nostradamus Factor* by Ingo Swann. Copyright ©1993 by Ingo Swann. Reprinted with permission of Ingo Swann.
- *The Body Electric: Electromagnetism and the Foundation of Life.* by Becker, Robert O. and Selden, Gary. New York: William Morrow and Company, Inc. 1985. 105 Madison Avenue, NY, NY 10016. [in process]
- *A Brief History OF Everything,* by Ken Wilber. Boston: Shambala,1996. 300 Massachusetts Avenue Boston, Massachusetts 02115. p. 176-77. [in process]

Index

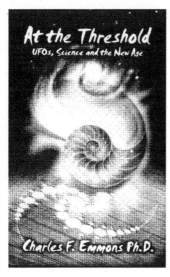

Place
Stamp
Here

Wild Flower
PRESS

Wild Flower Press
P.O. Box 190
Mill Spring, NC 28756